CONFESSIONS OF A TINDERELLA

ROSY EDWARDS

CENTURY

1 3 5 7 9 10 8 6 4 2

Century
20 Vauxhall Bridge Road
London SW1V 2SA

Century is part of the Penguin Random House group of companies whose addresses
can be found at global.penguinrandomhouse.com.

Penguin
Random House
UK

This book is a work of non-fiction based on the life, experiences and recollections
of the author. In some limited cases names of people, places, dates, sequences or the
detail of events have been changed [solely] to protect the privacy of others. The
author has stated to the publishers that, except in such minor respects not affecting
the substantial accuracy of the work, the contents of this book are true.

First published by Century in 2015

www.randomhouse.co.uk

A CIP catalogue record for this book
is available from the British Library.

ISBN 9781780893877

Typeset in Melior by Palimpsest Book Production Limited,
Falkirk, Stirlingshire

Printed and bound by Clays Ltd, St Ives plc

Penguin Random House is committed to a sustainable future for our business,
our readers and our planet. This book is made from Forest Stewardship Council®
certified paper.

CONFESSIONS OF A TINDERELLA

For Anthony, Fiona, Benjamin and Sam

ACKNOWLEDGEMENTS

First and foremost, my undying gratitude goes to my friend and superlative agent, Marigold Atkey, without whom this book probably would have been written, but certainly not by me. Without your kindness, time, advice and harissa chicken, I wouldn't have made it; I owe it all to you, Maz – a diamond-shod elephant is in the post. Huge thanks also goes to the fantastic team at David Higham, especially Alice Howe and Emily Randle.

Next, thank you to the powerhouse of support and enthusiasm that is my editor Francesca Pathak, whose kindness and patience never waned, even when I sent through my latest draft late. Again. I cannot thank you enough: your knowledge, instinct and keen eye has made this book so much better than I ever could have. Thank you to everyone at Penguin Random House, particularly

Philippa Cotton and Lindsay Davies – oh, and a big shout out to Roger.

I would still be merrily ensconced in manic schizoid defences without the advice and friendship of Isla Tulloch, Coralie Lasvergnas, Sophie Barrett and Sabrina Meakins, and the guidance and support of everyone at Birkbeck and A Space, as well as Jessica Mayer-Johnson. Special thanks goes to Richard Austen, who is one of 'those' teachers and who turned me on to writing in the first place, and thanks, always and abundantly, to the renal and dialysis teams at Guy's Hospital (especially those who have migrated to the Evelina Children's Hospital) who have made staying alive a whole lot easier over the years. Mr John Taylor remains forever and always in my mind and this book is written in his memory. Nick Hicks-Beach and Kate Stables, you have been wonderful in so many ways, and your advice on things literary and beyond is constant, and so very much appreciated. I am also very grateful to the National Theatre and Southbank Centre for providing quiet, comfortable – and free! – space where a novice writer can hone her craft.

Will, Ian, Izzy, Kirsty, Stu, Phillipa, Jamie, Hannah, Zara and Lizzie, you wonderful people: thank you for all your encouragement along the way and much more besides. DM: I can happily confirm that you are definitely – and now legally – not a Nazi. Thank you for the pulled pork, the chai lattes and Juan Mata's blog; you sat beside me whilst I wrote and believed in me when I didn't. This book is for both of us.

acknowledgements

Limitless, shameless love and thanks go to: Amir and Ella Al'Ajooz, Amy Baker, Clare Brenton, James Buckey, James Chapman, Justin Coaley, Ben Cooper, James Dalton, Heidi Gazeley, Steven and Cathy Geraghty, Tom Hand, Pippa Hare, Rachel Hodges, Olly Hodges, Mike and Bev Newman, Mia Reakes, Andrea and Gavin Schaller and Hannah Simmons, and especially Alex Cooper and Joanne Pickard. To Maisy Harman, for always being there in the middle of the night, whether you're across a hallway or an ocean; to Mark Goodwin, for being my creative guru and for being more excited about this project than anyone, and to Adam Crudgington – if it doesn't work out with JD, the deal still stands; thank you for every single one of the last twenty-four(!) years. Anna Newman, you are my heartbeat and my biggest inspiration; you are always in my mind but too little in my shower. Kat Baker, Katie Chapman, Siobhan Geraghty and Fiona Robertson, my Crazytown Crew, my loudest cheerleaders, my loves: you are the most talented, beautiful women I know and it is a privilege to have my life bound with yours. Lastly, to Ellie Sykes: thank you for all your help and ideas, many of which can be found in these pages; thank you for looking after me when I couldn't look after myself; thank you for the hug you gave me, that one time. You are my person. There aren't enough fucking pens in the world, mate.

My final, most wondrous and mighty thanks go to my family. Benjamin and Sam, the tallest, most beautiful brothers I could wish for: you are more gifted than I shall ever be, thank you for keeping me safe in the middle. And lastly, my parents, Anthony and Fiona: I owe you everything, and every ounce of my love. You have guided and comforted me far beyond the writing of this book and for once, words are not enough.

MOVING

Here are some facts about hummus:

1. Hummus originated in the Middle East, where it is often eaten for breakfast.
2. The main ingredient in hummus is chickpeas, also known as garbanzo beans.
3. High in protein and low in cholesterol, hummus is nutritionally beneficial (unless you eat it in the same industrial quantities I do).

I have learnt a lot about hummus since The Couples and I started coming here: Eser, my favourite waiter, smuggles me extra portions, I think because he feels sorry for me, and he likes to give me facts about it from time to time. According to statistics – and these are from the Internet, so they're true) – Monday morning is the most common time for people to kill themselves, presumably as Sunday evening is so unremittingly depressing. We frequently come here on Sunday nights, The Couples and I, and as the sole Single in our group, Eser believes me to be particularly at risk.

'The Couples' is my shorthand and slightly disparaging way of describing my closest friends who happen to delineate into pairs – Sophie and Ollie, Kate and Bob. In fairness, they don't act couple-y (i.e. they don't copulate on the table). Bob's real name is also Ollie, but it's too confusing for everybody to have a boyfriend called Ollie so we decided a long time ago that one of them had to be called something else; Kate's Ollie thus became Bob, as his last name is Roberts but 'Rob' didn't sound funny. My real name is Rosamund, which I can only assume was my mother's way of punishing me for the abrasive journey I took down her birth canal, though I have insisted on Rosy from the moment I could talk. I am also ginger, 5ft 1in and soft at the edges from all the hummus; I have enough embarrassment in my life without 'Rosamund'.

Tonight's topic for discussion is house prices. Over the past few years, our conversations have been slowly changing to reflect the vast difference in our lives compared to how they were in our early twenties, before the reality of independent, urban living beat the joy and optimism from our hearts. We used to effuse about our challenging new jobs and plan adventures for the weekend; now we all deride the jobs we hate and grumble about micro scooters. At seventeen, my mother assured me that, one day, I would listen to Radio 4 – on purpose. I remember laughing at her senile ways. But then something happened just after my twenty-fifth birthday and I awoke one morning to find that Radio 1 repelled me and I wouldn't mind making jam. I recently turned twenty-seven; I am not ashamed to admit I find Radio 4 charming. I love *Desert Island Discs.* I think Barry Cryer is hilarious.

We are talking about house prices because Kate and Bob are in a position to buy, and spend their free time looking at property porn online instead of Twitter and actual porn like the rest of us. That they can even consider buying a house is so outlandish to me that they might as well be buying a mermaid – I still balk at paying £3.20 for a soya chai latte (doesn't seem to stop me buying them, though). As I load flatbread with hummus (from my personal stash), Bob says: 'We're almost priced out of Clapton.'

'Forest Hill?' Ollie asks.

'Going up.'

'So we're looking a bit further north now,' Kate interjects, 'on the Haringey ladder.'

'It's unbelievable what you could have got with the same money three years ago.'

'Three bedrooms instead of one.'

'Which is in a cupboard,' says Sophie.

'And a kitchen that's not also a bathroom,' I add; I like to join in. I know as much about buying a house as I do Chinese papermaking.

Bob says, 'And a garden,' and places his hand over

Kate's. 'We'll find somewhere. I wouldn't have thought about Southgate before.'

'They have a Costa there now,' says Sophie.

'I prefer Caffè Nero,' I say, 'the lattes aren't great in Costa.'

'You can't move somewhere that serves sub-standard latte,' says Ollie, and we all laugh as though it's a joke.

Eser has to have a colleague help him deliver our food: we've gone for a wide-net approach and ordered a selection of meatballs, koftas, griddled aubergine and steaming bowls of rice pilav with the intention of sharing. The problem with being Rosy, singular, however, is that I end up stuck on the odd seat at one end of the table, and tonight the good stuff has pooled at the other; the lamb is severely depleted by the time it reaches me. Conversation wanes until all we're doing is endorsing cumin and repeating the phrase: 'You have to try the . . .' before it peters out, and there follows three minutes of rapid, silent ingestion. When social norms return, Bob and Ollie fall into a discussion on football about which Sophie, Kate and I have little knowledge and less interest. Sophie tops up our wine glasses. 'Did you both get the "save the date" for Cassie's wedding?' she asks. Kate nods. I received it too: I can picture it now, at the bottom of my underwear drawer, on the premise that if I can't see it, I won't have to think about the wedding and this will somehow equate to my not having to go. I give a vague half-answer to which Kate immediately responds: 'Is this because of Charlie?' and I wish I hadn't said anything at all.

Sophie throws Kate a glance like, *shut up* . . . it is

incredibly unsubtle – it's like she's doing a skit. Kate bites her lip.

'Do you know if he's bringing her?' I ask.

'I don't know,' says Sophie. 'Cassie didn't say.' I have been friends with Sophie for a long time – long enough that I didn't care when she threw up, on me, on my birthday; long enough that I instinctively know when she's lying. I assume Cassie did say, and that the answer was yes. To ease the tension I say, 'I don't think I'll get the time off work,' and we all relax. Cassie is technically Sophie's friend (they were at primary school together where they used to practise kissing, a detail Sophie remembers selectively) and she has a unique way of giving compliments that make you sort of . . . hate yourself (on my hair: 'I'd love to be ginger, just for a day, just to see what it's like'). I'd rather spend the travel/accommodation/present money on someone I actually like and/or see more than twice a year. Plus, it turns out weddings are not the fuck-fest, rom-com wet dream that single people are encouraged to believe so they won't bail last minute and ruin the seating plan. I could deal with this, however; I could force myself to go, were it not for the fact my ex-boyfriend Charlie will be there, along with his new girlfriend.

Charlie. I liked his name before I liked him and afterwards, when we'd fallen in love, I loved the way our names sounded together: *Rosy and Charlie, Charlie and Ro.* We met through work: my old PR agency was leading a campaign for the production company where he worked; I used to sit in those meetings looking anywhere else but at him (I can recall to this day the location of every power socket in that room) and when his company invited our office for Christmas drinks, I only went because my colleague Pip forced me; that was the first night Charlie talked to me. He texted the next day, which I remember thinking was a big deal at the time, after years adhering to bullshit two-day rules. I couldn't believe I had almost turned down the opportunity to go, but if I had the chance again . . . I don't know. It seems like another life.

The conversation moves on as we work our way through the rest of the food; we meander through holiday plans (Sophie and Ol: Istanbul; Kate and Bob: France; me: weekend at my parents, possibly), the Middle East, Saturday night TV, flavoured vs plain nuts and the extortionate expense of train travel; we've all been friends for so long, one topic flows into another. Sophie and I met on our fourth day of university and we both met Kate on the sixth but because three years together was not enough, we all moved to London after graduation and shared a succession of houses until, one by one, we moved in with our other halves. I was so thrilled for my friends when Ollie and Bob arrived and it was Kate and Soph who carried me through the first few months after Charlie when I couldn't carry myself.

Eser hovers as we pick at the scraps until finally we sit back, sated. It takes him three trips to clear the table and when he returns for the final time he is clutching dessert menus. I wouldn't mind some baklava – I'm about to suggest it when Ollie pipes up, suggesting we get the bill and a round of coffee. Ours is a utilitarian friendship group: I'll buy a Crunchie on the way home. The bill comes first, quicker than any of our food, and Ollie calculates an equal split on his phone; he announces what we each owe before he and Soph begin their traditional post-dinner debate about whose turn it is to pay (she got the shopping on Monday but he settled up with the cleaner); they both argue in their own favour which I've never understood as it's pretty much the exact opposite of the stance I'd take. I place my card on the pile; I really hope it doesn't get declined – it would be the Topshop summer sale all over again. And then come the taxis.

As the group member that lives furthest away, earns the least and would be paying for a taxi from solely my own pocket, I watch as my friends huddle over their phones and tap away on taxi apps whilst I flick packs of sugar and listen to their muted mutterings: '. . . cheaper than last time . . .', '. . . less than fifteen minutes, it always is . . .'. This is the bit I hate.

'How are you getting home, Ro?' asks Ollie.

'I thought I'd wander down to the Tube, it's pretty close.'

Ollie frowns. 'Will you make it?' I've been glancing at my phone all night (calls – none; texts – none) but have consistently failed to look at the time: it is 12.20 a.m. This place stays open until 1 a.m. on Sundays, a detail I should have remembered after last time and my £37 taxi (it was more than my share of the meal). 'I'll get the night bus, it's not a problem,' I say breezily, which I hope successfully hides the fact it's a problem. The bus takes double the time of the Tube journey.

'It's what, a five-minute walk to the stop?' asks Kate.

'Sort of closer to fifteen . . .'

'But it has stopped raining,' says Ollie, 'that's lucky.'

Eser brings the coffee. I didn't order one in a silent baklava protest and in retrospect I'm glad: if getting home is going to take longer I want to get going. I stage a yawn, that pre-empts a real yawn, and tell my friends I'm heading off. They erupt into a pleading chorus, imploring me to stay, but I am already on my feet.

'At least let us drop you at the bus stop,' says Bob, as I pull on my parka and sling my rucksack on my back (I'd been aiming for nerdy chic with the rucksack; the result has been more twelve-year-old exchange student, especially in conjunction with the parka). I reply that I'd like the walk: Eser's generosity means I am now physically 42 per cent hummus and the restaurant, pleasingly warm on arrival, feels stiflingly hot. We say goodbye amidst a flurry of kisses and I push through the glass door out to the street. Ollie was right about the rain; it must have stopped a while ago and the pavements shimmer and steam under the yellow glow of the streetlights.

I unzip my coat and as I start to walk and tune into the mundane hum of the late-night traffic, it's a relief after the surround-sound chatter and dropped dish crescendos from the restaurant. I can picture my friends, finishing their coffee, making the taxis wait with purring engines; they'll soon be unlocking their front doors and feeling their way along hallways for lights; brushing their teeth and hurriedly pulling off clothes; jumping into bed and curling round each other. I miss that part of being with someone. And the sex, I miss that a lot. God, I really miss the sex.

I don't realise that I'm lost straight away; it is a gradual understanding that sweeps over me, like flu, and only becomes full-blown certainty as I look around and don't see anything I recognise. I took a left out of the restaurant then veered towards the church, but I'm thinking I should have turned right out of the restaurant and not veered anywhere. Charlie would know where to go. He'd get out his phone and show me the map on his phone, hugging me from behind: 'Think about it, Rosy,' he'd say, 'we're here and we need to get *there* – why would we turn left?' Then he'd laugh and kiss my neck, and he'd tell me I was an idiot before leading us off in the right direction; I would clasp his hand and follow him because I trusted him. I followed him, even in those last few months, right up until he was gone.

I can't get a Wi-Fi connection on my phone and retracing my steps would only be an option if I could remember what those steps were. I jiggle my phone in my hand. It's late, if I phone her she's going to be pissed off; however, as my best friend since our first year of uni she is also duty bound to forgive me, and she should have thought about these sorts of scenarios before she signed up for the role. I find her name and hit 'call'. She answers on the third ring. 'Yes?'

'I'm lost.'

'Where are you?'

'Well, I'm lost, so I don't know.'

'All right, where have you been?'

'The Turkish place; now I'm trying to get to the bus stop and I can't get Wi-Fi and it's dark . . .'

'OK, slow down.'

I take a deep breath as per BF's instruction and listen to the clicks of her laptop keys as I exhale. I feel better for just hearing her voice.

'Right, what road are you on?'

I take a few steps forwards, squinting at the street sign up ahead. 'Corrance.'

'Corrance, OK . . . can you see a church?'

A large, grey-stoned behemoth towers above me from across the road with lattices of stained glass in the windows and a spire reaching far into the sky. I'm going to take a punt. 'Yes.'

'If you walk round to the front, you should come to a small green and if you cross over and walk left a bit, you'll be able to see the main road – please tell me you can get to the bus stop from there?' She sounds bemused, as though being lost whilst standing 100 metres from your target is a physical impossibility – for me, it's an almost daily reality. I got lost at school once, having already been there for two years. If I could have any super-power, it would be the ability to navigate. Or the ability to teleport, thus negating the need to navigate entirely.

'How was dinner?' BF asks as I set off.

'Nice . . . lots of chat about houses and holidays. Which is interesting, but sometimes a bit . . .'

'. . . shit?'

I smile. 'Yeah.'

She says, 'Well, if you will *insist* on dying alone . . .' which makes me laugh.

'It's not that, they don't make me feel excluded. It's just that all the talk of houses and holidays reminds me just how far away I am from that stuff.' Even I can hear the sadness weighing down my voice. I don't despair at being single, but in the last six months I've had a growing sense of being . . . left behind. BF replies, 'Yeah, me too,' and I can hear the sadness in her voice too, which makes me love her more.

Then she says, 'Look; sod it.' She checks I know where I'm going then tells me she'll ring tomorrow; we say goodnight and hang up. I cross the green as she said to and come out on the main road where things look more familiar – especially the fucking Turkish place that I can make out down the road to my left. I turn right. Bloody geography.

It's half past one by the time I get home. Oona, one of my two flatmates, is still up, sitting on the sofa reading today's paper with her laptop perched on her lap and the TV on in the background.

'How was dinner?' she asks as I walk in.

'Nice, thanks.' I go through to the kitchen for a glass of water. Remnants of what I presume were once strawberries and bananas are smattered on the side and splash-backs and coat the innards of the blender jug that is in the sink. I pop my head back round the door. 'Has Harriet . . .?'

'I've left a note on her door.' My second housemate, Harriet, is a joy to live with until she goes on one of her rampant juicing fads, at which point I want to go on a rampage of my own. I must remember to text her tomorrow and warn her about Oona's note. Oona is . . . a challenge to live with. In the single year since I moved in, she has twice threatened to get me evicted, instituted a loo-roll ration and launched a failed bid to sell the TV because Harriet and I 'only watch trash'.

I fill up my water glass and tell Oona I'm heading for bed.

'I'm going to Dublin tomorrow but I should be back on Sunday,' she says, which I pretend is her saying 'goodnight'. Oona works in finance; beyond this, I don't know what she actually does, though from the handful of anecdotes she's told me it involves travelling and shouting at people. Sometimes she fires them. Harriet is a primary school teacher, which has been a lot easier for me to grasp and sounds relatively interesting, especially compared to my own job as a PR account manager, and as I need to start doing it in seven hours' time I should really go to bed.

* * *

I am exhausted. I couldn't sleep last night (I blame the hummus) so whilst on the bus in, I determined that my coping strategy for this morning would be to not really do very much. It is almost 10 a.m.; by this time I should have cleared my inbox, written and sent out the daily media round-up and started the trawl for online coverage of our latest campaign. So far today, I have managed to cross off two items from my seventeen-point to-do list (thirteen of which have rolled over from last Friday), the first of which was: ~~get coffee~~, and instead of doing the work I am paid to do, I have elected to stare at my computer screen and replay an episode of *'Allo 'Allo* in my head.

'Rosy.' I jump at the sound of Helen's voice. She is standing over me with, thankfully, a look of amusement. My boss is twelve years older than me and the mother of two children, yet she has advert-grade shiny auburn hair, wears lipstick *every day* and owns a selection of designer coats that combined are worth six months of my rent. I know that today's offering is from Max Mara because I check the labels when I hang them up. Helen is in late and carrying a gym bag (so expensive I don't recognise the brand) which means she has been working out with Dermot, her ex-Marine personal trainer. 'How was it?' I ask.

'Ugh,' Helen sighs, 'horrific. Apparently Arsenal lost yesterday and I think Dermot took his frustration out on my quads. He made me do squats until I collapsed into the foetal position.' I offer to make a cup of tea and Helen accepts with such gratitude I wonder if I might get a raise. I go as far as brewing her a mug of herbal tea (looks like piss, smells like piss) and bring it out alongside my own normal-person brew.

'Perfect, thank you,' Helen sighs, reclining back into her chair. 'I moan, but he is really very good. I'm back to the weight I was before I got pregnant with Sylvie, maybe even a bit less.' She swivels round to me. 'I got another voucher for a free session, you should use it, I keep telling you.'

'Dermot would destroy me.'

Helen laughs. 'That gym is packed with good-looking men, though,' she says, turning to her computer, 'you might meet someone.'

I focus on my screen. I can't fault Helen's logic: in her exclusive, £120-a-month gym, I'd imagine you can't swing a kettle ball without hitting (also injuring) a muscular, attractive man – the type that pulls off a sheen of sweat with the same panache as a Savile Row suit. Unfortunately I don't earn as much as Helen, nor am I married to her stockbroker husband, so the gym I go to is run by my local council and costs me £45 a month. There are no frills and that includes the men. My gym is the ideal venue to meet someone if your type is a fifty-year-old with a comb-over and a paunch; the same applies if you're into married men, steroid-pumped meat-heads or the guy that works out in a shell suit, emitting an ungodly aroma. Young-ish, good-looking-ish guys do turn up occasionally though my chances of meeting one would be greatly improved if I could be arsed to go more than once a month. I would like to be fitter and in better shape; I used to run three times a week up until my final year at university but since arriving in London my activity level has decreased in direct correlation to a rise in my general mooching-around time.

By mid-morning, Helen has gone out for a meeting

and Pip, my go-to procrastination buddy, has been on the phone for the last fifteen minutes with no sign of getting off soon. I bring up the press release I should be editing and try to concentrate. Helen's edict about the gym has been playing on a loop in my head since she said it; over the course of the last hour, it has somehow transmuted in my mind so that now all I can hear is my thin, rich, married boss telling me that I shall never meet a man unless I get my fat arse down to the gym and will instead be destined to a life of singledom and despair. I wouldn't mind being like Helen; I'd like to be the sort of woman who wears Max Mara coats and actively enjoys mugs of steaming weed juice and I certainly would not object to having her abs. The thing that stops me from spitting in said weed juice is that I know how hard Helen works for it all. I abandon the press release to pinch my stomach and pull out at least a centimetre of flab, three if I stretch it, which I do in sadistic fashion.

*　　*　　*

I have concluded I am obese. Instead of going to Pret for lunch and buying whatever I can grasp before my arm gets ripped off in the scramble, I opt for a small selection box from the good sushi place and imagine a brownie for dessert. Back at my desk in the late afternoon, my to-do list is only three items lighter and all I can think about is how inert my lifestyle has become: I sit here for roughly eight hours a day and the most exercise I get is the short walk to and from food-selling shops. On weeknights, I swap my office chair for my sofa, watch TV and eat dinner; otherwise, I meet BF or Kate and Sophie for Happy Hour cocktails that are as calorific as the double cheeseburgers we consume before stumbling home. And the weekends are my cheat days.

At half past four, I stop even pretending to look like I'm busy and text BF.

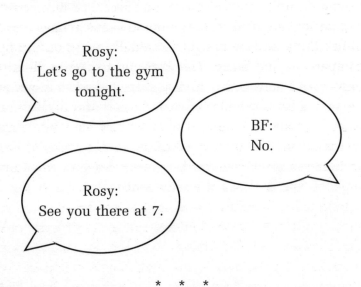

Rosy:
Let's go to the gym
tonight.

BF:
No.

Rosy:
See you there at 7.

*   *   *

In reality, I find going to the gym no different from going to a club. You have to pay to get in and if you were hoping for a genial drink, a sit-down and a chat, forget it; high-energy chart hits thump overhead and everyone sweats and jiggles along, though only a handful look graceful doing so. Perspiration hangs heavy in the air despite the air conditioning and men and women of every persuasion swig from their drinks, checking each other out. BF fills her water bottle as I look around, scrunching the hem of my T-shirt in my hand – I'm sweating, even though so far all I've done is walk in. I'm not sure I'm really right for the gym. The dress code for the girls seems to be short, tight and skimpy – I've come as a mum's first post-partum night out. I wish my leggings didn't sag so badly at the knees. My slim, toned gym sisters are clad in tops from designer ranges that I didn't think anyone bought to actually work out in; by comparison, my faded *The Earthquake Album* T-shirt looks like I salvaged it from a skip. I used to come to the gym a lot, particularly when I was with Charlie – he went a lot and encouraged me to – and my confidence increased in line with my fitness; in the wake of our split, my sense of self-worth has recovered but my lung capacity has not been the same since.

BF heads off toward the cross-trainers so I step on to a treadmill, press some buttons and try to at least look like I know what I'm doing – it's moving, which is a good start. I peek over at my neighbour's machine; the display reveals he is running at 13.5 km per hour but his feet, snug inside some performance-enhancing trainers of the future, are pounding the belt so hard I would never be able to keep up. I increase my incline and up the speed slowly until I feel my leg muscles start to tug; this leaves me at a pitiful 7.3. I push my head-phones into my ears and adopt a jaunty, nonchalant jog that I think clearly says 'warm-up'.

OK: I'm jogging. This feels good, this is bearable – and

if I hang my towel over the display nobody can see how slowly I'm going. I have the timer set for a twenty-minute run and I have so far run for . . . forty-five seconds. I search around the room for BF and spot her on a cross-trainer by the wall. Her ponytail bobs around like a cheerleader's and whatever sports bra she is wearing is doing wonders for her rack; it has not gone unnoticed by the weight-lifting heavy in front of her but he is double the size he genetically should be so not really her type – BF strides on oblivious. My hair does not bob, just as my breasts do not incite anything beyond perfunctory interest, though I've yet to see anyone whose interest I'd seek. A guy who could be good-looking is on a bike in front of me but I'm basing this on the back of his head and I've been fooled by an attractive skull before.

By the sixteenth minute it is only pride keeping me going but I power on through until my twenty minutes of hell are over and step off the treadmill to find my legs are now made of seaweed. 'I need to stretch out,' I say to BF as she wanders over; when I look at her, she is already gazing at the mat area.

'You should stretch next to that guy,' she says, 'the one in the blue shorts.' I follow her eye line to the mats where the man in question is bending over so we spend a few moments collectively objectifying him by staring at his arse. When he stands up, I note eyes the same hue as his shorts, a slightly upturned nose and a thatch of blond hair that's nicely cut but would be nicer without the oil slick of gel. Beads of sweat have rolled half way down his short neck, which he wipes away with a towel.

He's not what you'd call tall but neither am I; he is lean, though, and holds himself well. BF prods me in the waist. 'You should say hello.'

'Why?'

'Because he's good-looking.'

'Relatively,' I add, glancing round at his competition. BF is looking at me, her eyes wide with optimism. I think about Helen; her husband is not very tall either.

I walk over. Gym mats make me queasy if I think too much about them; I pick one up by the edges and overlay it with my towel, hoping it will afford me some protection from the years' worth of sweat infused into its surface. As I'm rolling it out, it suddenly occurs to me that Fit Gym Guy and I are the only two people here and placing my mat so near to his is farcical, and probably fucking irritating – it's not a great start. He is lying on his back with his right knee pulled up to his chest, so I get down on all fours and do some leg lifts. He extends his arms out into a crucifix, twists his body to stretch his back and turns his head in the opposite direction to me.

I kneel back on my heels and look for BF but I can't see her, so I embark upon the stretching routine I learnt in Year 9 netball, starting with slow head turns (to the left; middle; to the right; middle) that Miss Armond insisted were the key to a decent chest pass. Fit Gym Guy is still on his back, using his left leg as a lever to stretch out his right with his gaze concentrated on the ceiling above. I roll my shoulders and windmill my arms. Eventually he sits up in a perfect L shape, back straight, legs flush to the floor (I only ever *think* I'm doing that pose) so that finally we're essentially facing each other. If I'm going to make eye contact, this is my chance – yet I need to get his attention. So I lunge. Abruptly.

In a way, this works: his eyes snap towards me, gifting me the opportunity for a coy yet friendly smile, but I've overestimated my lunge trajectory and thoughts of him must be repressed in order to simply survive. I want to look over, but if I stop concentrating on my elected patch of wall I'm going to topple over, most likely on top of him. The only way out of this is down, and it is not a graceful descent.

When I look back over he is oblivious, stretching forward to his toes, so I lie on my side and pretend to do a sort of leg-lift thing that I hope looks like exercise. I have a long way to go before I'm fit enough to fit in at the gym. This is where I come to escape: it is the ideal place when I want to jam my headphones into my ears and pretend I'm in a music video and/or training for the Olympics; being here is also preferable to yet another night spent watching shit TV in my pyjamas. What it is not is a good place to meet men: I feel only relief as Fit Gym Guy rolls up his mat and I don't have to pretend I'm good at exercise any more or try and introduce myself to a man in child's pose. I stretch out one final time and when I stand up I see BF has been cornered by the weightlifter. I watch until my inaction becomes cruel and I go and pretend to be her life partner.

* * *

I thought the flat was empty when I came in but as I'm dumping my bag, Harriet (my non-Fascist, second house-mate) calls hello from her room and I go through to find her on her bed, painting her toenails. 'How was the gym?'

'Painful.' I lay back on her bed beside her; I've decided to ignore the fact my legs are hurting as much as my pride. To casual observers, of which gyms boast plenty, my pathetic attempt to talk to Fit Gym Guy must have been risible; I could have just said 'hi', or 'how's it going' or 'don't these mats make you want to be a bit sick in your mouth' – anything but the lunge; the sheer absurdity of it makes me wince. I can feel Harriet looking at me. 'My boss told me the gym is a good place to meet men,' I say, closing my eyes. 'It really isn't.'

'Are you trying to meet someone?'

'Hmm?' I open one eye, then both.

'I think I might know someone if you're looking. I could set you up?'

My eyes, barely open as they are, narrow further still. Being set up with my friends' friends who are 'hilarious' (read: wacky, intensely annoying) or 'so sweet' (ugly) based on the sole criterion that we are both single is a perennial problem of being single. The last time Sophie tried (Josh, 32, her sister's housemate) I was almost inter-ested until I asked if she would date him herself. 'God, no,' she had laughed, 'no, I think he's pretty dull.'

'Is it a friend of James's?' I ask Harriet, propping myself up on my elbow. On reflection, I'm not sure dating a friend of Harriet's boyfriend is a wise move: James wears running trainers with his jeans.

'No, I did my training with him, he's called Craig.'
She stands up and gets her phone, hobbling in preservation of her wet toes. 'He broke up with his girlfriend a few months ago and when we were chatting last week he sort of hinted he was ready to start looking again.'

'"Sort of hinted"? He doesn't sound like he's looking very seriously.'

'No, he's great,' says Harriet, concentrating on her phone, which I note doesn't answer my question. I know that she is looking for a photo of Craig to show me and I know what's going to happen: he's going to have two heads or sixteen nostrils, or he'll be a foot shorter than me, or five taller. He'll have hair down to his waist or a swastika tattooed on his forehead; I don't know what it will be yet but I know I won't fancy him.

'OK, what do you think?' Harriet asks, passing me her phone.

I am surprised – I was wrong on all counts: Craig isn't monstrously deformed or an evident bigot, his hair is a good length and he looks to be normal height with a warm, friendly expression. Unfortunately, Craig, I would guess, must be forty-five if he's a day. I glance up at Harriet, who is waiting for my reaction, tense with hope. 'I think he might be a bit old for me, Haz.'

Harriet reaches out for her phone; she says, 'Oh, really?' and I can hear the disappointment in her voice. She looks down at the picture. 'He is a bit older but he's such a nice guy, you'd really get on – he's in PR, like you.' Craig is almost twice my age, not my type and we are only compatible because we have a similar work-life, though

I hope not, because if I'm still a lowly account exec at forty-five I'll move to Fiji and start again. I don't think it's a love match.

'I'm not sure I'm looking for someone,' I tell Harriet. 'Not proactively, anyway.' Essentially, this is the truth. When I am out with The Couples, I sometimes think it would be nice to be with someone, and if a man falls into my lap (so to speak) I won't turn them down. But seeking someone out seems like a lot of effort – I wouldn't know where to start.

'He's just such a nice guy,' says Harriet again, locking her phone. They always are. I am not at the stage where a date with Craig appeals.

Not yet.

2.

THE HANDSOME CABIN BOY

At work, as I was telling Pip about Harriet's matchmaking service, she nodded along, listening attentively, and when I reached the end, said: 'Ooh, I've got someone I could set you up with,' then dove into her bag for her phone. It's as if the words 'single' and 'set up' work together to inspire a Pavlovian response that renders people incapable of not offering me a date.

'I'm not sure, Pip,' I say, 'I'm not really looking . . .'

'His name is Elliot. He's an ex-boyfriend but from a million years ago so it wouldn't be weird. We've just always kept in touch – in fact Geoff isn't too keen about it so you'd be doing me a favour if you guys hit it off.' This is what I am now, apparently: a beard to appease colleagues' husbands. Pip thrusts her phone at me (I wish phones would go back to just being phones some-times) and I look down to see she has pulled up his

Facebook page and clicked through to his photos. She motions for me to scroll.

My big brother, whom I still call Bru (even though I am not three any more and don't have to rely on monosyllabic nicknames) once told me that it takes just one tenth of a second to form a first impression of someone. At the time, I remember thinking this was ridiculous: how could you do any more than snatch a glimpse of a person in that instant? You'd barely have time to take in their features let alone form an assessment of their character. What if they were frowning? You might assume said person to be grumpy and belligerent when in fact they were well known for their sunny disposition. You'd make a first impression but it would be wrong. I told Bru he was stupid and that he should shut up (I was eleven at the time) but I can hear him saying it now as I look through Elliot's pictures. I don't know if it's possible to form an accurate impression from pictures but if you can, I think Elliot looks . . . nice. He has dark hair and light eyes that crinkle when he smiles; if not a head-turner he is certainly good-looking, more Boden than GQ, but he has promise. From my own (consistent) experience, I am well aware that pictures can be misleading: for every good picture I have seen of myself there are seventeen that suggest I have a genetic deformity, but it's worth giving Elliot the benefit of the doubt.

'He is quite attractive,' I tell Pip. 'What does he do?'

'Something in insurance, I think? He's lovely, really kind and smart. Why don't I talk to him, and give him your number?'

It is quite a jump from scrolling through a man's Facebook page to real-life communication; I'm not sure it's one I should make. Then I am rarely sure about anything: I am not sure it was a good idea to spend £17 yesterday on shampoo rather than food; I'm not sure I can get away with crop tops any more and yet I continue to wear them; I've been working in PR since I was twenty-one and a fresh-faced graduate, ready to take on the world, yet I'm still not convinced I enjoy it. On this basis, I might as well date Elliot. I tell Pip she can go ahead, which makes her beam, and though she assures me she's messaging Geoff I think she texts Elliot then and there. I turn back to my to-do list, which appears to have got longer in the ten minutes we've been chatting.

I'd forgotten all about this conversation by the time Elliot messaged me four days later. I couldn't understand why someone I'd never heard of, texting from a number I didn't recognise, was making references to a *'slightly awkward situation!'* and telling me he thought he'd *'get in touch anyway!'* Then his second text came through:

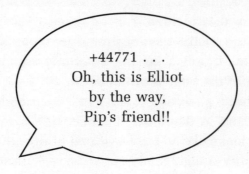

+44771 . . .
Oh, this is Elliot
by the way,
Pip's friend!!

. . . and it all came flooding back.

I replied, and we've been messaging back and forth for just over a week so it didn't seem inappropriate when Elliot suggested a date for tonight. The exclamation marks have remained a constant (slightly alarming) feature, otherwise we've stuck to neutral topics: yesterday he was telling me about his family's boat and the lasagna he made for his housemate's birthday, so I know he likes sailing and Italian food, and Elliot knows that I share these interests because I told him I did, even though both make me queasy. I have never been on a fix-up before and it's been such a long time since I've dated I'm unsure of the etiquette: I don't want to lie (more than I already have) but building common ground seems important in advance of our first meeting. Sophie and Kate are beside themselves with excitement: they have concluded Elliot is the man I shall marry and are in the final planning stages of a couples' weekend to the Cotswolds.

I'm dawdling: it's 6.45 and we're not due to meet until 7 p.m. Arriving ahead of time feels over-eager and being late is rude (unless you witness a minor road traffic accident and rush over to help; this was going to be my excuse. And sure, yeah, everyone was fine, it was a miracle . . .). Getting there bang on seven o'clock seems overly anal, however, so now I'm confused. I got off the bus three stops early and walked to kill time but it has started spitting, despite assurances from two different websites that it definitely would not rain. Putting my hood up looks like an overreaction but if I leave it down my carefully straightened hair will be steadfastly frizzed to shit. I opt for up. It's dark, cold and miserable – February, essentially – yet in spite of this, I have a warm sensation just behind my stomach at the prospect of meeting Elliot; it isn't dissimilar to the time I got food poisoning but I am confident that on this occasion it's excitement. It's not only my first date with Elliot but also my first proper date since Charlie and I broke up. I lay in bed in a panic two nights ago as it occurred to me I might have forgotten how to do this – Charlie and I were together for two years and though I've had a couple of one-night stands since, neither required much in the way of nuanced seduction (one barely required talking); however, as BF assured me, as long as I don't fall over or try to have sex with him in the first twenty minutes, everything will be fine.

I've been to the bar where we're meeting before; it was Elliot's choice and it's not a bad place, if a little lacking in character. There's five minutes to go until 7 p.m. but the spit is turning into full-blown rain and I'm not far from the bar – I can see raindrops bouncing off its illuminated sign ahead and as the lights are changing at the crossing I might as well go. If I speed up I can walk straight over the road; I like it when things like that happen. There are two people already stood waiting: a woman who is drenched, hopping from foot to foot and trying to shelter under her newspaper, and a man in a flimsy anorak that looks oddly familiar, but I don't know if . . . ah yes, that's it: Bru had one similar when we were kids. It packed away into a pouch; we used to compete to see who could stuff it in the quickest. He left it on the ferry on our way back from holiday in the Isle of Wight and he whined about it afterwards for a solid week until Mum cracked and bought him a new one that I don't recall him ever wearing; avid *Vogue* reader that I'm not, the resurgence of circa 1993 navy anoraks has clearly passed me by. Both the man and the woman are crossing when I get to the lights, with the woman sprinting ahead; Anorak Guy continues to check both ways as he walks, then he steps onto the pavement and walks towards the bar. As he turns to open the door, I see that it is Elliot. Elliot is Anorak Guy.

Did he see me? Is turning around at this stage appalling and spineless? Were the situation reversed and a prospective date spied me and ran, I would take to my bed and be unable to face my family again let alone another date . . . so, to sum up, yes, it would be appalling. I can't let an anorak put me off; it may not be to my taste but it doesn't prevent him from being charming and funny and even the most lacklustre wardrobe can be rectified by the love of a good woman and a trip to Topman. This could all turn out to be humorous fodder for Elliot's wedding speech.

I bowl through the door, soaking up the warmth that envelops me as I step inside. Elliot is leaning on the bar, studying the Real Ale selection, still wearing the anorak.

'Elliot?'

'Rosy?'

'Yes!'

'Ha! Good to meet you.' He is smiling broadly as he gives me a wet hug (this isn't sexy like it sounds) and

I feel myself relaxing slightly. We pull back and face each other in silence.

'Great place!' says Elliot.

'Yeah, it's good – I've been here a few times. It's not too loud and the drinks are pretty reasonable.' I sound like my father, which I don't think is a good omen.

'Yeah, it's brilliant.' Elliot looks around, nodding for no discernable reason, and smiling. I take off my coat in the hope he'll follow suit. 'Can I get you a drink?' he asks.

'Vodka and soda would be great, thanks.'

'Single or double?'

I opt for a double.

It isn't hard to find a table – only four others are taken – and I head for one in the corner as Elliot orders. He joins me, sets down our drinks and pulls off The Anorak to reveal a mundane but inoffensive grey shirt. 'That's a nice shirt,' I tell him.

'Thanks.' He sits down and sips from his flagon of Real Ale. 'I think I bought it for my Grandad's funeral.' He is still smiling as he says this. I leave what I hope is a respectful pause for Elliot's dead grandfather and ask: 'How was your journey?' which is the same thing my parents ask me when I visit home.

'Not bad – it was only six stops on the Tube. The Northern line.'

'That's a good line – I take it to work. It's so crowded in the morning, though.'

'It can get really bad, yeah,' Elliot nods. I nod. We sip our drinks. 'How was your journey?'

'Oh, fine,' I say, 'I got the bus. I only live up the road.'

Elliot laughs, I'm not clear why – I don't think I made a joke. Eventually it tails off. We lapse back into silence.

*　*　*

Elliot is talking about sailing: he's using terms like 'boom' and 'cleet' that mean nothing to me but I am so relieved that one of us is talking that I concentrate hard and ask lots of questions. (First question: 'What's a boom?' Second question: 'What's a cleet?') It is always a joy hearing anyone talk with passion, even if the topic is dry and incomprehensible; it also gives me a chance to study Elliot in more detail. His light eyes that looked luminous in his photos are more insipid in person; his smartly cropped hair is a month's growth from pudding-bowl and whilst his creased smile is endearing, I can't understand why he uses it all the time. Overall, he bears a good resemblance to his photos; his looks are not the problem. The reason I want to go home at ten past eight is because I don't fancy him. I knew it from the minute I saw him and I can't imagine I'm going to change my mind before I've finished my drink. I don't find Elliot engaging; I don't feel any sexual chemistry and I don't think we have anything in common beyond the fact we've both seen all of *The Sopranos*. I'm sure that one day he'll meet a fellow mariner (mariness?) and they will sail off into the sunset together, tweaking their booms and cleets as they go. The received wisdom is that you're supposed to 'know' when you meet The One and I think the same is true when you don't.

I'm suddenly aware that Elliot has stopped talking. I

want to say something – anything – and I'm trying to reach for words but there's nothing there. We smile at each other, or I smile at him – I suspect Elliot was probably smiling already. I sink the last of my drink.

'Would you like another?' Elliot asks, hands on his knees, ready to spring into action.

'Actually . . . I think I'm OK.' I frown, and nod, saying it with a puzzled inflection, as though it's something I have only just discovered myself. Elliot says, 'I might treat myself to one more,' and before I can say anything he is headed towards the bar having decided that another Real Ale would be 'just the ticket'.

*   *   *

Elliot is a slow drinker. Our date is starting to feel like that dream where you try to run but your legs won't move. We've eked out conversations about Christmas, hypothetical lottery wins and (more) box sets; it has taken us seventeen minutes and Elliot is a third of the way through his drink.

'Do you . . . have brothers or sisters?' I ask.

'No, only child I'm afraid,' Elliot says. I don't know why this annoys me, it shouldn't, but it just seems like another example of our intense incompatibility.

'What about you – brothers? Sisters?'

I tell him I have one older brother and that he's currently on a boat in the middle of the Indian Ocean.

'Is he a sailor?' Elliot sits up, alert. I almost feel cruel admitting he's a marine biologist.

'That's good,' says Elliot, smiling.

When he has (finally) finished his ale, Elliot asks if I'd like to go on somewhere else. It takes me a few seconds to process the question. Does he think this date is going well? Is he on this date? 'I've got a pretty early start tomorrow, I'm afraid,' I say, my voice thin and high. It isn't a lie: I want to be in the office for half eight to finish a report I told Helen she'd have by today. It's not the reason I want to leave, though.

'Sure, no problem,' says Elliot. 'Me too, actually.'

'Perhaps we should make a move?' I say, already getting to my feet. 'Do you have far to get back?'

'Just about six stops up the Northern line.'

'That's not too bad.'

'Yeah, no, it's fine. Shouldn't be too busy at this time.'

Out on the pavement Elliot says, 'You seem lovely, Rosy, I've really had a good time.' I look at him, looking at me. His light eyes are wide under his dark eyebrows and I notice his left hand pulling gently on the cuff of the Anorak. Then, before I can stop myself, and for an unfathomed reason, I say: 'We should do it again.' Elliot agrees; he'd love to meet up again, he says – he's free next week.

'I'll have to check my diary,' I reply, though I don't own a diary.

'No, that's fine. I could give you a text and we can arrange a night.' We hug goodbye and I walk off in the opposite direction to Elliot though it's also the opposite direction to my house.

I'm not sure what's just happened. Elliot said I was

'lovely' and it threw me. It's been a long time since a man who isn't my father has complimented me like that and I couldn't reject him, not outright, not with him standing in front of me; in hindsight, maybe asking him out for a second date was a step too far the other way. Elliot was boring and sexually unappealing, and the constant smiling was very unnerving by the end, but he was generally a pleasant man, undeserving of my cruelty. Except it will now be worse to reject him having led him on . . . shit. Dating is governed by a whole host of rules and conventions and if I knew them once, I've clearly forgotten them all, even if I did manage to avoid falling down. Let's see . . . spitting, hitting or racial abuse – presumably these are all things to avoid, as well as turning up in dirty clothes, or no clothes, or clothes made of latex. Offer to buy a drink, and not just for yourself. Talk; laugh; occasionally check that food isn't stuck in your teeth: these are the basics, surely, and I think I had most of them covered. But how are you supposed to end a date? There must be a way of saying goodnight that is kind yet definitive and allows both parties to leave with their dignity intact. Whatever it is, if I'm to have any more dates like Elliot, I need to learn it quickly.

3.

WHY SHOULD I LOVE YOU?

The internet: internationally recognised refuge for the awkward, the nocturnal and the garden-variety conspiracy theorist, and now my portal to love.

I should explain.

Elliot didn't text me. He still might but after six days it seems unlikely. Primarily, I feel relieved and if he does get in touch, I'll probably spend a while composing a reply that is kind and compassionate but that doesn't end with my accidentally asking him out again. I didn't expect Elliot to get in touch the day after we met, or even the day after that. But by the third day, I noted that I was checking my phone every so often, just in case; by Day 4, I could barely put it down. On the morning of Day 5, after a sleepless night spent analysing all the possible reasons why a man who wears an anorak didn't fancy me, I was forced to admit that part of me (a very small part; the word 'part' seems excessive, really – fraction might be better, or shard) was disappointed he hadn't got in touch and that, shamefully, it was not because I liked Elliot . . . but because I wanted him to like me. I am not proud of myself. Yesterday, I realised I had a choice: I could burn my arms with cigarettes to assuage my shame, or I could accept that if nothing else, my date with Elliot has triggered my wont for company rather than solitude, intimacy rather than a rapid finger-bang in the bathroom. I thought those feelings had died along with my relationship with Charlie – who knew Elliot the Anorak Guy would be the one to bring them flooding back? Therefore, as I can no longer trust my friends to match me up, I have been forced to contend with the issue myself, and this means the internet.

When I was seven, I planned, officiated and attended the wedding of my Ballerina Barbie to Willy, my anatomically correct boy doll. It was Barbie's third marriage: she had also wed a Captain Scarlet action figure of Bru's and my bear earlier in the year. Barbie went on to live a life of marital bliss with all three husbands because as a child, I had no reason to believe that love wasn't an eternal state, that marriages didn't last a lifetime or that they could only go ahead if both parties were single; I should take to Twitter and campaign for a Polyamorous Barbie to ease confusion for future generations. As Barbie and Willy danced at their reception, I assumed that I would grow up to (firstly, look like Barbie) get married, procreate and work doing my dream job as an artist/hairdresser/Aston

Martin test driver. I had no concept of 'dating'; I knew nothing of unrequited love or rejection. I had my first experience of divorce in Year 3 at primary school when (according to my mother's reconnaissance) Poppy Mason's dad had an affair with their nanny and her mum chucked him out, the sole consequence of which seemed to be that Poppy would get two sets of presents on birthdays and Christmas, a deal my friends and I agreed was pretty sweet and spent the next three weeks hoping our own parents would get divorced too. It wasn't until I hit adolescence and saw the dirty reality of a parental split that I came to truly understand how the solemn vows of marriage, much like puppies and murder sentences, don't always last lifetimes.

My own parents are an exception to the rule: this year they will celebrate their thirty-third anniversary and whenever I want to transport myself back to those Barbie-wedding halcyon days, I remember that Dad tells my mother he loves her every morning before he leaves for work. I respect and admire their achievement, though I don't understand it. How you stay with the same person for thirty-three years, I cannot fathom; if I think about it for too long I start to feel like I'm trapped in a lift and I have to recall Newton's Third Law (for every action, there is an equal and opposite reaction) which fills me with an equivocal sense of panic at the thought of dying alone and balances it out. Internet dating is the palatable Third Way: I can dangle my feet in the dating pool without having to plunge in, or having them torn off by a shark.

Seventeen kerjillion listings popped up when I searched

'online dating'. The sheer abundance of dating sites must mean it is crucial to pick the right one – I don't want to spend my hard-earned money meeting untenable morons. I don't actually want to spend my hard-earned money at all, but my research (ten minutes on a forum for the über-lonely; four minutes chatting to BF) suggests that eternal happiness comes at a price, and that price is £32 a month. After careful consideration, I have opted for Guardian Soulmates on the basis that *I* read the *Guardian* so if a guy has applied the same logic we'll have a lefty sense of righteousness as common ground and we can laugh over Tim Dowling's column as an icebreaker. It's not foolproof: I must stay vigilant for rogue *Telegraph* readers who've cheated the system and signed up by citing Al Gore and quinoa as their interests. Also, in all honesty, I only read the *Guardian* on the weekend. Mainly just the magazine.

As it transpires, choosing the site is nothing compared to the torment of trying to write my profile. I say *writing* . . . to be accurate, I am sitting in Caffè Nero, staring at my laptop screen. A coffee shop is a natural choice of venue for this onerous task, as in my head, writing a dating profile somewhere social makes it marginally less pathetic than writing it alone in my flat, although I'm down £4.20 (soya chai latte and a biscotti for sustenance) and have a feeling I am as pathetic as ever. The general hubbub is not helping my concentration either: whenever I come up with something, a barista fires up the milk-steaming machine and I lose my train of thought.

I sip my drink. I have chosen a table near the back, next to the wall, so that nobody can see what I'm doing, but looking around – and so far that's pretty much all I've done – I wonder how many of the people in here might also be active internet love-hunters. I wonder how many are single and would rather not be.

I'm wondering when everyone stopped calling the internet the World Wide Web.

Now I'm wondering if I want a toastie. I need to focus.

Surely nobody who is sane or over the age of four actually enjoys extolling their own virtues; I couldn't put my old winter coat on eBay without effusive apologies for the sticky zip, and describing myself in anything other than mildly self-deprecating terms makes my teeth ache. Although scanning through other profiles, it appears I'm not alone: '*Let's be desperate together!*' demands Sasha from Bow, as if by collectively accepting our pathos it will simply go away. Thirty-two-year-old Tony from Richmond wants us to tell our friends we '*met in a bar*' which is fine but makes me wonder why Tone doesn't just *go to a bar.*

Right. OK. OK. Let's see. I don't need a toastie. OK . . .

Hi! I'm Rosy, twenty-seven years young . . .

No. No exclamation marks. No whimsy. Delete.

Thanks for looking at my profile, you clearly have good taste . . .

I hold my finger on the backspace and watch the letters whizz away. I might need another chai latte.

The girls – of course. The girls are the key. If I scour what other girls have written, I can steal the best bits from each profile and create a hybrid Perfect Woman in my own image. First up is Anna, 28, from Dalston: she likes cooking roasts, playing Scrabble (she added 'LOL' to imply irony, but Scrabble is awesome so the LOL is on her), going to the gym, going to the cinema and going out with her mates . . . she is not averse, however, to a Sunday afternoon in the pub or having a glass of red in front of a good film. Becky from Islington likes cooking as well – her speciality is chilli. Daisy from Forest Gate is a fellow Merlot drinker; Justine likes to 'chill out and watch a good movie' – it always has to be 'good', as if these girls haven't all watched *Romy & Michele's High School Reunion* seven times.

My own big white box is looking bigger and whiter with every profile I read. I don't *dislike* the cinema, but I don't go as much since I found out a medium tub of sweet popcorn contains 758 calories – the popcorn is the main reason I go. I can't cook, unless stirring pesto into pasta counts, and after last week's display at the gym I can't in good conscience say that I'm into keeping fit. I like going out with my friends, but I also like watching *Masterchef* in my pyjamas whilst eating Special K out of the box, neither of which strikes me as a 'hobby'. My life consists of work, ready meals, seeing my friends and cleaning my flat; as it stands, it doesn't merit a glowing review. In fact, thinking about what I *do* do is making me all the more aware of exactly how much I don't; I'd like to go to gigs but I don't. I moan that the tickets are too expensive or my friends too apathetic but if I spent less money on manicures and take-away coffee I could afford it (though I would have to get new friends). I'd also like to run a half marathon and take guitar lessons. I'd like to actually go to all the exhibitions I currently only read about.

If I'm going to make a go out of this, I'll have to focus on my personality. I'm quite nice – that's the general consensus amongst my friends. What other characteristics do men want in women? Intelligence? Sense of humour? I don't know why, most women aren't funny; I guess trying to make a man laugh is preferable to trying to make him cry. Maybe if I look through all the men's profiles, I can extract the most common personality traits men are after and pretend I have them all.

'Laid back' seems to be popular – presumably this is code for: 'please don't shout at me for getting drunk like my ex used to'. 'Outgoing' and 'up for an adventure' also appear frequently and I'd like to think I'm spontaneous: last week I bought profiteroles, just because I fancied them. But I'd need to know the specifics of any 'adventure' before I decide if I'm up for it: a mini-break in the Cotswolds would be excellent; a surprise, all-expenses jaunt to South America and a month in a Venezuelan jail would not.

I take a fortifying sip of chai latte and begin to type:

> If you like death metal, animal sacrifice and marmalade . . . then you are probably not the guy for me . . .

I think I need a toastie.

* * *

People have been and gone. Men have translated *Beowulf*; women have written novels on laptops; a group of girls bought a round of flat whites and spent over an hour bitching about their friend Carly. Hours have passed, maybe days; I've lost track of time. I have, however, created/ borrowed from other people something that might be pass-able as a profile. This is what I've come up with/stolen:

> Do you like death metal? Animal sacrifice? The smell of rain and puppies? Then I'm not the girl for you.
>
> I'm outgoing, relaxed and always open to an adventure. I haven't drunk red wine since an unspeakable experience at a school disco, but I'll happily drink vodka and soda whilst you finish your bottle of Shiraz. When I'm not at work ruining PR for everyone, I go out with my friends, go to the cinema, go to the gym

> and plan my next backpacking adventure (I
> caught the travel bug after going to Cambodia
> – and amoebic dysentery!).
>
> If you read on past the first sentence, well done!
> And if you liked what you read, why not say hi.

If my amalgam method holds true, I am now officially
the most dateable woman on Guardian Soulmates, probably the internet. I've had to take some licence with the
truth: I didn't backpack round Cambodia so much as
spend a week getting pissed in Bali, and it wasn't dysen-
tery so much as a particularly severe hangover, but this
is an internet dating profile, it's hardly the time or place
for honesty. It's been a struggle and I'm running out of
energy for photo selection. Most people seem to have a
few close-ups where they're smiling and one or two
where they're doing their hobbies but as I don't have
any (hobbies/photos of me doing them) I upload three
from the limited selection on my laptop in which I look
the least grumpy. I want to go home.

* * *

The response to my profile has been unbelievable, by
which I mean, it is hard to believe some of these men
are real, functioning members of society. I had every
intention of waiting at least a day before I logged back
in to see if my profile had garnered a response but I

cracked, eight hours after I sat down in Caffè Nero. I was amazed to see that twelve messages had amassed in my inbox with my future husband undoubtedly amongst them. I don't know how many responses are considered respectable but I read back over my profile and winced until new wrinkles formed, so twelve felt like an achievement.

Unfortunately, I then read the messages. Poor spelling; slang; abbreviations; inexplicable use of apostrophes . . . the confusion around homonyms alone made me want to mainline vodka through my eyeballs. Tom from Hammersmith opened with: '*Hi Rosy, hope your having a good day?*' I have decided to give him the benefit of the doubt, however, having now read 27-year-old Francis's message: '*Hey babe u look soooooo sexy wanna get a drink sumtimes?*' Maslow's Hierarchy of Needs should be amended to include good grammar.

A week has since passed, messages have continued to come in and merely by the law of averages a few have emerged as possibilities. From BF's sofa, I log in surreptitiously whilst she's making us dinner (heating up pizza).

'Is that a dating site?' I didn't hear her come out of the kitchen; she is standing behind me, looking at the screen. I hit the cross to close the window, but it's too late. She hands me a plate. 'Were you messaging someone?' She grins. 'I think you'd better tell me.'

His name is Jonathan. He got in touch a few days ago and he is currently the most promising of the bunch. BF demands I show her our messages on the principle that if she's seen my vagina, she can handle my flirty banter; my protests are useless, so I select a snippet I'm happy for her to read.

Rosy	I don't play any team sports, no – although I was captain of my college cheerleading squad at uni . . .
Jonathan	Captain eh? Does that mean you got to go on top of the pyramid? I was deputy of my rugby team, not quite as good! ever fall off? bet u had some pretty skimpy outfits!
Rosy	The skirts were quite short . . . we had to be careful if it was windy. So do you still play rugby? Which position? My brother and Dad played back in the day so I *might* know what you're talking about . . .
Jonathan	don't get to play much any more unfortu-nately! Used to play a bit for my local team but work gets in the way and u have to make mid-week training to play in matches. I was kinda all over the pitch, not in the scrum. So what do u do for fun?
Rosy	Usual, I guess?? I see my friends a lot, try and get to the gym from time to time . . .

BF says: 'You told him about the cheerleading!' and once she has stopped laughing, adds: 'He sounds all right. Plays it a bit fast and loose with punctuation, though.'

I feel my jaw tighten: that's been concerning me and it's amplified now BF has picked up on it.

'Where does he live?'

This is my other worry. 'Debden? I had to look at the Tube map, it's somewhere at the top of the Central line.'

'And has he asked you out?' she asks.

'Yeah, for Friday.'

'He's given you a Friday?'

'Why do you sound surprised?'

As BF explains it: a Sunday coffee suggests apathy, mid-week drinks is code for, 'you're fit but we'll see' and men reserve weekend dates for girls they think have potential. When she's finished talking, I feel buoyed. Then BF asks where he's taking me. It's not a bar I'd heard of; at the mention of its name, BF arches her eyebrows. 'It's an interesting choice.'

* * *

There are lots of reasons why I rarely venture into Leicester Square, the first of which is that I'm not a tourist but even if I were I wouldn't come here: the area lacks the finesse and character that can be found almost anywhere else in London, and maybe I'm a snob but I don't consider the behemoth M&M store to offer much in the way of cultural capital. For every theatre and cinema in this part of town there is a shop selling Union

Jack junk or an over-crowded, over-priced bar that serves drinks notable for their atomic hue. It is to one of these bars that Jonathan is taking me.

He is waiting for me as I come out of the Tube and I recognise him straight away: he bears a passable resemblance to the six photos he posted on GS. He is tall and slim, which gives him the overall impression of just being *long*, with a smattering of stubble and shorn dark hair that is starting to recede. I've made my peace with a receding hairline (or 'advancing forehead' as my Dad put it when his started to go) because when you are getting on for thirty a boyfriend with a full head of hair is a luxury, not a right. As he leads the way to the bar, I'm starting to get the feeling you could view a hundred photos of somebody and still not have an accurate idea of what they look like.

He pulls open one of the heavy glass door of Letters Bar and I am immediately hit by a wave of noise, quickly followed by the type of cocooning heat you feel upon walking into a greenhouse. London – all of it – appears to be here: the space is packed with the end-of-the-week workers in moist shirts and loosened ties standing back-to-back with groups of giggly girls in tight skirts and vertiginous heels. Along the walls are booths lined in black pleather: in one, a group of students are drinking pints with their coats and laptop bags piled in the corner; two along, two dapper older gents are laughing with equally chic women, who are presumably (hopefully) their wives. A dead bottle of champagne bobs in the cooler between them and there's another on the go. They are too early for the post-theatre crowd and too late for the pre-, and though I am perplexed as to what drew them here, they look like they're having a good time. I wonder if they'll let me join them.

I'm amazed, in fact, that they can hear each other over the pumping Euro-club beats that seem to add to the density of the air. Jonathan is shouting something at me – I know this because I can see his lips moving and the veins straining in his neck, yet all I can hear is: 'Whamf-a-shtupa-alik.' I shake my head and squint: the international sign of incomprehension. 'Would you like a drink?' he yells into my ear canal.

'A vodka and soda please,' I shout back. I wouldn't say no to a lime wedge either, but the effort of asking outweighs the reward. I only have my date with Elliot as a comparison but if alternately shouting at each other is the only way we'll be communicating tonight it doesn't bode well for success. As Jonathan pushes his way to the bar, I spot something miraculous, the metro-politan equivalent of a desert oasis: an empty booth. Everyone else is too busy queuing or chatting or, at 8 p.m., too drunk to notice. Being short has resulted in much humiliation over the years (I was the first student up the scaffolding for the whole school photograph, for example; I was in Year 9 at the time, with two year groups below me) but being a child-sized adult in London has advantages, such as being able to fit myself into gaps on rush-hour Tubes, gaps that to the untrained eye (a.k.a. normal-sized people) look unfeasible. I like to think of myself as a type of Tube Ninja. Right now, it means I can weave in and out of the mass of bodies and claim the booth as my own. I spot Jonathan and wave, watching as he walks over, being careful not to spill our drinks and glaring at anyone with the potential for careless elbows.

He sets our drinks down and manoeuvres into the booth. We clink glasses and say 'cheers' and I go to take a sip just as Jonathan says, 'They do doubles as standard here.' It is all I can do not to gag as the sharp, sour tang of cheap vodka burns its way down my oesophagus.

I put it back down. 'I'll be drunk after more than a couple of these.'

'Let's bulk-buy then!' Jonathan cries and mimes jumping from the booth to flag down barmen.

I force a laugh at the prospect of Jonathan getting me drunk to the point of incapacity. 'I can't believe how busy it is in here.'

'Yeah, it's rammed; it's always like this on a Friday,' he says. Always? How often does he come here? The booth insulates us from some of the noise, but the effort of listening and making myself heard is causing tension to gather at the base of my skull.

A small plus is that the vodka is becoming more palatable the more of it I drink. 'You never told me what you do,' I shout across the table.

'It's a bit unusual,' he shouts back. Maybe he's a dolphin trainer. Maybe he's Willy Wonka. He says: 'I work in security at Gatwick.' He tells me about the 'hilarious' group of 'lads' he works with, all called Gaz, Baz or Daz from what I can make out; apparently they spend a lot of time looking at 'hilarious' videos on YouTube.

'What does your role involve?'

'Have you been to an airport?' Jonathan asks me, leaning in.

I pause. 'I have.'

'And you've flown, yeah?'

'Yes . . .'

'So, before you board you have to go through the scanners – you know which ones I mean? You walk through and they beep? My job is to scan all the hand luggage to see if anyone is trying to smuggle contraband on the plane. Anyone we think is acting a bit suspicious, we have the power to pull them over and search their bags.'

I lean in, too. 'What sorts of things are you looking for?' I laugh: 'Are men in sunglasses and trench coats too obvious?'

'Depends really,' Jonathan continues. 'Anyone acting suspicious, that sort of thing.' He is po-faced; either he's ignored my joke or not realised I've made one – both would be concerning.

'Right, sure.'

Across the table, Jonathan is leaning back, waiting for me to speak.

'I was just wondering, I mean . . . specifically? As in, do you look for a certain behaviour? Lack of eye contact or something?'

'Specifically?' He frowns; I look down at my glass and make a mental note never to fly out of Gatwick again. 'Not really . . . just if someone looks dodgy. A bit suspicious.'

'Right.' My glass now contains a murky mix of watered-down vodka and ice-cubes; I swill it round in the glass. I am officially 0 for 2 on my dating record. My apathy for Jonathan has not been instant like it was with Elliot but it has fermented over time, giving it a stronger bent. It's very confusing. Jonathan came across well in his messages: amusing, interesting – how has he turned out to be so different in person? However, as I'm here, I feel duty bound to make genial conversation until I can think of a reason to leave. 'So, what's the weirdest thing you've ever found in a suitcase? I bet everyone asks you that.'

'Handcuffs,' Jonathan grins. 'Bet you can't guess what they're used for!'

'I think I have an idea,' I chuckle.

'Sex games.'

'Right, yep, got it.'

'What are you having?' It doesn't feel like a question. Jonathan slides out of the booth and stands beside me, waiting for my reply.

'It's my round, isn't it?'

He smirks. 'Girls always do that.'

'Do what, sorry?'

'They pretend they're happy to pay – like, they take forever to find their wallets because they're waiting for the guy to be like, "I'll get this."'

I'm finding it hard to keep up. 'But . . . I really am happy to pay.' I shake my wallet in my hand.

Jonathan smirks. 'Don't worry about it,' he says and starts to walk to the bar. I don't know what just happened; was I supposed to pay? Or insist that I did? He calls back over his shoulder, 'I'll just get you the same again,' which is clearly my punishment.

*   *   *

The moment Jonathan asks me if I've ever had a three-some is the same moment I conclude that internet dating is not for me. I've only had two dates, one of which was not even from the internet, but between them, Elliot and Jonathan have made me want to throw my expensive, uninsured laptop against the wall. Jonathan is chatting away: I can see his lips moving but I've stopped listening; for the past three minutes I've been running through excuses to leave in my head. I could tell him I'm meeting a friend – but then who would arrange to meet a friend on the same night they have a date . . . if I'm going to blow him out, I need an excuse that is plausible and unassailable in case there are follow-up questions. Maybe there are only bad excuses, though. There's no call for good ones; people have to believe bad excuses because the alternative is accepting that your date finds you repellent and can't bear another minute in your company. I could resort to the classic 'early start' like I did with Elliot (not that it exactly panned out): it straddles the border between believability and all-out rejection. Really, what I should do is thank Jonathan for a nice evening and tell him I'm going home. But what if he doesn't get the message? I don't think I could bring myself to add, 'Please never contact me again.'

'Rosy?'

I snap back to attention. 'Yes.'

'Would you like to?'

Oh God – would I like to what? Go home? Or go back to Debden to drink cheap beer whilst Jonathan watches a prostitute called Cherry lick my nipples? On balance, no is the safe option. 'I probably shouldn't, I'm afraid.'

'Come on, one more round.'

'It's tempting . . .' I make myself look like I'm weighing up the options: another foul drink with Jonathan or heading home, buying a Wispa on the way and getting into my pyjamas.

'Come on,' he says and leans back hard so he thumps against the booth, 'don't be a dick.'

'I'm going to head home,' I say, firmer this time. 'Thanks, though, I've had a good time.'

'Seriously, you're going?' He sounds genuinely amazed.

'Fine. You're not that fit, just thought I might as well try.' With men like Jonathan, no is always the safe option.

When I get home, I climb into bed with my laptop and log into my GS account. There are nine unread messages in my inbox, three of which have spelling mistakes in the first line; I go through the rest one by one but they are all fairly nondescript. Up until tonight the unopened messages in my inbox held the same thrill as a pile of colourful envelopes on the day before my birthday; it's a buzz that wears off as you get older and realise that only a few of the cards, just like the messages, will be meaningful (it's the cards with the cheques in, by the way). The others might look all right but eventually they'll end up in the bin. I open my thread with

Jonathan and scroll up to the beginning, looking for any clues to suggest he's been a patronising, uncouth wanker all along. In his first message, he made a flirty reference to my school disco that made me laugh at the time but now I can hear him saying it: '. . . *and do you still do unspeakable things <u>without</u> red wine???*' Ugh. I scroll on; details that I'd initially found attractive – the rugby playing, that he likes to cook – are now redundant; they belong to the 'Jonathan' I created in my head: well-mannered, rugged yet sensitive, smart but not pompous . . . the Jonathan who I pictured cooking dinner on a Sunday night whilst I read the *Guardian* on our Habitat sofa with a glass of Sauvignon Blanc. Even had Real Jonathan taken me to a nice bar and made interesting conversation, instead of trying to get me hammered and calling me a dick, he wouldn't have matched up to the fantasy in my mind. I should have listened to my instincts: his laissez-faire approach to grammar meant it was never going to work. I select the thread and click to delete it. Guardian Soulmates wants to know if I'm sure, and finally I am.

4.

L'AMOUR LOOKS SOMETHING LIKE YOU

BF knows that the answer to any crisis, especially one concerning men and a desolate, loveless future, is a cold bottle of white wine, a family bag of Doritos (each) and a rousing recital of the Female Pep-Talk. At eighteen years and one day, women, all of us, wake up with The FPT instinctively in our heads as though we've been listening to tapes in our sleep for the last eighteen years (we also know how to quit smoking and some beginner Spanish). It covers many different facets of womanhood, from ageing to dating to which body parts you should never, under any circumstance, ever shave – and everything in between. As women, we recite relevant parts to each other whenever a fellow female is sad, vulnerable or lonely and its purpose is to relieve said female's anxiety thus restoring her capacity to function, i.e. to work, to date, to get out of bed (it depends on the crisis). It doesn't matter that The FPT is based on felonious half-truths and conjecture – 'Of course you won't die alone!' 'They'd be stupid not to hire you!' 'There's no way he's fucking the super-hot receptionist when you're so familiar and comfortable' – because that's not the point; the point is to show your friend/sister/cleaner that even if the world is about to screw her over, you'll still be there, cheering her on. This evening, BF is doing a sterling job (In regard to Jonathan: 'He said that? Cock. You're well rid') and the wine is having a suitably pacifying effect. We channel-hop in search of trash to watch, eventually landing on a film that involves Nicolas Cage driving a series of cars around a city at high speed. I'm getting quite into it; Angelina Jolie has just popped up. BF is sitting beside me, tapping away at her phone.

I deleted my GS account. A promising thread with a guy named Owen fizzled out, and with scant few messages coming in it was too much effort for so little reward. It's been a week since, and despite the odd low moment of Googling 'single all-female retirement communities' whilst two thirds of my way through a bag of doughnuts, I'm content with my decision; men and women have been copulating for centuries without a laptop, the internet isn't the only way to meet men. I'm sociable; I go places and sometimes the places I go have men in them. I should go to more bars; I can offset the financial outlay and potential liver damage with the assurance that eventually, I shall definitely meet a man who is attractive, intelligent and (for a reason I have yet to decide) desperate to get married.

I know it works because that's how my parents met. Dad was at a bar celebrating his colleague's birthday and Mum was there too, having been persuaded to go by her best friend Liz, who is now my godmother (had the story ended differently, she'd now be 'Liz, that lush Mum can't stand'). Dad claims he spotted Mum as soon as she came through the door and waited all night for the opportune moment to approach her; Mum insists that he spent most of the evening looking at the barmaid's breasts and it was only a serendipitously timed toilet trip that saw them meet at all. Dad was sent abroad with work not long after, and he wrote her letters, one every week.

'I wish people still wrote letters,' I say to BF.

'Hm?'

'Nobody writes love letters any more. If a man wrote me a letter, I'd be, you know . . .' I click my fingers. 'Done.'

She looks up at me briefly and says, 'I don't understand what you're saying,' before returning to her phone.

I hear keys turn in the front door. Oona walks into the living room and flops into the green chair, still wearing her coat. I ask how her day has been, though I suspect I know the answer.

'Long,' she says, 'very tiring.'

BF looks up. She says, 'Hi . . .' then stops, because she can never remember which of my housemates is which. It doesn't matter: Oona says a curt hello in response and it's clear she can't recall BF's name either. There's a chance she never learnt it to begin with.

'Whilst you're here,' says Oona, levering off each of her heels with the opposite foot, 'don't forget the council tax comes out this month.'

'I've already put the money in the account,' I tell her/ lie.

'Does Harriet know?'

'I'm sure she does.' I hope she does. None of us wants a repeat of the Water Bill Disaster from last autumn.

Oona rests her head against the side of the chair and turns her attention to the TV. 'What on earth are you watching?'

'It's a film about cars. With Nicolas Cage.'

'Is it a documentary?'

'I don't think it is.'

Oona makes what might be the vocal equivalent of a shrug and gathers up her bag and shoes. 'I'm going to take a shower then go to bed, so if you could make sure the TV is turned down . . . I'm up early tomorrow, so I might not see you until the weekend.'

'OK. Night, Oona.'

'Goodnight.'

'Night,' says BF, my ambivalent echo. There is no sign of her venturing towards her own home; instead, her phone seems to have become a hypnotic vortex from which she cannot look away. I say her name and get nothing, so I give her a shove and demand to know what the fuck is so interesting. 'You've been on your phone for ages. Are you texting someone?'

'No.' She smiles and finally meets my gaze. 'I'm on Tinder.'

'What's Tinder?'

'It's amazing, you should get on it.'

'I still don't know what it is.'

BF shuffles towards me and holds out her phone. On the screen, a bearded man is peering out at us wearing a striped beanie and holding a guitar with his name and age listed below: he is Bryan, and he is twenty-nine. At the bottom of the screen there is a green heart and an ominous red X.

'What do you think of Bryan?' asks BF. 'Fit or not?'

I lean in closer to the screen. 'I don't feel strongly either way . . . why? Does it matter?'

'Yes, that's the point. On spec, are you attracted to him?' BF taps his face and four additional photos pop up: Bryan in a pub; Bryan with a dog; here's Bryan with his friends, who all look much like Bryan himself.

'I suppose, if I had to say . . . he's not really my type.'

'No, not mine either,' says BF, and she swipes her thumb left across the screen; in a split second, Bryan disappears and is replaced by Travis, 30.

'Where's Bryan?'

'He's gone.'

'Where?'

BF sighs and turns to me face-on. 'Tinder is like a supermarket of men. Every time you swipe, a different man pops up and you can decide whether to Like him or move on.'

'How do you Like someone?'

'You swipe to the right instead of left.' BF continues flicking the screen left, discounting faces so quickly they become a blur, muttering, 'No, no, no . . .' as she goes. Then she stops; a gorgeous man – blond, tanned, clear green eyes – stands in board shorts beside a glistening turquoise pool, a beer in hand and a wide, bright smile spread across his beautiful face. The man is called Ed and he is twenty-seven.

'I like Ed,' I say.

'Me too,' BF agrees, 'so instead of swiping left, we swipe him right.' LIKE, writ large, flashes momentarily on the screen; Ed is gone and the next man (Colin, 30) fills the screen.

'But where's Ed gone? Does he know you Liked him? Can you get him back?' I can't stop my questions pouring out. Before BF can answer, the screen changes again: suddenly Ed's picture is spinning towards us below the words: 'You have a match!' This must be good because BF beams.

'So now we've matched,' she explains, 'because we both Liked each other – and in answer to your question, no, he'd never have known I Liked him otherwise. It means we can start messaging each other; you can't do that unless you've matched.'

'I wish Guardian Soulmates had that feature.' I twitch at the memory of Mani from Tottenham, for whom my rebuttals seemed to serve only as encouragement. BF continues swiping. Justin, Amir and Gavin all fly away as she swipes left, left, left. 'They could be the loves of your life,' I say.

'They're not.'

'How do you know?'

BF looks at me, her right eyebrow cocked. 'You just do – you said you knew as soon as you saw Elliot.'

'Yeah, but he was standing in front of me, in the flesh. And we had a real date that confirmed it – you're looking at these guys for half a second at most.'

'I just don't think they're attractive, then.'

'That's quite shallow.' BF shrugs and turns back to her phone. I look at the TV. Vinnie Jones has turned up.

I'm not sure what to make of Tinder – it looks alarming. My mother would hate it; she'd lump it in with the celeb-rities who dare fall in love. 'They've only known each other for ten minutes!' she rants (I've taken to leaving the room if I think there's a chance she's about to engage with media of any type). 'It's not a wedding, it's a publicity stunt.' She refers to them all as *those female pop stars* (despite many not being pop stars at all) and says they treat their marriage vows like their live shows – 'just miming the words'. My mother worries that marriage is becoming disposable. She and Dad had a rough couple of years when I was in my late teens; Bru had left for university by then and at first he didn't believe me as I recounted their arguments and the subsequent days of silence down the phone. Neither of my parents would talk to me about it. After one particularly painful weekend (a plate was thrown) I sat with Mum as she did the ironing and asked if they were going to get divorced. 'When storms come,' she said – I remember it so vividly – 'you batten down the hatches, you don't move to another country.'

'But what if it's a tornado?' I had asked her. 'An affair tornado, because somebody had an affair?'

'Nobody's had an affair,' she told me sternly. I watched as she folded one of Dad's shirts with mathematical precision. 'You do your best. You muddle through and you remember why you said your vows in the first place.' The idea of an app that encourages you to discard someone based on your one tenth of a second impression would be anathema to her. Dad wouldn't care so much, especially if there's cricket on.

I look over at BF who is still men shopping, the lucky ones dropping into her basket, the rejects presumably relegated to the Tinder equivalent of the wheelie bins out back in hope that a Freegan might fish them out at 2 a.m. As I watch, she matches with a man named Jose and it's only then that I see it – I didn't spot it when she matched with Ed: once all the spinning, tapping and mutual lust is affirmed, Tinder has a question for you: 'Keep playing?' I repeat the phrase to BF, who nods sagely. 'It always says that. It doesn't mean anything.'

Is Tinder supposed to be a game? If so, the prize is . . . what? A shag? A boyfriend? A trip down the aisle? BF blitzes through the endless stream of faces as if they are nothing more than carefully arranged pixels rather than actual men who laugh and fart and pretend they're not crying at the end of *Toy Story 3*. From my side of the sofa, it looks like the least romantic way to find love I've ever seen.

5.

HOUNDS OF LOVE

Something is ringing. It's either my phone or the smoke alarm in the kitchen alerting me to an inferno that is tearing its way through the flat; I heard it in my dream but now I'm awake and the noise is happening here too. Fortunately, my phone is glowing in the darkness so though I'm awake unnecessarily I am not about to die. I reach for it, fumbling on the bedside table until my hand chances upon it. 'Hello?'

'WE'RE ENGAGED!' someone yells, as I recoil from the handset. 'Bob asked me to marry him!'

After nine years of friendship, Kate's faint Welsh burr is instantly recognisable but in my drunk-sleep state I squint at the screen just to check. I try to say, 'That's amazing!' but it must come out as drunk-sleep noise because Kate replies, 'What? Shit, did I wake you?'

I come to and heave myself up to sitting, then turn

on my lamp; my alarm clock reads 12.37 a.m. 'No! Well, yes, but I'm awake now . . . Kate, that's wonderful, that's so wonderful – I'm so happy for you.'

'Thank you!' she squeals. 'We've only just got home . . . we went out for dinner and he'd been acting strange all night and then he suggested we walk back instead of getting the Tube even though I was in heels . . .' The proposal story tumbles out of her mouth: it involves a walk along the river, romantic lighting of some kind, a bench, a bottle of champagne that had been secreted . . . it ended with a large diamond which is sort of the point of the story. Plus their everlasting love, etc.

The relief in Kate's voice as she says 'the ring is beautiful' is audible down the phone. The thought of receiving a bad engagement ring choice (*Abhorred of the Rings* as I once, hilariously, dubbed it) is a spectre that has long haunted our Fantasy Wedding chats: your boyfriend plans the perfect proposal only to open the box and reveal a shocker of a ring: a coloured gem, say, or a *princess* cut . . . the horror.

Kate starts telling me about her ideas for the dress, the venue and the cake; we talk about Bob and his general amazingness and decide on a planning schedule, to commence immediately. Several years ago, Kate and I stood in the corner of a Christmas drinks party thrown by our uni friend Barrett and reminisced about his wedding to Isla the Psychotherapist – he had been one of the first of the group to get married. Kate had said: 'You get together, you fall in love, you move in together, then he asks to marry you – that's just what happens.' Kate met Bob six months later; she knew at a year that she wanted to marry him and though she's had to wait a further five for him to ask, everything happened just as she said. 'I'm so thrilled for you, Kate,' I tell her as our conversation winds down. 'I am really, really thrilled for you.' I tell her I love her and she says it back before we hang up and my bedroom is dark and still. It's close to half one; I want to go back to sleep but my mind keeps drifting back to the drinks party and the surety in the way Kate said, *'That's just what happens.'* We were interrupted by the start of the limbo competition soon after and then I got drunk, but I remember feeling unsettled. And I feel the same, lying here, in the darkness, thinking of Kate, my parents – even Harriet, and the confidence in the way she presented Craig as if to say: *'Here's a man – now what's the problem?'* To me, the idea of relationships, and love, and the convention of marriage with its assertions of forever . . . these are arbitrary concepts, intangible, inscrutable, and yet the standard by which they are measured is concrete: you *just know*; they are *The One*. I remember now what I was thinking, just before the music came on and a mop was proffered for a limbo bar: *life isn't a straight line.*

In the morning, my bus – the same bus I get to work every morning and have done, day in, day out, for the last three years – is on diversion. The traffic is backed up too, so I'm going to be late despite having left my flat early. Then when I looked in my hand mirror to check I hadn't got toothpaste on my top I saw that one of my earrings is in situ, but my other lobe was vacant. I have to scramble through the detritus in my bag to find my phone. I take it out and check Facebook. Kate has posted her engagement news with a photo of the ring – it's stunning – along with two others: the first is of her and Bob the first night we all met him and the other is one I took of them last week when we all met for a drink. Bob looks older; Kate looks thinner. Fourteen congratulatory messages have amassed under Kate's status in the past ten minutes; most of the names I recognise, though there are several I don't and these mystery girls (the messages are almost exclusively from girls) have written things like, 'Welcome to the club!' and 'I'll give you my contacts book!' They must be her 'other' friends – her married friends from work and yoga. Either that or Kate's been admitted to the Freemasons. She's got Sophie and she's got me – why does she need more friends?

Talking of whom: Sophie has left a message involving emojis and multiple exclamation marks – it's the only message to which Kate has replied: '*It'll be you next.*' I read it three times. Kate's right; we all know it won't be long before Ollie proposes, even Sophie, but I can't stop staring at the words. First Kate will get married, then Sophie, then they'll both move to the suburbs and get pregnant and they'll never invite me round in case I get my single, promiscuous sex germs all over their kids. When I look out of the bus window, I have no idea where I am.

*   *   *

Despite being late, I've had a productive morning: five items have officially been crossed off my to-do list, which

I feel warrants a celebratory trip to the Big Sainsbury's for lunch. I take my time perusing the aisles, weighing up the pros and cons of various flavours of Monster Munch, and after fierce internal debate I opt for Roast Beef, plus a chicken noodle salad, a small box of sushi, Diet Coke and a small packet of nuts. My last decision before heading back is the chocolate. I've whittled it down to a choice of five; I don't allow myself hardcore chocolate bars often so it's essential I make the right decision. I pick up a Twirl, then put it back, letting my fingers hover above the Galaxy, but a Galaxy feels a bit fancy for today. A Twix? I take it, put it down and ponder Maltesers, then grab the Twix and a Twirl and run to the checkout before I stop myself. I eat the Twirl on the way back to the office so that it doesn't count. At my desk, I pick at the rest of my lunch and take a quiz on Buzzfeed to find out which Disney Princess I am; I end up with Cinderella so I keep taking it until I get Ariel from *The Little Mermaid*.

I've deliberately saved the Diet Coke for the inevitable 3 p.m. slump when, for reasons beyond my under-standing, it is physically painful to keep my eyes open and I have to shy away from important tasks (I learnt this after I sent a journalist an email that had been meant for Charlie; fortunately the journalist and I were friendly, otherwise I would have been fired on the content of the first two lines alone). I text BF, asking if she's seen Kate's news; she replies straight away saying that she has and thinks it's great, though not a surprise. She asks if I'll get a plus one to the wedding; I think of how the vein in Kate's forehead bulges when I skew the numbers at her dinner parties. I text back and say yes.

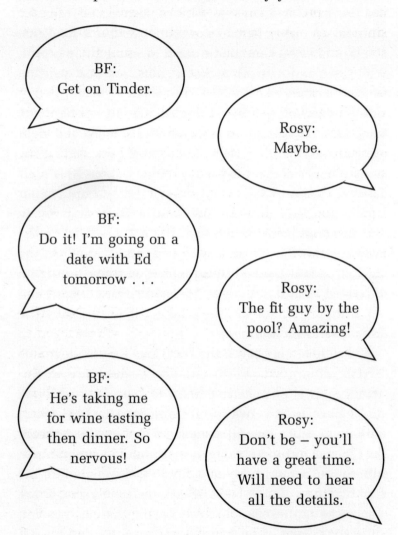

I stash my phone and turn my attention back to the report I've been working on for the last three days, which has yet to prove of any interest. I've wanted to be a writer since I was eight years old, when an author visited our school and I found out that writing was something people will pay you to do. I have since discovered that *other* people – people like my boss, for instance – will also pay you to write, but instead of stories they want reports about the press coverage you've garnered for each of your clients over the quarter . . . PR is not quite what I dreamed about as a little girl. Still, at least I'm writing something. As an adult, I dream of having a mansion and tits like Kate Upton: you have to make the best of what you've got.

It takes me three hours (and two cans of Diet Coke) to finish the report, plus another hour to proofread it, but I get it done. When Helen makes overtures for a cup of tea I jump up, desperate for respite from my screen.

I stare at the kettle, waiting for the water to boil. I already know what's going to happen: BF will get together with Ed and a few months later they'll be in love and rarely out of bed. Kate will throw herself into the wedding and because Sophie is next in line she'll get sucked in too; meanwhile I'll be sitting at home eating tuna from a tin and my friends will shun me because I'm single and/or I've stopped washing. They might take pity on me occasionally and invite me to hang out but the conversation will be about the merits of bridesmaid dresses in navy vs midnight blue and I'll be forced to sit in the corner, quiet and hungry because I left my tin of tuna at home. I should get a hobby, something solitary.

The kettle comes to the boil just as I hear my phone beep . . . or I thought I did; when I check it, there's nothing new, just my messages with BF. I re-read the last one she sent: *Get on Tinder.* It seems like Tinder is everywhere: I've seen people swiping on buses, in cafés, right under my nose – the swift thumb-swipe motion is so distinctive I don't need to see the screen to recognise a Tinderite at work. A few days ago, I stood behind two girls who were discussing it whilst in line at Caffè Nero. The first was complaining about the dearth of attractive men on Tinder of late; her friend agreed, then recounted her most recent date, starting with: 'I think he turned up drunk.' The first one decided she wanted a muffin but they just kept chatting away so it was ten minutes before I finally got my chai latte. Tinder is seeping into my life whether I want it there or not.

I take the tea through to Helen and sit down with my own cup and check through my inbox: no new messages. I look at my phone – nothing. Even the junk in my personal email is thin on the ground today. Facebook is vacant but for the constant wave of messages for Kate, twenty-nine so far, a constant stream of elation and love that is growing by the second. It's not that it isn't warranted: Kate is one of the kindest, smartest, most considerate people you're ever likely to meet, as is Bob. Yet as I read through – Congratulations! Well done! You can finally relax! – it's starting to feel as if getting married is some sort of huge . . . achievement. *No need to worry about spinsterhood – you're getting married! Today, you are a woman-wife, my friend!* I couldn't be happier for Kate – I am delighted that she and Bob are so in love they are ready to make that commitment; I'm just yet to be convinced that marriage is the peak of a woman's success.

My phone beeps as I'm putting on my coat to go home. I rush to check it to find a message from my bank, reminding me about the prospects for my ISA. On the bus home, I download Tinder.

*   *   *

I had steeled myself for a protracted registration process, but simply by downloading the app I was up and running on Tinder; it pillaged my Facebook identity thus giving me a profile picture and making me available to see and be seen. I flick through my first set of faces slowly, examining each one in turn, taking time to go through each man's photos rather than swiping either way based on the display model . . . although some do get an outright no: like Freddie, who was nigh on twenty stone with hair longer than mine. Adam, John, a guy calling himself Tex . . . I give them all due consideration but ultimately swipe them left. A couple could have gone either way, and I have no doubt that most of these men are smart, polite and interesting, but at thirty-four, JD has been the youngest so far. I keep swiping in hope that some more age-appropriate men might appear, but then Tinder slams into reverse and gives me a glut of 'men' in their late teens. I scroll faster, but only Ali and Lee are closer to my own age. Tinder is broken. Maybe it's messing with me.

Although . . . did BF mention something about changing her preference settings? I had thought she meant from men to women, that she was experimenting and that I should give her space to bring it up as and when she was ready, but it dawns on me that perhaps she was referring to age as well. It takes me a while to find my settings but yes, preferences for both age and location can be adjusted. Narrowing down my age bracket is tricky: twenty-five to thirty-five is a nice, round decade but twenty-five strikes me as quite young. Starting at my own age of twenty-seven is the obvious solution but how old to go up? Thirty-five? What if the love of my life is thirty-six? It's such an arbitrary decision. Lines must be drawn somewhere, however, and it's better to take my chances with twenty-seven to thirty-five-year-olds than risk being harangued by middle-aged men or ending up being single forever. Setting my location range is far easier: 3 km from my current location. I don't want to schlep across town every time I want to have sex.

With my settings confirmed, Tinder finally gives up the goods: the guys come thick and fast and despite my cautious approach to Liking, I get my first match, with Seb and his *Vogue*-worthy cheekbones. He sends a message instantly, saying hello: hearing the ping from my phone results in the same sensation I got from licking a battery in Year 5 science. We start to chat: basic stuff – where do you live, what do you do – and six messages in, he mentions that all my pictures are the same, adding: '*Not that I don't like them!*' Sadly it's too late for Seb: he's all but forgotten as I scroll back to my profile and

flick through my available photos: he's right. Four identical shots of me with a wreath of flowers in my hair
taken at a party last year; it's a rookie Tinder error. I see
now that Tinder steals but one Facebook photo for your
main profile shot and you have to do the rest. Photos
are the main event on Tinder – there's a lot riding on
my choice. I want to project that I'm fun and popular,
so I need a shot where I'm surrounded by friends,
although not one with my better-looking friends standing
too close. And none where my smile has caused my
right eye to scrunch up to half the size of my left, even
if it does discount at least 50 per cent of my back catalogue. No photos that make my upper arms look fat or
my face unduly round; nothing in which I look drunk
so most of my uni ones can go (even though I'm probably only drunk in about half of them). I was dying my
hair blonde for the last year Charlie and I were together
but three days after he left I walked up to the high street
and bought a packet of Oreos, a bottle of vodka and a
box of home hair dye in Dark Passionate Cacao. It was
my attempt at the 'fuck-you' makeover that sees most
girls surface from the pit of heartbreak as a prettier,
slimmer, chicer version of their former selves. I managed
to emerge as the gothic meth-head version of myself.
Sadly, any photos in which my hair is not its natural
ginger should probably be discounted, lest I fall foul
of the Trade Descriptions Act. This leaves me with a
total of eight viable pictures; I'll post the first four,
gauge the response and rotate until I find the most
seductive combination.

6.

ALL WE EVER LOOK FOR

Tinder is addictive: *The West Wing* addictive, chocolate-coated pretzels addictive. My journey to and from work – usually a forty-nine-minute stop-start hell ride featuring screaming children and racist pensioners – has become a voyage of tranquility as I swipe and Like away. It's been four days since I joined, in which time I've had twenty-three matches and fifteen messages. There are several strong contenders but my current front-runner is Patrick who had me at hello:

Patrick:
I've been thinking
hard about what to
say to impress you.

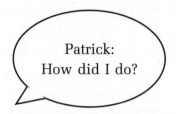

Patrick:
How did I do?

We've been chatting non-stop for four days. He's into sport, and he likes travelling, and he usually chooses fish over meat in restaurants like I do. We like the same movies and he goes to gigs of the bands I've always wanted to get into. I have another promising match in Graham who works with children and shares my love of Nineties dance, but a third, Mark, started off strong before his messages became intermittent and my interest waned. With so many other people to talk to, loss of momentum is fatal on Tinder. This is just one of the many things I've already learnt in the short time I've been in the Tindersphere. There is, it seems, a right and a wrong way to use Tinder; generally, most people swipe until they see someone attractive, Like them and hope for a match. This is the wrong way of using Tinder. Only since becoming an avid Tinderite myself have I discovered the Rules and one must adhere to them to avoid a date with Boring McHalitosis of This-Is-Going-Nowhere-Under-Lyme.

The First Rule: Explore *all* available photos before swiping right; this rule is essential, yet so easily forgotten in the midst of a frenzied swiping binge.

'*But he's hot!*' you cry before recklessly nudging him right. There will be consequences.

The Second: Swipe left anyone whose profile is black and white, as it means they are ugly. Monochrome is more flattering than colour. The subject knows this, he knows *you* know this, but he remains hopeful that a good B/W profile shot might lure you in. Anyone who has all his photos in B/W should be avoided at all costs.

The Third: If a man is wearing a hat, he is bald. Now this need not be a deal-breaker – look at Jason Statham, Taye Diggs, Stanley Tucci (Stanley might be a personal choice); I know lots of girls who are unfazed by a follically challenged man – I know some who actively seek it. But don't underestimate the significance of a hat, as it is also indicative of ginger hair (again, not untenable: look at Damian Lewis and . . . just look at Damian. Also, I'm ginger).

The Fourth: Swipe any man who describes himself as 'cheeky'. Just because.

The Fifth: This was something BF flagged up and, arguably, it's the most important rule of all. If a man is not standing next to anything, he is short. The key here is scale: it's helpful if the man is next to an inanimate object. Something common like a post box is useful as it provides instantly discernable perspective.

Several other, less subtle rules also contribute to Tinder success: if a guy has taken a selfie of his torso, he is a moron. The same goes for any man with a photo of his penis, except he is both a moron and a perverted pillock. And there are patterns, which the discerning Tinderite can use to work out what a guy is like from just five photos.

Men do not choose their photos arbitrarily. A single man must prove he is kind and not psychopathic and the best way to do this is to hold a small dog or, better yet, a baby. All women are desperate to get married (all of us – remember, it's our life ambition) so to get a girlfriend men must imply they share this goal (they can renege at a later date) by posting a photo of themselves at a friend's wedding – this will also prove a man has friends. To labour this point, he will load up his profile with confusing group shots that make it hard to discern which one he is (NB: he's usually the least attractive one). He will show he's adventurous (ski shot) and enjoys travel (beach shot) whilst demonstrating he is outgoing (festival shot) and has a sense of humour (fancy-dress shot) . . . at the very least, he is seeking to prove he doesn't spend weekends playing X-box and eating cereal in his bedroom.

I've been adhering strictly to the Rules of late and in combination with the rapid swipe technique I've developed I almost miss Liam, but I spot him and stop just as I'm about to resign him to Tinder purgatory. My thumb hovers over his face, smiling out from the screen, making me smile back. It's a photo I took when we were at a festival a couple of years ago: he is wearing sunglasses and has the remnants of cheap day-glo face paint smeared across his cheek; it wasn't that sort of festival, but we'd drunk too much cider to pull ourselves back. This is not an issue I've encountered before – what's the rule for when you see a friend on Tinder? If we match, is that weird? But what if we both know the other is on here, yet only one of us Likes . . . without knowing the etiquette, I'm better off engaging in off-Tinder contact so I switch to texting.

Rosy:
You're on Tinder!

Liam:
Then so are you!

Rosy:
Busted. What do
you think?

Liam:
Reserving
judgement so far.

Rosy:
No fruitful
matches then?

Liam:
Can you really tell
if you like
someone after a
few messages?

> Rosy:
> That's why you
> have to arrange a
> REAL date.

> Liam:
> Hm . . . sounds like
> a lot of
> commitment . . .

I met Liam when he started as a junior account executive six months after me; he got fired after a further eight, his pared-down approach having done nothing to ingratiate him to the MD, whose name I can never remember. Liam is the archetypal Tinder demographic: chatting up girls whilst watching football is Liam's dating ideal. Yet energy is required even in the Tindersphere, especially if you're a man – just as I would rarely approach a man in a bar, I rarely make the first move on Tinder.

Liam asks about work and I fill him in on the office gossip (highlight: Short Martin's yoghurt was taken from the fridge – the culprit remains at large) and he tells me about the wreck of a vehicle he's most recently devoted himself to renovating. He is keen that we should catch up properly and I am equally enthusiastic in my response, yet we both sign off without setting a date. 'ASAP'; 'really soon'; 'I'll text you tomorrow' . . . this is the paltry level of commitment I extend to my friends these days, as if a host of potentially better offers are just on the horizon or I'm waiting for a life-saving organ transplant for which I must be available AT ALL TIMES. Neither is true, yet these days tying oneself down to a pre-arranged time and location seems to hold some nameless dread. I reopen Tinder and browse through Liam's photos. He has posted two photos of himself with friends and one in which he is holding (what I hope is) a chicken, but there are no puppies, no adrenaline shots on a mountain and no idyllic beach scenes; it's just him, with his T-shirt tan and thick hair flopping over his eyes in that slightly disheveled way he pulls off with aplomb. He half smiles and he doesn't turn on his full beam until he really likes you. I have never seen someone so at ease with themselves as Liam, so content to just be. He is one of those people who feel more present in the room once they've left it; when he talks to you, it's like he's sharing a secret. But the women of Tinder won't know this; they might focus on his creased shirt and crooked nose and instantly swipe him left. I feel angry thinking about it, and sad. I feel sangry. I could never date him myself; after three years of platonic friendship, I know too much about him.

I am on the verge of sleep when my phone beeps.

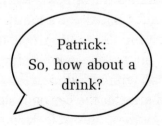

Patrick:
So, how about a
drink?

7

MOMENTS OF PLEASURE

I am lost. I shouldn't be because I've been to this area before, plus I have a map on my phone showing me where I am, where the bar I was supposed to be at five minutes ago is, as well as my location in relation to said bar, but it's saying I'm almost outside it when I'm clearly not. Getting lost is my thing, the same way other people are really funny or great dancers. I get the same feeling when I'm lost that anyone else might experience upon being told they're going to prison for a crime they didn't commit; time marches on in spite of my need for it to stop or rewind and I become gradually consumed by a darkness so black and dense I have to sit down and put my legs between my knees. I take to the pavement to do so now; it is from this low vantage point that I notice the small, muted sign for the bar on a side street opposite. Patrick, presumably possessing the navigational skills of a normal person, is waiting at a table to the side of the bar, studying the label on his beer bottle as I rush in.

'I'm so sorry I'm late,' I gush, the way you might apologise to your lover, or someone you've just hit with your car.

'Don't worry, I've only just got here myself,' says Patrick, though I note his beer is all but finished. He leans in to kiss me hello. He has hazel eyes that are so wide they are almost circular and for a second, as I gaze into them, I feel like I'm lost again; the warmth resonating from his body is making me unbearably hot.

'Can I get you a drink?' he asks.

'I'd love a . . .' I begin, except I can't think what I'd love; my mind appears to have emptied of cogent thought.

'A glass of wine? A beer?' Patrick seems relaxed, so hopefully he is unaware of the abject panic happening in my head. I keep thinking *a shot of tequila*, which isn't helping.

'A spirit?' he prompts. 'Like a gin and tonic or . . .'

'Yes! A gin and tonic, that would be great, thanks.' Patrick has to come past me to get to the bar and I catch the scent of his aftershave as he passes. It almost makes me forget I hate gin and tonic.

* * *

'A lot of us came down to London together after uni and my friends Sophie and Kate and I lived in this soulless flat that was essentially a corridor with rooms off it, which of course we thought was amazing . . .' I am talking quickly and I'm talking a lot; it has been this way for the last twenty minutes and I know I need to stop, yet I am still doing it. I've covered my job, my family and my deep, enduring love for Amy Poehler; I've offered up analysis on the Middle East, daytime television and animal rights. Patrick has bought another round of drinks in the time I've been talking. The more I talk, the more he listens – it is both his downfall and his merit. He is such a good listener that I am pouring myself into him just so he'll keep his round eyes trained on mine. Through his shirt I can see the outline of his toned, muscular chest and it has been the catalyst of a fantasy involving Patrick, sweaty and topless, toiling in a wheat field. I think this might be the other reason I'm still talking: I am scared Patrick is too attractive for me. I need to try and impress him with my mind.

I conclude my latest Homeric anecdote and take a breath. 'My round,' I say.

'No, sorry,' says Patrick, raising his palms to me. 'First date prerogative: the man pays.'

'Then I'm overruling you.' I pull my wallet from my bag. 'What would you like? If you don't tell me, I'll guess and you probably won't like the outcome.'

Patrick laughs. He thinks I'm funny. Unless it was a pity laugh? 'I'm not going to argue. Just another beer, if that's OK?'

'It's my pleasure.' I float to the bar. So maybe it is possible to 'know': I knew outright that Elliot and

Jonathan were wrong and it's no different with Patrick, just the opposite feeling.

Back at the table, we get into a conversation about music and specifically bad music, the music you hide in a playlist called 'Songs for Mum's birthday' in case someone stumbles across them. I've confessed that Ace of Base's seminal work *Happy Nation* is one of my most-played albums – I've never said that out loud. Patrick laughs, again. It is definitely not a pity laugh.

'Now you have to tell me yours.'

'You can't judge me,' he says.

'You didn't judge me.'

'Well, not outwardly . . .' Patrick slides his eyes to the floor, feigning derision. He leans towards me conspiratorially. 'OK . . .' He waits a beat then, deadpan, says: 'Enya.'

The corner of my mouth twitches. 'Seriously?'

'Seriously.'

'I . . . well . . .'

'Oh God, I know . . .' Patrick laughs, which is a sound I am growing to love; I let myself join in as he tells me he got into Enya through his mum and decide this is our first official in-joke. 'Enya' can be the code-word for all the secret, guilty passions we share; Enya's *Greatest Hits* will feature amongst the pile of presents I'll buy him for his birthday; we'll play her for the first dance at our wedding. I watch his Adam's apple bob as he takes a gulp of beer, then he excuses himself to the toilet like he's apologising ('I don't like leaving you at the table by yourself'). He bounds up the stairs two at a time.

I rest my chin in my hand and giggle. My first Tinder date is also shaping up to be the best date I've had, ever, bar none. My first date with Charlie doesn't come close: he took me to a house party with all his friends – it was barely classifiable as a date. But this, with Patrick, this is real. We are grown-ups, having grown-up drinks, in search of a grown-up type of relationship somewhere down the line. We're not being buffeted by drunk people or drowned out by music and I'm not bored (Elliot) or mildly repulsed (Jonathan) and desperate to go home. In fact going back to my flat is the last thing on my mind.

*   *   *

The shots were Patrick's idea: he came back from the bar carrying our drinks, plus a shot of sambuca for each of us. I detest the taste of aniseed in all its guises but when Patrick counts to three I throw it back; this way, he will know I'm fun. And funny. I'm definitely drunk as we launch into a conversation about cars; we weave in and out of topics, talking about everything and nothing and for the whole time his eyes are fixed on mine and he never takes them off. At some point, I notice that we're both leant forward with our elbows on the table and our hands lightly folded atop one another – a mirror image of each other. As an experiment I reach up and brush my nose; ten seconds later, Patrick does the same.

'One more?' I ask as Patrick drains his glass.

He groans. 'I would love another . . .' But . . . 'but I'm catching a flight tomorrow and I need to be at the airport horribly early, so I probably shouldn't.' His last night in the country and he's chosen to spend it with me! The thought of him leaving, though . . . I can feel my stomach drop. 'Are you going anywhere nice?'

'Does a hotel in the middle of nowhere count? It's a work trip so no, not really. But I won't be away that long, thank God.' I take this to mean: *I want to see you again very soon.*

'I shouldn't lead you astray, then.'

His wide eyes grow wider still. 'Now I'm very tempted,' he says, and I dissolve. I want to lead Patrick astray. I want to do a very wide range of things to Patrick; I've never felt so much chemistry, been so instantly attracted to a man. This has been such a brilliant night; Patrick is brilliant. Tinder is brilliant too. As am I. As is life.

He told me he would text me as we hugged goodbye – and he has. Back at home, I was searching for a saucepan to make noodles, trying not to wake whichever of my housemates may be in, when my phone beeped:

> Patrick:
> Hi Rosy, hope you got home safe? Thanks for a great evening, don't know what my signal will be like where I'm going but I'll be in touch soon!

I pick it up to reply – then stop and put it down. I should leave it until tomorrow; I don't want to seem over-eager. Although if his hotel is in the middle of nowhere and his signal is bad he might not get it – then he'll probably think I don't like him and lose interest. And *he* texted me, less than an hour after we parted ways, so to not reply would be rude . . . I pick my phone up and write out a text. I've made it back fine, I say, and it's me who should be thanking you; have a safe flight, I hope you don't hit turbulence. I may be drunker than I originally thought (I did attempt to put both my legs through the same hole in my pyjamas) so I reread what I've written to check for misspellings and super-fluous % signs. My thumb hovers over the X key; Patrick didn't put a kiss so I probably shouldn't either. I add one. Then I delete it. I hit send and go back to my noodles.

Three minutes later, my phone beeps again. I grab it; the message isn't from Patrick but a guy called Andrew, checking to see whether I'm still up for our date tomorrow. I set my phone down and try to recall who Andrew is – men have been starting to amalgamate in my head recently. Tinder has really capitalised on the medium of the photograph but men all look the same to me, especially the ones with whom I match: they have dark or slightly less dark short-ish hair, come in regular height and wear a standard uniform of shirt/T-shirt with jeans – my type is essentially men who look like other men. Unless our messages veer off from the formulaic exchange about jobs, location and favourite bars then their faces get reabsorbed into the Tindersphere like a hamster eating its young. Without an in-joke or an interesting detail (unusual job, webbed feet etc.), a man's face is nothing but well-organised pixels. Andrew's face is still at pixel stage in my head but he must have piqued my interest somehow if we've not only moved on to text but I have also agreed to a date on the day after meeting Patrick. Fuckity fuck bollock bag. I fork a mound of noodles into my mouth and open Tinder to find my message thread with Andrew. It's brief, standard fare: I asked about his job, he asked where I live and he's made a comment about his housemate that is funny without being cruel. In his pictures he looks attractive but un-extraordinary.

I need to make a decision. I could text back and postpone; it sounds far better than cancelling. I could reply tomorrow, saying I've got stuck in the office or that I've been feeling peaky all afternoon and think I'm coming down with . . . tuberculosis. Can I do that? If a guy sacked me off with so little finesse without giving me the benefit of at least one date I'd be mortified. And if my father found out, I'd be disowned: years ago, he forced Bru to weed our aunt's lawn when he 'forgot' to send a card thanking her for a birthday present. It is just one date, and with Patrick away . . . I could stay for one drink, two if he's pleasant, then get home for an early night.

Rosy:
Hi Andrew, yes still keen
for tomorrow. I'll be free
from 6:30, so let me
know when and where.

I close the thread and go back to my message from Patrick: *Thanks for a great evening* . . . he'll call in the next two days; he wouldn't have sent a text like that otherwise. I smile. Some noodles fall out of my mouth.

8.

EXPERIMENT IV

Either London is getting weirder, or I am growing older and less cool with every passing year (do people say 'cool' now?). When I arrived in the city six years ago, a night out involved happy hour at All Bar One, the long, cold queue for a sticky-walled club and a McDonald's on the night bus home. This no longer seems to be the case; now you're barely allowed to own an Oyster Card if you don't know the password for the latest street-food/art/sushi pop-up or haven't sipped a gunpowder cocktail out of a watering can; there might have been a ten-minute window, sometime back in 2009, when I was on board but it was likely a serendipitous coincidence. When I go out-out these days, I'm either too progressive for the retro twists or too antiquated for the modern bents – I don't know which but I know I don't get it, whatever 'it' is, and the venue Andrew has chosen for our date is a harsh reminder that, even at twenty-seven, I am already egregiously un-groovy.

I'm in deepest East London, far beyond the relative commercialism (read: safety) of somewhere like Shoreditch. I took an overground train to a station I've never heard of and now I'm walking down a bustling street of Turkish cafés and Jamaican stores, unconvinced that a super-awesome-trendy bar could be anywhere near here. I check the map on my phone: my blue dot is almost atop the red marker; surely, this cannot possibly be. After one last check for a message from Patrick, I lock my phone and slide it back into my bag. The signal must be bad wherever he is, and without knowing where he's going I can't account for a potential time difference either.

I drift up and down the street, scanning shops and doorways, until I bump into Andrew. 'Thank God,' I say instead of hello, 'I can't find the bar.'

'Ah yes, it's hidden,' he says. 'Good to meet you, Rosy.' His stubble rasps against my cheek as we kiss. Andrew is the opposite of Patrick. He has dark hair against pale skin in contrast to Patrick's fair hair and freckles; Patrick seemed to radiate ease whereas Andrew is precise. The black rims of his glasses sit centrally on his face and his shirt, buttoned to the top, is crisply ironed. He leads the way, back where I came from and says that we're not far; I notice his speech is slightly accented and it's surprising though I don't know why. When I look at Tinder photos, I might imagine how tall a man is or the way he dresses; I never think about the way he might sound. 'Are you . . . Scandinavian?' I can't pinpoint where he's from, my guess is Sweden and this seems like the least offensive to ask if I'm wrong. Which I am.

'I'm Dutch, actually.'

'God, sorry.'

'It's fine, I get that a lot.' He says this in a way that makes it sound totally not fine.

It's little wonder I couldn't find the bar; officially, Andrew explains, it doesn't exist. We are walking down the road when he stops, apropos of nothing, and raps on one of the ordinary-looking residential doors that are nestled between the shop fronts. It is opened by a bouncer; a chandelier glints where an Ikea lampshade might once have been. A pretty, young blonde girl hovers at the bouncer's side, holding a clipboard. 'Hi guys,' she says in bouncy, kids' TV-presenter cadence, 'have you booked?'

Andrew affirms that, apparently, we have; he gives her our names and she scans down the list. 'Andrew . . . yep, great, got you . . . and Rosy . . .' She isn't speaking. Time is passing. The bouncy blonde continues to look. Please, God, let my name be there. I'll give you my soul, Lord, my Mulberry bag (the real one), anything you want, but please let me get in: I don't fare well with embarrassment. Should I ever fall down an escalator, I'd rather land at the bottom in a crumpled, dead heap than have to stand up and try to laugh it off.

'Yep, Rosy, here you are. Brilliant. You can go on down guys, have a great night.' I exhale, and doing so brings such a sense of relief that I must have stopped breathing. I follow Andrew down the narrow staircase and offer up a final prayer: *Thanks for getting me in, God; if you*

*could also make this not be a masquerade, S&M orgy
I'd be very grateful.*

At the bottom of the stairs, I am surprised (and
relieved) to find that we are in the middle of a compact
but bustling bar and that the internal walls have been
knocked down so the bar stretches from the front of the
building to the back. Shaded floor lamps emit a muted,
yellow glow that fades into shadowy nooks and corners,
creating a warm and intimate feel – I could catch the
scent of my grandmother's pot roast at any moment. It
is like I'd imagine a Victorian garret to be, and everything
is mismatched, from the chairs to the tables to the modern
artwork hanging on the walls . . . everything apart from
the clientele, who are clustered round the rickety tables
sporting what I would term identical 'hipster' style
although I don't think you're supposed to call it that any
more. There is an abundance of plaid and facial hair,
and that's just the girls.

We go to the bar. Andrew turns to me and says, 'Take
your pick,' gesturing to the liquor display that looks like
a quaint apothecary I once visited with Kate when we
went out to Swansea to stay with her parents. In times
of stress and confusion, human beings gravitate toward
that which is familiar; I'm getting those feelings now,
and am gravitating towards vodka mixed with soda and
possibly lime. However, from Andrew's watchful expression I garner that a pedestrian choice will only embarrass
us all. I look across to the barman. He is dressed like
the fifth member of a Barbershop Quartet. I ask what he
recommends.

'First time here?' he asks, to which Andrew answers quickly, 'Not at all.' The barman strokes one manicured sideburn. 'We have some specials tonight, my pick would be the Fred and Ginger.' He slides over a piece of thick card on which three drinks have been printed in type set with their ingredients and the price listed under each. The Fred and Ginger comes second: it costs 8.5 (pounds? Buttons? What?) and consists of **gin, lemon, ginger**.

'That looks good,' says Andrew. He slides the menu back and sets off towards the tables.

'We don't need to wait for our drinks?' I say to the back of his shoulder as I scuttle along in his wake.

'They bring them over,' Andrew replies with a gentle smile; it could mean either *you're adorable* or *you're a bit simple.* Andrew is quite impassive, it's hard to tell.

The barman brings our drinks in tumblers – holding out for a martini glass was clearly folly. Andrew holds up his glass and says, 'Cheers' and I clink it with my own, making the pale yellow liquor slosh up the side. I take a sip, and have to fight the urge to spit it back out again. The first 'hit' is of gin (a lock in a sock to the temple, prison-style, might be more apt) followed by a mega thwack of eye-watering lemon before the ginger burns a rivulet down my gullet. I want to throw up, yet feel strangely like I already have.

'Like it?' asks Andrew.

'Mmm,' I nod. Then I sneeze five times in a row.

* * *

We are forty minutes in and for much of this time I've been trying to establish the source of the odd chirruping sound I've heard every couple of minutes since we sat down; finally, I have worked out that it is coming from Andrew. He makes this weird grunting-clicking sound in his throat as though he needs to cough or have an operation of some kind. It was quite subtle at first and blended in with the background noise of hipsters talking about their hipster affairs and the experimental jazz that wafts softly out of the speakers, but then I couldn't stop hearing it and now I can focus on nothing else. When I think it's stopped, he does it again. I've started to wait for it.

'How did you get into PR, Rosy?' Andrew asks me.

'By accident; I sort of fell into it. I temped at a firm in the summer after my second year at uni and they offered me a junior role just before I graduated.'

'And how long have you been at your current place?'

'Three years.' The phrase resonates round my head: *three years*. It is a long time by any standard; in PR years, it's forever, especially if you don't happen to love PR. 'What about you?'

'I started off in media recruitment but I got a tip-off from a friend about this start-up . . .' The start-up has one of those ridiculous names so beloved by the media sector and Andrew announces it like there's no earthly way I won't have heard of them, but I must look as confused as I feel.

'You don't know them?' he asks, frowning. 'They're a specialist production agency.'

'What do they specialise in?'

'Media production.' Andrew blinks at me. 'Didn't you say you worked in media PR?'

'The name kind of rings a bell,' I say, hearing only silence in my head. I've finished my drink; now seems like a good time for a second. I look down at the candied lemon peel at the bottom of the glass and briefly consider eating it.

'Anyway,' Andrew goes on, 'I was there for a few years and in my role I was dealing with a lot of advertising guys who made me see I was suited to that world, so I applied for my current job.'

I grin. 'And how did that work out?'

Andrew frowns behind his glasses and shakes his head, as if trying to rid himself of an itch. 'I got the job.'

'Yeah,' I say limply, 'I was . . .' Then I tail off because explaining the joke seems worse than letting Andrew think I'm an idiot.

Andrew says, 'Hm,' and click-grunts twice.

I stand up. 'It must be my round,' I say, and there is no Patrick-esque leap to stop me. 'What would you like?'

'Another one of these, thanks.'

'Cool.'

I panic at the bar and end up ordering another foul Fred & Ginger for myself too, hoping it might be more palatable on the second go round. Back at the table, two sips in, it hasn't proved to be. I've adopted a new strategy that involves letting Andrew talk, lest I should embarrass myself further by daring to ask questions and/or make jokes, and it seems to be effective because Andrew likes to talk. I'm getting a good insight into the world of advertising – he tells me he worked on the campaign for the toothpaste I use.

One of my major gripes with modern society is that people now think it's OK to look at their phones during social interaction. Andrew has shown no compunction about doing this; he placed his phone on the table at the start of the evening and has been checking it intermittently throughout. I don't know when it became acceptable to do this; I wouldn't take out a book and start reading the moment my date started to talk, so how is it permissible to browse Twitter on your phone mid-conversation? I wait until Andrew goes to the toilet to check my own, but it is a pointless exercise: no missed call from Patrick, no text. Although he did say he'd call *in the next day or so* – that suggests a window of roughly a week, and this is only Day 2. And though I was the last one to text, seemingly making it Patrick's responsibility to continue the chain, *he* was the first one to text *me* so maybe it's technically my turn to initiate contact.

I type: *'Hello You!'* then delete it.

'How was your flight . . .?' No – too prosaic.

'If you're reading this, at least your plane didn't crash!' . . . Perhaps it's best to abstain until I can come up with the perfect message. I look up and see Andrew making his way back towards me so I put my phone away.

*   *   *

There are only so many times I can pretend I'm *au fait* with the band/restaurant/conceptual artist Andrew is talking about and I'm coming up on my limit. I might have already gone past it, I don't know. Andrew is the 'cool' equivalent of the *nouveau riche*: you can tell he didn't grow up cool but has stumbled upon it in his mid-twenties and lacks any of the self-assurance required to pull it off. I wasn't in the cool gang at school (I referred to it as the 'cool gang', for a start) not because I was unpopular – I got on with everyone; I was sort of an omni-friend, if you will – but because I lacked confidence; it's a trait I recognise in Andrew. I read somewhere (probably *Stylist*, which I remain adamant is written exclusively for me as my own, personal life manual) that we are drawn to people with similar insecurities to our own, attracted, I assume, by a sense of familiarity that equates to safety and comfort. I don't see Andrew and I becoming familiar any time soon.

Not long after Liam got fired, when he was still gigging around chi-chi bars in North London, we'd been talking one night about his set list, which included a song by Pixies, and I had questioned its suitability. I remember Liam shrugging before he said: 'You can tell if the crowd aren't into it, so at that point I just play the stuff I like.' I am thinking of this story when Andrew asks if I've thought beyond PR. I tell him I'm considering a move into tree surgery. He doesn't laugh. I have a violent premonition of sitting across a dinner table with Andrew on Date No. 2, trying to feign interest as he explains his belief that George Harrison was the superior songwriter in The Beatles.

I have no future with Andrew and he clearly feels the same: at 9.45, he looks at his expensive watch and says, 'It's getting late.'

'Another drink?' I say out of ritual.

Andrew looks down, then up, then he fiddles with his glass. 'I've got an early start tomorrow, for a work trip abroad. So I have to catch a plane. And I probably won't be around for a few weeks after. I'm going abroad.'

It is like I've been smacked in the tits. The breath in my chest dries up, the world around me dims. It feels like I am wheeling through three of the seven stages of grief at breakneck speed: shock and denial; unbearable pain; anger at Patrick for lying . . . except, no, Patrick can't have lied, he wouldn't. Andrew is the one who is lying and for someone who works in advertising he's terrible at it, but Patrick probably *is* on a work trip – this is just an unfortunate coincidence. I force air into my lungs and try to corral my thoughts. OK. Don't panic. Logically, there is no reason why Patrick won't get in touch – we had a great date, he was eager to come back. And in all honesty, even if he has landed, and does have signal, texting immediately would be a little . . . desperate; Patrick is not That Guy. This is stupid fucking Andrew's fault: just because he made up a half-arsed excuse, it doesn't mean Patrick has too. Fuck Andrew.

Fuck.

We finish up and I follow Andrew back up to the street and, after another prickly and chaste kiss, we say goodbye (forever) and I head towards the station. I check my phone as soon as Andrew is gone: the screen is blank. Hard as I try, I can't stop the fourth stage of grief seeping into my bones: it is utter, soul-consuming loneliness.

9

RUNNING UP THAT HILL

Two minutes. Keep going.

A little over a minute. Don't stop.

Ow. Fucking . . . ow.

I am watching the timer tick down, something I was warned by a gym trainer (who just 'happened' to be walking past the other week, and just 'happened' to have some personal training slots left for a bargain £50 a session) that you should never do as it makes time pass slower until all you can think about is the pain and how much you want to stop. He was right. But if I can just keep running for nineteen more seconds . . . eighteen . . . seventeen . . . then I never have to step foot in a gym again. I can have cookies for dinner. I can live in a house made of cookies.

In the last seconds, I slow the treadmill to walking pace and wait for my breathing to ease from 'manic/

hysterical' to 'pretty knackered'. I felt OK after my first workout on Monday but now my body is in revolt at undergoing two sessions in the space of a week. Numbers like these are what make up my gym experience. Forty-five, for instance: the number of pounds sterling per month I lose whether I come or not, so I might as well come. Two: the number of visits per week I need to make my investment worthwhile. Fifteen: the total number of minutes I have spent on the treadmill, and the same again on the cross-trainer makes thirty. Nine: the number of minutes I spent on the rowing machine before I had to roll off into a heap on the floor. I can do twelve squats with 3 kg free weights, ten press-ups if I think about bunnies instead of the pain in my biceps and I can run for twenty-five minutes, at 9.2 with an incline of 1.5. On a good day.

Once I've completed my allotted hour I usually take a shower, get changed and treat myself to a fancy apple (Pink Lady – Galas and Braeburns are really more of your everyday apples) and eat it on my way home as the late-finishing workers are emerging from the Tube. Because I'm high on endorphins, I have to make my face say, *I'm one of you* rather than, *I just did exercise so I am better than you.*

Tonight, with one hour and ten minutes to my name, I leave the gym area clutching my water bottle, sweatshirt, towel and iPod; things are slipping perilously as I pass the pool but I manage to reach the changing rooms just before everything topples out of my grasp. My water bottle bounces off the bench and rolls under the lockers. I get down on my hands to retrieve it, carefully avoiding the wet patches left by the Lil' Fishes under-six swim class, and reach around in the darkness until my fingers come across it and I can pull it out. Back at the bench, I am sorting through my bag when a woman emerges from the shower with one towel tucked around her body and another artfully perched on her head; she opens the locker two down from mine, then discards said towels so that she is four feet away from me and naked bar a pair of floral flip-flops.

Oh God. OK. If I just stand still . . . Close proximity to naked strangers who I am not about to have sex with makes me excruciatingly uncomfortable, like the time I accidentally touched my examiner's knee during my driving test and in a misguided attempt to normalise the situation touched it a further three times. Part of me wants to look at her but I fear I might end up on a register of some sort; instead I opt for the occasional (swift) glance in her direction under the pretence of looking at the clock. This woman can't be much older than me, early thirties maybe, yet her body is so superior to my own it's no wonder she drops her towel at will. The first thing I notice are her arms: whereas mine look like gammon when I squash them against my ribcage, hers are firm, strong and delicately contoured by sinewy muscle under the skin. Her stomach is long and flat – *flat* flat, not with a bulge at the bottom like mine – and the skin is smooth so that when she bends over to dry her legs it ripples into a delicate concertina. I see her arse when she turns round; I didn't think women had bums like that outside of porn or magazines (usually porn magazines). It's taut and shapely; it doesn't jiggle when she walks and there is only the slightest hint of cellulite around the bottom where the bum stops and the thigh begins (the infamous yet largely unknowable 'arse-leg' region). My arse does not look like that. I have her anti-arse.

Suddenly, she turns so that she is facing me and I look away, but not before I see it; I see her vagina. I don't know how mine compares, never having examined it in detail, but based solely on pubic hair I'm a poor relation. BF and I frequently discuss at length the problems inherent to creating and maintaining a perfect landing strip so I can only assume Naked Girl has taken a course to achieve such a precise, streamlined result, though she has dark hair that contrasts against her skin, making for cleaner lines; my hair is red and, as I was forced to repeat to my male classmates during Years 7 to 9, yes, I have red hair *everywhere*. The best thing to do with ginger pubic hair is to shave it all off.

Naked Girl and her snatch start towards me and are gathering pace. I fixate on the inside of my locker and try to take my bra off under my running vest but my fingers fumble over the hook and eyes as I feel her pass behind me. She grabs a handful of tissues before wandering back, then, mercifully, flip-flops off to blow-dry her hair.

It's not easy to assess your own level of attractiveness, but a useful gauge is to assess yourself through the eyes of others. For instance: I have dated men that my friends consider to be attractive, therefore I must be of roughly an equivocal standard. I get chatted up in bars sometimes and nobody has ever shouted at me to put a bag over my head as I'm walking down the street. I do what I do, I look how I look and work within the boundaries of my aesthetic limitations. In isolation, I am not ugly . . . the problems start when I am held against another girl and it becomes clear where my aesthetic limitations end and hers begin. Up until a moment ago, they ended four feet away from where Naked Girl was standing. *If you had a body like hers*, says my beleaguered self-esteem, *then Patrick would have been in touch and arranged a second date*; it has been a fortnight since our first one and I've heard nothing since. But then objective reality kicks in, countering that surely he Tinder-Liked me based on my looks, therefore Naked Girl probably isn't his type.

Hot and naked isn't a man's type? says Self-esteem.

Don't be facetious – you know what I mean, argues Reality.

Then that's worse – I am his type and he still didn't go for me.

Yeah . . . (Reality scratches its ear). *I don't know what to tell you about that.*

I swaddle myself in my towel and head to the showers. A full-length mirror hangs on the wall and, having checked nobody is around, I unfold it and look at myself. Mum describes my complexion as Celtic, which is a kind way of saying pasty/milky/translucent. I think I might look fat.

I know how much you weigh, says Reality, *you're not fat.*

I dunno, argues Self-esteem, *your dating record is pretty poor, there must be a reason . . .*

Those guys were all losers!

Even Patrick?

Especially him, the liar! Then he . . . Self-esteem, what are you doing? Seriously, fingers in your ears? Wow. That's super mature.

I shake my head so the voices stop. Maybe Naked Girl is on Tinder, maybe she isn't; in the end it doesn't matter because hundreds of other girls just like her are. I head into the shower and stand under the hot stream of water. I need to lose weight, not a lot, maybe just half a stone, but I need to lose it quickly because for every second I'm sweating off the pounds in the gym there are Tinder matches being made. What if all the good guys get taken while I'm buying my fancy apple treat? I'll be left with the dregs which will inevitably be men named Howard who have little dress sense and fewer social skills. And to stand any chance of shedding this half stone quickly, I'm going to have to diet, too.

I pad back to my bench, pull out my tangle of clothes from my locker (I knew as I shoved them in I'd regret doing it) and dry off. I want to lose this weight properly so it doesn't creep back two-fold; I'm not going back to that cayenne-lemonade monstrosity, not after last time, not after the fainting episode in Zara. I should give up carbs: it's effective and I'd see the impact within days, so no pasta, no potatoes, no bread. Although I could probably still have a sandwich at lunchtime – two small slices of bread won't make a difference, nor will the occasional biscuit, which I need to make it through the 2 p.m. lull. Oh, and it's Pip's birthday on Friday so I'll have to have a slice of cake otherwise I'll get moaned at and called a fat-shamer behind my back. It happened to Lena from HR after she declined the brownies at the Christmas do.

Wait . . . what am I saying? I'm not even fooling myself any more, I can't forego carbs – I love them too much. We go way back, carbs and I: on those interminable Saturday nights in by myself, it was pizza that kept me company. After Charlie, when I was crying for the fourth time in the day, mac 'n' cheese dried my tears (with added diced bacon for the really black days). And when I got promoted, or when I got that haircut that BF said made me look a bit like Emma Stone, how did I celebrate? By finishing the last of the potato gratin my parents left when they came for Sunday lunch. I'm sorry, carbs – we always hurt the ones we love the most, but I'll never let you go. I'll come up with something else, I promise. There has to be another way.

10.

STRANGE PHENOMENA

I'm hungry. Oh sweet Lord I'm hungry, so hungry that I can't go to the loo because the toilet roll is looking increasingly tempting. I'm also drinking three litres of water a day to trick my stomach into thinking it's full, so peeing is a prerequisite roughly every seven minutes. This is all Sophie's fault.

Sophie subjected me to the section of the Female Pep-Talk concerning Appearance (sub-section: Weight) when I told her about my weight loss plan; it's along the lines of, 'You're beautiful as you are/You don't need to lose weight/I'd kill for your legs.' I listened dutifully and gave all the right responses ('Thank you/I want to be fit, not thin/I'd kill for YOUR legs') but Sophie could tell I was going through the motions. Eventually, she said: 'Do the 5:2. My cousin lost a stone.'

'Don't you have to starve yourself?'

'Well, they don't market it that way . . . you can have 500 calories on "2" days.'

'I just ate a cereal bar that had 196!'

'You should probably avoid those.'

For all my reservations, I've taken Sophie's advice and put myself on the 5:2; I've given up cereal bars, along with sugar, which in turn means I have also given up feeling happy. On my fast days (which, ironically, go interminably slowly) I have a banana for breakfast, miso soup with broccoli for lunch and a grilled chicken breast and salad for dinner that I season with my own tears. It will be worth it. This half-stone is my keystone: it is the crux to building my confidence; my confidence will entice men, then I'll get a boyfriend, thus freeing up mental space to (somehow) improve my job and I shall henceforth be deliriously happy for ever and ever and ever.

I have so far lost 2 kg and as a reward I'm meeting BF for sushi and, if I can resist temptation for another four hours, possibly a glass of wine. In the meantime, I have seven items left on today's to-do list to be getting on with.

'Do you want a coffee?' Pip asks, stretching out and yawning. I would love a cup of coffee, but I can't drink it with any less than two sugars. Coffee now, or wine later. I have to choose. I choose wine.

'Could I have a cup of herbal?' I try to say it quietly but Helen still hears and swivels round in her chair.

'Did you just ask for herbal tea?' she grins. 'And after all your little comments . . .'

'I thought I'd try it,' I mumble, busying myself with the papers on my desk.

Later, my phone beeps.

BF:
Ed is a dick.
Looking forward to
a drink.

BF is at the bar when I arrive. I join her at the table where a bottle of wine is already chilling in a cooler; looking at her, I can see that she's been crying though she's tried to redo her make-up since. We make a half-hearted attempt to talk about work and the new handbag BF is sporting but I rush us through because I want to know what's going on.

'Fucking Ed,' she says by way of a prelude. This is the first time I've heard her refer to Ed in anything other than glowing terms; their first date led to a second, then BF took him to the cinema, then Ed made her dinner. It all seems to have been going swimmingly, but when I described their budding romance to Pip last week, she rolled her eyes. 'It's always like that in the beginning,' she muttered darkly.

'He's fucking grumpy,' BF continues, 'all the time. Like, I spent the evening at his yesterday and he barely said a word.'

'Is he stressed? Didn't you say he's a banker? That's got to come with some pressure.'

'Yeah, he does have a lot on . . .' BF looks down at her glass, twirling it between her thumb and forefinger. 'But it's always been that way. This is new; it's like I piss him off just being there.'

After a few minutes, BF says: 'I really like him,' and then nothing for a long time. I'm not sure how to respond, so I don't say anything. I don't think I'm supposed to.

'God, he's such a dick,' she says, her aimless musing now infused with anger. 'Men don't talk about their feelings, fine, I get it; we don't need to light candles and get out a guitar. It would just be nice if he could say, "Hey, look, this is happening, it's a bit shit, sorry I've been in a mood for two weeks" . . .'

'Two weeks?'

BF shrugs a shoulder. 'About that.' Ed sounds like a prick. I don't say that either. 'Are you guys still having sex?'

She makes a face. 'Yes, that's all we do. He won't speak to me but he's more than happy to . . .' She makes a different face which gives me the gist. Then she sits up, exhales hard and demands we change the subject. 'Let's talk about you,' she says, and asks about my love life. I'm not keen on this change of direction as it means having to tell her I have a date on Friday, and in the circumstances, it would sound like I was gloating. Instead, I say something vague about swiping and Liking, matching and messaging, the general ebb and flow of Tinder.

'That's good,' she replies, only half listening, then takes out the bottle from the cooler and tops up both our glasses. I feel a pang of guilt at having more than half a glass but I push it away because friends drink with their friends, when their friends are sad. I'll make tomorrow a 4½ day.

* * *

My date is with a man named Doug. We have been messaging for ten days and he is taking me out for dinner; I've had to jiggle my 5:2 days around to ensure this one is a 5 but at this stage I am simply excited about eating. From his pictures I see that Doug has good teeth and he comes across as refined and witty in his messages. There is one small issue, however.

If you want an accurate, contemporary picture of London, read *Game of Thrones*; watch *Gangs of New York*; recall how Mufasa told Simba not to go beyond where the light touches. For one of the most progressive cities in the world, London is essentially feudal, divided into distinct tribes along the lines of the compass, each with their own philosophies, past-times and dress code. And, above all else, they rarely mix. To the North are The Lifestylers: they work in media, they buy artisan bread and the new mothers of the tribe frequent Wi-Fi-enabled cafes *en masse* so they lactate and then blog about it. In the East the vibe is creative, the culture is underground and the clothes are second-hand or buttoned up high. Tattoos are prolific, transport involves a bicycle or the Overground and if you aren't involved in a pop-up/ start-up/mash-up then you better get out of Dodge. The West is where the money is thanks to the influx of foreign investors who use their £10 million mansions as summer homes. Westees dine out rather than in, send their children to exorbitantly priced prep schools where a lost boater will earn you detention and social standing is determined by how well one wields a lacrosse stick. The Westee young are well groomed and impeccably mannered but prone to recklessness (at Bedales one could get away with murder) because money affords spontaneity. Think *Made in Chelsea* if they all didn't live in Fulham.

The South is a mixture of all of the above with handfuls of Australians thrown in for good measure. The south west is pretty public school but things get grittier as you travel further east; the kind of Tinderites I tend to go for fixate on Clapham with its newbie graduates or Brixton where things are a little more grounded. Of course, London's archaic social structure has implications on its dating scene. The temptation to break across boundaries is ever enticing: Clapton looks very exotic when you're stuck playing fucking ping-pong in Baron's Court. But it is unusual – nay, inadvisable – to date outside your tribe; when Andrew invited me to the Tundras of the east, I never thought I'd make it home again. And this is in essence the problem with Doug: he lives in Chelsea. I must have been Tindering on a bus passing through but I've been bingeing of late so I probably swiped him right and thought no more about it. I do not fit in out west. I've been to the King's Road on occasion, usually in search of a McDonald's or a bus to take me home, but otherwise the area is a strange, mysterious place where all the girls wear fedoras and the men look straight through me. I've told Doug that I'm southern so he must be OK with it to have asked me out, but we are going west for our date. He messaged me the name of the restaurant – it's very French, and when I searched it, the cheapest starter on the menu was £8.50. I am all for gender equality and I like to think I pay my way, but as it's Doug's choice, on Doug's patch and it's dinner rather than drinks – unusual for a first date – then I assume it's Doug who'll foot the bill.

*   *   *

Doug has offered to pick me up in his car. I'm waiting for him outside the Tube, but as I don't know what car he drives I am steeling myself every time a BMW or Aston Martin comes past. Except every car in this part of town is a BMW or an Aston Martin. I contemplate buying a pack of cigarettes – I'm an occasional Nervous Smoker – but Doug is due any moment and he might turn out to be one of those eugh-God-smoking-is-gross-my-grandad-died-of-lung-cancer types.

Having been expecting a face in a driver's side window rather than a bipedal man, I don't recognise Doug until he's so close he can't be looking for anyone else. We do a two-cheek kiss, something I've done hundreds of times, yet I choose this occasion to make a superfluous 'mwah mwah' sound. I really don't fit in around here. Doug is tall and stocky, the build of a scrum half. His hair is thick and wavy and run through with wax that somehow doesn't stop it falling into his eyes.

'Rosy, you look lovely,' he says. He is lying. I've haven't seen one girl walk past who isn't 5' 9" or over, size six or below and devoid of long, glossy blonde hair; I am short, ginger ('strawberry blonde' according to Mum) and am wearing my only good jeans ('your sex jeans', BF calls them) with a T-shirt I salvaged from Kate's latest wardrobe purge. At least I'm wearing my leather jacket, the one that makes me cold and generic at the same time. I am clearly not Doug's usual type; still, if he is disappointed he has been bought up well enough not to show it.

'I'm parked just around the corner,' he says.

I've seen cars like Doug's before – on *Top Gear*. It looks like a Ferrari but I haven't had time to check, and now I am standing in front of the door with the sinking realisation I don't know how to open it. There doesn't appear to be a handle.

Doug says, 'Would you like me to . . .?' and makes his way round to my side of the car.

He presses something, or unlatches it, or possibly the car knows and responds to him like the one in *Knight Rider*, but it flies wide open and almost knocks me over.

'Jump in,' says Doug.

I don't 'jump' in so much as tumble. The car is so low that there is no graceful way of getting inside bar a simultaneous crouch-and-topple manoeuvre that relieves me of my last shred of dignity. I manage to get seated but when I turn to shut the door, I see that it is now very, very far away. I try to reach out and grab it but I am nowhere close. Placing one foot back onto the pavement for stability, I perform a sort of leaning/grasping gesture that sees me miss the handle by a country mile and almost fall out of the car in the process. The only way I can reach the handle essentially means getting *out* of the car, but it's been a trial to get this far and I can foresee problems with closing the door if I'm not inside. I go for one last attempt, swinging both my legs onto the kerb and pushing myself upward into a semi-squat; I just about get a grip on the handle but I've misjudged the amount of exertion required to close the fucking thing and fall backwards, landing on the seat with a thud.

Doug, who has watched the whole charade, looks bewildered and frightened. 'Shall I come round and shut that?' he asks. Fantastic. *Again*, Doug is forced to come round to help me and Bonus Humiliation Points for having to sit like a child whilst he slams the door shut, then gives me a thumbs-up through the window. Mercifully, when we get to the restaurant, no one is around to witness my ungainly exit. We walk inside where the *maître d'* greets Doug like he is a regular, but my parents went somewhere equally fancy for their thirtieth anniversary and apparently they do that to everyone. He shows us to a large, square table covered in heavy, white linen and darts behind me to pull out a plush, upholstered chair. This is definitely the right haunt for a guy whose car doors are inoperable. The waiter appears with the wine list, which he gives directly to Doug.

Doug peruses it for a while before peering up at me. 'Red or white?'

'I only drink white actually.' It happened when I was sixteen, the 'unspeakable red wine incident', and I haven't been near the stuff since; the smell alone makes me nauseous.

Doug chooses something German and unpronounce-able and hands the leather-bound folder back to the waiter. He looks at me. 'You'll like it.' I'm tempted to tell him, I know, I drink expensive wine like water; instead, I smile and give an approving nod.

I look down at the menu. There is no guarantee that Doug won't ask to go halves (if he can afford a parking permit in Chelsea, he can afford dinner, but you can't assume these things) so I should opt for one of the more reasonably priced dishes. Unfortunately, there aren't many of them and I doubt olives followed by soup is going to endear me to Doug, who is browsing his menu with a distinct lack of impetus. 'The scallops are good,' he says, not necessarily to me.

'I think I'll start with salmon and then . . .' I drift over to the Mains. Monkfish for £32? Does it come with the keys to a one-bed in Balham? 'The halibut with capers. That looks nice.' Except I fucking hate capers.

* * *

I definitely don't fancy Doug. He's attractive and I like how he's dressed, not because it's expensive (though I imagine it is) but because he looks smart and it makes me think he's made an effort. I like that he's courteous, too, and confident, but I could never date a Doug; he's too brash, too sure of himself and in my experience, men like that often have a swell of insecurities lurking just below the surface.

'Do you ski?' he asks as our starters are cleared away. I shake my head.

'My whole family skis, we all love it.' Doug tops up my glass. I can't pronounce the name of this wine and I'd have to sell a kidney to afford a bottle but I'm having no difficulty drinking it. 'So what would be your ideal holiday?'

'Sunshine; a beach; good books.' I smile at the memory of my last holiday, a week in Crete with Charlie, when we were happy – or I was. 'Skiing seems like too much exertion to constitute a holiday.'

'Skiing is an *incredible* holiday! A group of us have just come back from Verbier – we had a great time, great time. You should try it.'

'Did you see any Royals?'

Doug frowns. 'You're maybe thinking of Klosters.'

I'm not thinking of anywhere; I've just seen pictures of Prince Charles in a ski suit, I've no idea where he goes.

*   *   *

I am half way through my halibut (I managed to scrape the capers off) and we're onto a second bottle. Doug, meanwhile, is five minutes into a detailed exposition of his ex-girlfriend. Exes aren't first-date fodder as a rule so I assume Doug is drunk. I know that I am on my way; there is something about wine that gets me drunker than anything else, but getting drunk on dates with men like Doug is dangerous because of the risk I'll mistake his pretence for charm and think I'm in love with him, so I'm trying to have a prophylactic glass of water for every one of the delicious, delicious wine. 'She used to model,' Doug is saying, still on the ex, 'it's a different world.' I'm starting to feel that I know Doug's ex-girlfriend better than I know him; so far, I know she works 'in property' (read: estate agent); she was a reserve for the GB women's hockey team; her middle name is Heidi and all of Doug's friends thought she was 'hilarious'.

'Why did you two break up?' I ask.

Doug pushes his hand through his hair. He seems to shrink a little in his chair. 'I was working a lot and she was going through some stuff . . . we never saw each other, basically.' He looks down and a shadow passes across his face; it's so quick it's barely there but it carried with it all the sadness, regret and hurt – all the feelings that settle behind your stomach not just after a break-up, but after you get dumped. I wore the same expression for three months after Charlie.

He catches himself and in a moment he is big again, back to the Doug I have known and loved (read: met) for the last two hours. 'It was a good thing really because I never got to see my mates.' He loads up his fork with steak and shoves it in his mouth.

'What do they do, your mates?'

'Rockwood's a broker; Tank is a lawyer; my mate Forcey does hedge funds, though not very well!' Doug guffaws. Such banter. Doug does something with money, too; he told me what it was but with no frame of reference and too much wine the information has gone. Something in insurance? Whatever it is, it obviously pays well – I needn't have fretted about the bill. When it arrives, tucked inside a leather wallet, Doug picks it up reflexively and glances over it before sliding a black credit card into the wallet.

I should have had the monkfish.

*   *   *

Coffee was proffered but Doug declined for both of us, an opinion I wholeheartedly supported as my stomach was straining against my top, and whilst Doug has been entertaining and generous company I've had my fill of him, too; I'm not sure what Doug makes of me, with my under-stairs inclinations and grammar-school education. Classless society is a fallacy. It is on this date, anyway.

I check my watch as we get up to leave. To my dismay, it is almost 1 a.m.; I huff (accidentally) and it makes Doug look over and ask what's up.

'I didn't realise it was so late, I've missed the last Tube.'

'Just crash at mine. I'll be very well behaved.' He makes a sort of growling noise that makes me shudder.

'That's OK, I'll book a cab.'

'Rosy,' he says with a slight slur in his voice, 'my flat

is literally two minutes down the road. Book it from mine, then you can go when it arrives.' We walk out of the restaurant onto an otherwise deserted street; if my choices are to wait here, by myself, at 1 a.m., or to go back to Doug's, I know which one is safer . . . but it is really cold so I guess I should go back to Doug's. I follow as he leads the way; the wine has added a slight sway to my gait.

I stop, abruptly. 'Where's your car?'

Doug laughs. 'One of the waiters parked it back at mine, I gave them the keys.' He looks back at me over his shoulder. 'I'm a regular there.'

*   *   *

Doug's flat is two-parts OCD neat freak, one-part serial killer. Patrick Bateman would be right at home. The flat is open-plan and the vast whiteness of the walls is broken up by colourful contemporary art. A large, L-shaped sofa in dove grey dominates the lounge area whilst a pristine kitchen in chrome and black runs the length of the top of the room and looks like it's never been used. A 42-inch plasma stands firmly atop a black, lacquered cabinet that Doug opens automatically using what I thought was the TV remote but transpires to control the blinds, the lighting, music, internet and, possibly, the TV. Framed photos of Doug and his friends are dotted around the room: Doug wearing a beanie and ski goggles in front of a sparkling piste; Doug looking tanned and larking around on a white sand beach; Doug in sunglasses and facepaint, swigging bottled beer at some festival or other. It is his Tinder profile made real. I walk over to the wide French windows and peer through the glass: there is a balcony beyond which I can see the outline of the city lit up for miles.

Doug is choosing music when I look back, scrolling through a menu that has appeared on the TV screen. He selects a track, something indie and mellow that comes out of speakers I can't see; I sit on the sofa, careful not to soil anything with my pauper fingers whilst Doug goes into the kitchen to make drinks. I take out my phone and book a cab. Usually, they turn up before you've got your coat on but tonight, of course, it's saying the car won't be here for twenty minutes.

'Here you are,' says Doug, offering me a glass of what looks upsettingly like gin and tonic. I pass it under my nose: it's gin and tonic. He sits beside me and says, 'Cheers' so I feel obliged to take a sip. My stomach gurgles. Then it makes a groaning noise. I don't know if it's the wine, or the fish, or the excessively rich chocolate pot I didn't need for dessert, but in conjunction with this final hit of gin things are starting to churn. I'll be going to the loo the second I get home . . . my stomach creaks and lurches. Fuck getting home.

'Can I use your bathroom?' I ask, on my feet before Doug can answer; I'm moving as he calls out that I should use his en-suite. In any other circumstances, I might have taken the opportunity of being alone in Doug's room to gawp at his watch collection laid out in two perfectly uniform rows, or to inspect the tower of DVDs stacked precisely in a cabinet below a second flat screen to check for anything that might suggest Doug has a penchant for spiking girls' drinks and handcuffing them to radiators. I notice a set of skis leaning against the far wall and beside them a small set of free weights neatly stacked in their cradle, otherwise the room is bare bar the large bed that is made up to hotel standard.

However, the current circumstance being what it is, that is all I have time to take in; I only just manage to pull the screen doors shut behind me and yank down my underwear before nature runs its course. And runs. And runs some more. I use all the muscles at my disposal to keep the evacuation quiet but my bowels have their own agenda and no amount of clenching can negate the sounds I'm emitting as I violate Doug's spotless porcelain. I hope the music is drowning this out. After what feels like an ice age it looks like I have mercifully run out of fluid; I sort myself out and flush (twice) before staggering to the sink to wash my hands and face and lay my head on the cooling marble of the counter. I'd had the foresight to grab my bag before fleeing the sofa so I muster the energy necessary to stand upright, root around in its depths for my perfume and give the bathroom a few woefully inadequate spritzes.

I study my reflection in the mirror behind the sink. Black mascara has smudged around my eyes, which against my pale skin gives me the look of the recently exhumed. I wet some loo roll and use a slick of soap to wipe off the worst, but there's nothing I can do for my hair: all the shitting must have made me sweat because the front tendrils are slick against my forehead and from my crown backwards the hair is frizzed and matted. I smooth it down with my wet palm but that still leaves the glow of my puffy cheeks that are pink from exertion. In short, I look like shit and there's a very real chance I might smell like it, too. There might be a hair tie in my bag, I thought I saw one . . .

Suddenly, the screen doors fly open. 'What the fuck are you doing?' My head snaps up at the sound of Doug's voice and I see his face glaring at me in the mirror, his hulking figure stark against his dark bedroom behind.

'You're doing coke, aren't you?'

I barely manage to catch my breath before he storms in; I should say something but everything feels ten times harder because I have no idea what Doug is talking about and I'm probably dehydrated. 'What?' I croak.

'You've been in here for ages. I know you're doing coke. My ex and her fucking model friends used to . . .' He tails off. He is looking for something, his eyes darting around the bathroom. 'Where is it? In here?' Before I can react, Doug snatches my bag off the counter and starts rifling through it; a tampon springs out and lands on the floor behind him.

'Stop it!' I yelp and reach for the bag, but Doug drops it before I can get a grasp.

'What have you done with it?' he demands; then, before I'm aware of what's happening, he comes towards me and starts patting me down.

'Are you fucking joking?' I smack at his hands as they grope my waist, my thighs, the pockets of my jeans . . .

panting, he stands tall with a twisted look on his face; I can only presume he's angry at having failed to find the *imaginary drugs* about my person.

'I don't want you snorting fucking cocaine in my bathroom,' he growls. I bend down to my bag and shovel the spilled contents back inside, tampon and all. 'You've been in here for the last ten minutes – what the fuck have you been doing?' As I stand up he is staring at me, waiting for an answer.

Now, here is a conundrum. I can either: a) admit to having just had a bout of explosive diarrhoea or b) go along with Doug's gift-wrapped get-out clause and let him think I am a coke fiend. Opting for the former does mean I shall have to subsequently perform hara-kiri to cleanse myself of the shame. However, choosing the latter means letting Doug think he's right. Neither appeals. There has to be a third way; I glance around, hoping my surroundings might provide inspiration. I see the toilet. Of course. 'I was sick.'

'As in . . . throwing up?' Doug looks confused.

'Yeah. I must have drunk too much at dinner and then we had that gin . . .'

'I thought you only had a sip?'

Crap, too much . . . I could say it was something I ate but I sense that insulting the restaurant might be a worse offence than snorting coke off his sink. I say: 'I don't really like gin,' and look down at the floor. It occurs to me that not only is this the truth, it was probably the gin that tipped me over the edge and if I had just admitted that I didn't like it in the first place, we could have had a pleasant end to a not unpleasant evening. But as it is . . . I glare at Doug. 'So I wasn't snorting coke, but I appreciate the accusation, cheers.' Nothing detracts from a lie like righteous indignation.

I push past Doug and march down the hallway into the living room.

'Would you like another drink?' Doug asks, following me in. I look at him – or this version of him, anyway, I've seen about five of them this evening. The question is surreal, but based on the last twenty minutes, anything is possible. 'My cab will be here in a second.'

'Why don't you stay?' He comes up behind me and massages my shoulders. 'I don't have to be at work until nine.' I release myself and turn to face him: his fury has been replaced with a placid expression and a suggestive smile plays on his lips. Maybe his mother didn't love him enough, maybe he was bitten by a dog and is yet to move past it, but Doug is clearly a psychopath and I want to go home.

My phone pings. I don't look at it before I say, 'My taxi's here.' I'll take my chances on the streets if it's not.

'That's a shame,' Doug says as he walks me to the door, on which I have never been so relieved to see a prominent and obvious opening mechanism. 'Why don't I give you a ring tomorrow?' I make a humming sound by way of response, inching ever further along the hallway; I'd be within my rights to tell him he's mental and demand he never contact me again, but that would be rude, and it's not how we do it in the south.

11

AERIAL

The couple across the bar are on a date – the first, I would guess, and if not, they are doing the world's best impression of two people who are on a first date. He is wearing his work suit but carries no bag: he's optimistic, keen to meet her, and has prioritised the date over the gym. Her skirt, meanwhile, says 'office' but her top and heels (donned in the loos, along with a fresh layer of make-up) are meant for a night out. I am too far away to hear what they're saying, but overall I don't think it's going very well: she is leaning forward, fluffing her hair then tucking it behind her ear with a coy half-grin but he is sitting back and occasionally stretching his arms as if merely sitting at the table is causing him to cramp up. In the time I've been watching, he has done almost all the talking; I see her mouth move as she attempts to interject, but it doesn't prompt him to stop, so they both end up talking at once. When she can get a word in, his expression becomes serious and he nods, like she's killed the joke. Cue copious amounts of hair twirling from her and a hefty sip of beer from him, after which there usually follows a period of silence. Maybe she's not funny. Maybe he's mean. The one thing I know for certain is that observing a first date is vastly preferable to being on one.

I am killing time whilst I wait for BF and Ed. There has been an about-turn on this front: having arranged to spend the evening with Ed last week, BF arrived at his flat to find that his chilly hostility had thawed; he had made dinner and set the table with candles, and he told BF he liked her hair. Later, he insisted that she be the one to choose the movie they would watch snuggled up in bed (where he 'didn't even try to have sex', BF told me, 'which was really thoughtful'). So, I asked when she rang on Monday: what's prompted the change? BF posited something vague about his work project coming to an end before admitting, eventually, that she didn't know – nor was she keen to ask, she was simply happy that things were better. That was when she suggested I meet him. I've agreed because I love BF, BF thinks she might love Ed and therefore I am duty bound to at least make a go of tolerating him. My hope is that in meeting him face to face, I shall be swayed from thinking he is an unreliable shitbag.

From behind me, I hear BF saying my name and I turn to see her coming towards me with her hand clasped in Ed's.

'Hi!' she says brightly, piling her bag and coat onto a stool, 'sorry we're late, we . . .'

'Totally my fault,' interrupts Ed. 'It's great to finally meet you, Ro, I've heard so much about you.' He holds out his hand for me to shake and uses it to pull me in for a double-kiss, a smacker on each cheek. 'What would you girls like to drink?'

'A glass of white, please, sweetheart,' says BF. They both turn to me, waiting for my answer; I am still reeling from 'sweetheart'.

'Er, yes, wine – if that's OK?' I feel dazed: here is Ed, in the flesh (and very attractive flesh at that) and BF, my BF, reduced to his saccharine side-kick. Now his chivalrous offer of drinks . . . there's a lot to take in. Ed plants a kiss on BF's lips before heading for the bar.

'So?' BF grins in anticipation of my appraisal.

'He seems nice.'

'I know.' She giggles, and looks over to the crowded bar where he's already being served (how has he done that?). I use nice to describe lots of things; the cup of tea Pip made me earlier was 'nice'.

'So everything's going well with you guys?'

'Really well,' BF enthuses. She begins to say something else, but Ed is coming back to the table, clutching a bottle of wine for BF and me and a beer for himself. He sits next to BF and cinches his arm round her waist, adding another kiss to her cheek. She appears to become viscous at his touch; if she could climb inside him I think she might.

'How was your day today, Ro?' Ed asks me. The shortened version of my name is the purview of my closest friends, but BF must use it around him and he's presumed that's what I like.

'Fine thanks, nothing much to report.'

'You work in media PR, yeah?'

I nod.

'A friend of mine works for Irving Metcalf, he's called Rich Hutchinson – do you know him?' This is what happens when I tell people I work in PR: they assume I know *everyone else who works in PR.* The same thing happens to my Scottish friend Al: everyone thinks Scotland is the size of Slough, he told me, and that all Scots know each other.

'I can't say I do.'

'I should introduce you, he's great, you'd really get on.' I catch BF's eye; she flicks up an eyebrow, like: *double date . . .?* and I force a smile in reply. Thank God Ed is here to organise my woeful love life. I sound bitter. Am I bitter? Ed nuzzles BF's neck and I watch as her face lights up . . . she looks happy. It's been a long time since a man has lit up any part of my anatomy. I'm probably jealous: the sense of unease I get from being with Ed is my sublimated envy at wanting an Ed to call my own.

'Are you ready to date again, after Doug?' BF asks.

'Who's Doug?' chirps Ed. I was happy to share Doug with BF but I am wary of telling anyone else . . . unfortunately, my thoughts on the matter are null and void for BF launches into the tale on my behalf. I know she's not doing it to be malicious, or to laugh at my expense (kindly, she fudges the part with the uncontrollable diarrhoea) – she's doing it to impress Ed. She concludes with the showdown in the bathroom and when I look at Ed he is all but crying with laughter. Personally, I don't find it as funny, but then I've heard the story before.

Ed turns to me, reaching across the table to touch my arm. 'Ro, that is hysterical.'

I nod. 'I am a hoot.'

'Have you got any more dates lined up?' BF asks.

'Maybe. I've been messaging a guy called Archie.'

'I can't wait to hear about it,' says Ed, presuming, perhaps, that all my dates end with drug busts in Chelsea bathrooms.

Ed has a determined interest in my dating history, it turns out; he wants to know all about Jonathan and why it didn't work out with Patrick and Andrew; he grimaces throughout my précis on Elliot and concludes: 'What a loser!'

'No,' I say, as my eyes narrow, 'he was a nice guy, just not right for me.'

Still chuckling, he says, 'As if he wore an anorak!' and I wish I hadn't talked about Elliot at all. 'Anyway,' Ed goes on, 'I'm sure you won't be single for long, Ro.'

'That's what I keep telling her,' adds BF, although I can't recall her doing so.

I wouldn't mind getting off this topic. Fortunately, asking Ed about his work does the trick as it turns out that Ed likes to talk about himself – a lot. He is still going half an hour later, though I am no wiser about his job and his several hundred friends have all got muddled in my head.

'Right!' BF plants her hands on the table. 'Another bottle, Ro? And what are you having, sweetheart? My round.'

'Honey,' laughs Ed, 'that was a £40 bottle of Chablis – did you suddenly get promoted or something? I'll get this one as well.' He sounds grudging.

'Ed,' I say, throwing a quick glance at BF, 'I'm happy to get it.'

'No, Ro, don't be silly. Your friend just has expensive tastes.' With this, he pats 'my friend's' head – he *pats* it – and strides off to the bar. I look at BF. She laughs. I don't.

'That was a bit . . .'

'What?' The look on her face is one of innocence; she must not have noticed, or perhaps she doesn't care, that her boyfriend has just degraded her and insulted her career. Because he definitely did do that? I'm worried that I'm looking for reasons to dislike Ed, like I'm treating Ed as a face on the Tinder screen, swiping him left for an arbitrary reason rather than taking the time to get to know him. However, it is also still possible that he is simply a massive, massive jizz monkey. At no point does the Female Pep-Talk recommend telling your best friend that you think her boyfriend is a jizz monkey. I wonder how an observer, watching Ed and me meeting for the first time, would rate the experience – there has been little to no hair twirling and few laughs (not from me, anyway). You can't ask BF, her opinion is not reliable – she likes Ed. Overall, I think you would have to conclude that it hasn't gone very well.

*   *   *

Music, Shakespeare tells us, is the food of love and who am I to argue with the man considered by most as the greatest playwright of all time? He is wrong, though. When it comes to love, music is fine, if having your breasts fondled to Drake is your idea of romance, but music is not the food of love; food is. Food is the food of love.

Recently, most of my Tinder conversations have detoured towards food but it's my own fault for setting my age parameters at twenty-seven to thirty-five; if I could face the prospect of frottage with someone born after the Gulf War (the first one) we could chat about our favourite bands, or the best places to go clubbing, if people still call it that. When you reach dating middle age, however, nobody goes 'clubbing' any more – it's all bars and pubs and nights in with friends and everyone is talking about their favourite restaurant/take-away/hangover junk food (there is a correct answer to all of these, by the way, none of which is KFC). This is how it's been with Archie. My date with Doug could well have put me off Tinder – nay, dating . . . nay, *men* – for decades. But it's been a couple of weeks since it happened and things move on quickly in the Tindersphere; I've chalked it up to a dating anomaly and with the presumed guarantee that my dates can't get much worse, Archie seems like a safe bet. I Liked Archie because he's clean-shaven, reassuringly tall and I liked his shoes, and a man's shoes tell you all you need to know. Archie's were expensive. It sounds shallow to want a man with money and if you prioritise it above other characteristics, like 'doesn't drown puppies', it is. But when your boyfriend says he's going to treat you to dinner, it's nice not to end up at Madras Palace for the all-you-can-eat Sunday night buffet. Again.

Archie's messages have all been articulate and interesting – unlike Steve, 31, who enquired succinctly if I wanted 'sum fun tonight?' or Callum, 29, who sent me a selfie of him wanking. We've been through our jobs (he does something involving an online start-up), where we live (he's south like me) and downtime activities but yet again, food is back on the menu. Food is a good topic for Tinder: it's a common ground and accessible yet whimsical enough to discuss with someone who exists solely as words on a screen and five photographs. My 5:2 eased into something closer to 6:1 as we chatted about the best places we've eaten in London: Archie chose the expensive, exclusive Nobu whilst I plumped for Viajante based on the one time I went (years ago) and the fact I saw Matthew Williamson having a fag outside.

Archie:
So where's next on the to-eat list?

Rosy:
I've always wanted to go to The Shard – the views are meant to be amazing.

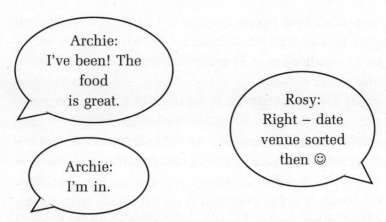

I had been half-joking (who puts a smiley face emoji unless they're joking?) but Archie wasn't: he texted yesterday to say that if The Shard was what I wanted then to The Shard we would go.

It's one of those extra-dark, cold, hair-frizzing, drizzly Friday evenings that make you yearn for British summertime, all eleven days of it, and I am waiting for Archie outside London Bridge station. Meeting here was my suggestion and it is proving one of the dumber of my consistently dumb ideas because there are several different entrances and exits and I'm pretty sure I'm shivering outside the wrong one. I am also wearing my stupid leather jacket again, purely for aesthetic reasons, because my parka makes me look like the seven-year-old nobody wanted to hold hands with at school (I left my rucksack behind at least). And so far, my first impression of Archie is: he's not here.

I can't bear waiting for dates. Initially, there is the shame and societal reckoning that comes from having (possibly) been stood up; this is swiftly followed by simmering irritation that he couldn't be arsed to arrive on time when I've inhaled hairspray to set my make-up *and* worn heels, and it is rounded off by a burst of withering self-revulsion that I'm relying on a phone app to try and find a boyfriend. I'm shuffling round in a half-circle to keep warm and because of this I come to realise that Archie is not so much late as standing behind me. I recognise him instantly: not only is he more attractive than in his photos (which is the opposite to almost every other date I have been on so far), he's also a tad shorter, which I realise for anyone other than my pint-size self would be disappointing.

'I came out of the wrong exit, I'm so sorry,' he says before pulling me into an embrace.

'So did I.'

'In that case,' he says, whipping out an umbrella and offering me shelter, 'we both came out of the right one.' I laugh, almost in spite of myself, and it's a real one, not my fake laugh that comes out of the side of my mouth. I edge a little further towards him.

As our dinner reservation isn't for an hour, Archie suggests we head for a bar he knows nearby, a plan I'm all for until we get there: a queue at least fifteen-strong is being kept in check by a surly bouncer and the girls, bare-armed, bare-legged (some hearty souls are both) are doing the shivery-hop I last performed on a night out in Newcastle where coats are illegal. I grimace and look over to gauge Archie's reaction. A queue, in the rain, can be toxic for a first date, plus I feel the same about the cold as I do about the Third Reich and grapefruit (not keen).

'We should be able to go straight in,' he says.

'Do you have mob connections?'

He smiles. 'It's all about who you know.'

I'm glad that I'm getting to know Archie.

He strides up to the bouncer. They have a quiet conversation. The bouncer smiles – a rare sight, like a leopard in the Savannah – then they shake hands and Archie gestures me over and guides me inside before pulling open the heavy, wooden door. I am assaulted with pumping beats as I walk in; I'd term the music 'dance' in the same way my grandma referred to anything with more than 100 BPM as 'disco'. The place is packed with the young, beautiful and moneyed; girls totter round in micro-dresses sipping bellinis through straws whilst men in handmade shirts and gleaming shoes look on.

Invoking my Tube Ninja skills, I weave through the throng in search of somewhere to sit. There are no chairs; instead, brown leather cubes surround the tables so I awkwardly perch whilst Archie disappears off to the bar; when he returns twenty minutes later, it occurs to me I never told him what I wanted so it is a relief to see him clutching a matching set of cocktails.

'The bar is a scrum,' he says, taking a seat on an opposing cube. 'Who knew everyone wants to get drunk so badly?' The cocktails are very small, which suggests they were very expensive and probably means they'll be very good; when I take a sip, they are. This is an extraordinary place for a first date and we're still only at pre-dinner drinks; as for The Shard, I barely knew what I was suggesting when I mentioned it and I'm amazed that Archie took to the idea so readily. It makes me think of all the men on Guardian Soulmates who cited 'up for an adventure' as a desirable quality. Perhaps Archie is no different. Maybe that's why he Liked me back.

*   *   *

'*The Poddington Peas*,' says Archie.

'They were excellent. *Playdays*?'

'Which stop?'

'Tent, obviously.'

Archie nods, concurring. 'I'd turn over if it was the Patch stop.' He grins at me. Good teeth – tick.

'There was this one show,' he says, taking a sip of his beer (I've stayed loyal to the cocktails, costly as they are), 'where kids went up in a lift and there was . . . a face, I think? . . . giving them instructions. And they had to get out on different levels . . .'

'And take part in weird games! Yes! In one they had to swim in a bowl of alphabet soup and find letters to spell a word. I loved that show.'

'I can't remember what it was called and all my friends claim they've never heard of it.'

'Mine too! They say I conjured it up during a night of debauched drug-taking.'

Archie cocks his eyebrow. 'Is that . . . something you're into?'

Shit – this could be Doug all over again. I've dabbled over the years but I'm never sure what the right answer to this question is: he might think I'm square if I say no. Then again – Doug. 'Not especially,' I venture.

A middle-aged man in a shiny jacket lands upon a nearby cube and is joined by a twenty-something blonde with dark roots and strappy pink stilettos. She could be his daughter if it wasn't illegal for fathers to touch their children in that way.

'Quick trip to the gents if you don't mind.' Archie stands up and throws a look over at our new neighbours. 'I'll let you all get acquainted.' I watch The Blonde, now on Daddy's knee, listening to him talk as she circles her finger on his chest. It's sweet, intimate and utterly gross all at the same time.

A late-night dinner reservation sounded oh so romantic, but I'm starting to regret having only had some toast before I came out – I'm starving. I have an emergency Tracker bar in my irritatingly small bag but I'll need to wait until my hunger peaks if I'm going to eat it. I take my phone out to check the time and am amazed to see it's 9.30 p.m., meaning that Archie and I have been chatting and drinking for over an hour when it feels like we've been here for ten minutes. There is something appealing about Archie. I like his dark eyes and the roundness to his face that softens him, in contrast to his lithe and muscular body. I hadn't detected a stellar sense of humour from his messages but I've belly laughed four times so far this evening. He has been in the toilet a while now and I've finished my drink. I look down at my phone as it rests in my hand. My thumb is hovering over the Tinder flame.

Tindering whilst already on a Tinder *date* is morally sketchy; if you want to get meta about it, perhaps this shameless act is symbolic of the wider Tinder experience, namely that there is always someone else, and potentially someone better, out there. I'm not dissatisfied being here . . . I am just intrigued to see what else might be on offer. I flick past Henri, Jimbo, Alexander and Christopher, before coming to a dead stop at Amit. Amit has written a tag line at the bottom of his profile. Why would anyone choose to write anything if they didn't have to? Writing my GS profile was the worst part of my internet dating experience and that includes my date with Jonathan. Just for that, I flick Amit left. I look up and see Archie weaving his way towards me so I stow my phone away and smile as he catches my eye then sits down, apologising for having been so long. I tell him not to worry and stand up – my round.

*   *   *

Archie looks at his watch. 'Time for dinner.' I'd forgotten all about eating the Tracker. The Shard is a short walk back in the direction we came from but already it looms above us, lit against the night sky and almost impossibly tall. Having lived in London for six years, I've had the pleasure of watching the glass tower push up from its foundations to over 1,000 feet into the air, so stepping into the foyer is a thrill in itself but I've long yearned to ride up in the lift, like a child who is perpetually too short for Space Mountain.

'This is incredible,' I breathe as we step inside.

'We're not moving yet!' replies Archie, giver of shelter, provider of warmth. He hits the button for the thirty-first floor and we start our ascent, a grin of idiotic glee spreading across my face as the earth falls away from under me. Archie smiles back at me as one might humour an elderly relative.

At the restaurant we are greeted by the *maître d'* who leads us to a table in the middle of the room; subtlely, politely, Archie asks if they might happen to have an alternative by the window, because when you are thirty-one floors above London, the only place to be is beside a (securely fastened) window. Being suave – tick. And it's worth it, because even at night, the view is breath-taking: London fans out to the horizon, a vibrant, twinkling toy-town beneath our feet.

We order wine and peruse the menu; when the waiter returns, Archie orders lamb whilst I opt for fish. I can feel Archie looking at me as he fills my glass; I am giddy after one sip. I look back and my eyes meet his – I can't take my eyes off him, in fact. Bread comes and we nibble at it and talk about the marathon Archie ran last year; he is contemplating another. I am not. Should I need to outpace killer bees or nuclear fallout I *might* run twenty-six miles, but it's tentative either way and it would take the motivation of death to make me bother.

Any doubts I'd harboured about eating a hearty meal so late at night evaporate as a plate of monkfish cooked with saffron and orange is set down before me and the aroma floats up to my nose; I take my first mouthful and it is love at first bite. 'This is amazing,' I say to Archie. He is still watching me as he says, 'It really is.'

It is as though being 300 feet in the air has heightened everything. It is so late (the last time I checked it was well after midnight) and the food is so delicious; even the wine seems colder and sharper than I'm used to. There is something magical, something dreamlike, about being up here, as though we are floating as the city sleeps below us; Archie and I could be the only people awake in London, in the country, perhaps even on earth. I watch him, watching me. In this dream it's like we have already fallen in love.

'Let's have a nightcap,' Archie suggests as the waiter arrives to clear our empty plates (I have to hold back from licking mine). *A nightcap:* it sounds so wonderfully old-fashioned, which makes it wonderfully romantic in turn. We retire to the bar, where Archie procures a whisky for himself and doesn't laugh at me when I order a vodka and coke; after the cocktails, after the food and a bottle of wine, it's the only thing I can countenance drinking, though it is not quite the stuff of nightcaps and antiquated passion.

We talk, talk, drink and talk: about the box sets that kept us up half the night, about the bands we like and the songs that take us right back to our big moments . . . we fill each other with our histories and, when Archie asks if I want children – how many, favourite names – it's like we've instinctively laid the foundations of our future.

Whether it's due to the excess of alcohol or altitude, the boundaries of first-date conversation seem to have melted away and something about being here, now, with Archie, makes me want to confide: I tell him about my turbulent adolescence, complete with references to the promiscuous years I'd rather forget and whilst I look away for the more sensitive parts, Archie's gaze doesn't deviate from me once. In return, he tells me about his work; he's an underwriter and says he never feels as clever as his colleagues, that he's waiting for his incompetence to be exposed. His left hand rests on the bar as he talks. With my eyes locked on his, I slide my right hand from my glass towards his, stretching my fingers infinitesimally. He glances down and I freeze, but in the next second our fingers are entwined, and my hand is grasped in his, and we stay like this until my heat is his heat, his skin is mine and I can't tell where I end and he begins. I don't want to let go. He strokes my thumb with his and any desire to swipe on Tinder dissolves; there is nowhere I'd rather be but here, nothing else exists but us.

It is only when the barman politely 'suggests' we solicit our bill that we realise we are the last patrons standing (sitting, technically, though definitely still drinking) and it is time to make our descent back down to earth, which is not nearly as fun as travelling skyward. It is dry but cold when we leave The Shard and I snuggle into Archie as we pass through London Bridge and back out onto the street; the station is barely recognisable without the noise and hoards of bustling passengers. As if we are in a generic rom-com, Archie sticks out his arm and hails me a cab that miraculously happens to be passing and miraculously happens to be free. Things like that don't happen in real life . . . but nothing about tonight usually happens for real. As the taxi starts to slow, Archie pulls me in to him and kisses me, slowly and softly; it is so welcome and warm that I don't want him to stop, but when he pulls back and smiles, his forehead resting on mine, I know that it's only a break in the midst of whatever is starting. He opens the door for me then leans in to say goodbye, but the word has nothing to do with an ending. On the journey home, I rest my head against the window and replay the night's events: the rain; the food; the warmth of Archie's body and his lips against mine. At our wedding, we should serve monkfish.

* * *

The next day, at Sophie and Ollie's for lunch with Kate and Bob, my phone pinged with a text from Archie just as Ollie placed a lasagne on the table. 'Something interesting?'

'I went on a date last night.'

'A good one?' asked Sophie.

'A *very* good one.' My friends listened in rapt attention as I described the details of the night: the cocktails, the food, the view – and I spared nothing when pronouncing my feelings on the company.

Kate squeezed her lips together. 'He sounds like he could be . . .'

'I know.' I giggled and piled carrots on my plate. My

phone pinged again. Archie wanted to know if I had plans for Monday. Kate and Sophie squealed.

We talked about Kate and Bob's wedding over dessert. Weddings usually trigger in me a sense of merry ambivalence; the joy I feel for my friends is shamefully tempered by the prospect of attending alone, again. On this occasion, as we discussed the merits of a DJ vs band, I felt a flash of smug elation, for the only thing better than the contented security of true, long-term love is that time at the beginning when it's fresh and intoxicating, for you know once it's gone you can never get it back. By the time Sophie served coffee my jangly zeal had settled into a more civilised sense of inclusion. I found myself thinking of Kate's comment in reply to Sophie's congratulatory Facebook post: *You'll be next.*

On Monday morning, having recounted the whole dream-like experience for a second time to Pip, I was scrolling through my inbox when my phone pinged: I beamed as I opened Archie's message.

Archie:
Morning you! So I've been thinking about a name for our dog and I've got it: Fat Bitch! How hilarious would it be to shout that out across the park?!

It took me a second to take it in; I read it again. I couldn't remember any conversation we'd had about getting a dog, but whenever I tried to remember specifics from the date I kept seeing candlelight and roses and Archie in a dinner jacket. Were I ever to get a dog (unlikely – I'm a cat person) 'Fat Bitch' would not rank highly on my list of preferred names; I must have been quite into the idea on Saturday.

I was about to reply when Helen pushed through the door, wearing her Lanvin jacket with the sharp lapels; she announced the firm had made a last-minute decision to pitch for a client previously thought to be untenable – and the pitch had been scheduled for Friday. All thoughts of Archie were lost as I sat down with Helen and we combed through a revised schedule for the week. When I got back to my desk, Archie had texted again:

> Archie:
> We could get her a
> name tag inscribed
> with 'A&R's fat
> bitch!' LOL

I had fleetingly wondered if the first text had indeed been meant for me but this confirmed it was. Nor was this 'joke' the result of Archie having a spontaneous brain injury, nor was it going away.

Four minutes later:

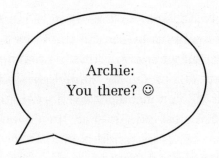

Archie:
You there? ☺

I replied the moment I could, which wasn't until lunch, and explained about the pitch. Archie apologised and suggested he buy me dinner; we texted back and forth as I ate my sandwich and gradually he returned to the Archie of Friday and I started to feel excited about seeing him in the evening. If you're not prepared to give someone the benefit of the doubt, Tinder is not the dating app for you.

Pip picked up the last of my call sheet so that I could go to Boots and spray myself with perfume samplers before heading to the restaurant Archie's chosen, but she needn't have bothered because Archie is late. I'm sitting at the bar, about to order myself a drink (from the cocktail list I've now memorised, having been reading it solidly for the last ten minutes) when the door swings open and here he is, wearing a near identical outfit to the one he wore on Saturday. I smile as he strides towards me, just as dashing as I remember him. He perches on the stool next to mine. 'Hello gorgeous,' he says and kisses me on the lips, 'how are you? Would you like a drink?'

'I was thinking about one of the house martinis.'

Archie scans the menu. 'Mm, good choice.' He calls the barman over and orders, adding a glass of red for himself. The waiter tilts his head, already contrite; in thickly accented French, he apologises that they have run out of lime so house martinis are off the menu.

Archie turns to me. 'Would you like something else?'

'I'm hungry if I'm honest,' I reply, 'maybe we could eat?'

He snaps the menu shut. 'Fine! Great.' Archie jumps up and takes my hand to help me down.

Our table is a cavernous booth. Archie cups his hands round his mouth and pretend shouts, 'You're so far away!' Before I can respond he hooks his arm around my waist, slides me towards him and proceeds to nuzzle my neck as his hands run amok over my body, finally coming to rest around my arse. I laugh and shove him but this only seems to encourage him and he grips me tighter.

'Someone's wearing a thong,' he whispers into my ear and snaps the elastic of my underwear, which hurts.

'I didn't have any clean pants left.'

'Dirty girl, eh?' he purrs. I want to vomit.

I order lamb chops. I don't like lamb chops but I like the other options less. I look over at Archie dissecting his steak and wonder exactly who it is I'm looking at. Is this honestly the person I thought I was falling in love with just yesterday? It's like Perfect Archie is gone and replaced with . . . Arnie, Archie's evil, gauche (though equally attractive) twin brother. Out from the flattering candlelight of the most romantic date of the century, I can see the Real Archie and the differences are blinding. I prod at my chops, half-listening to Archie's chatter and some of it is quite funny (as long as his comment about Belgians definitely was a joke). But in my head I am thinking about home. Every time he asks if I'm OK I lie and say yes because I can't tell him about the crushing disappointment that's pulling me under. I can't tell him I feel lonelier with him than if I were here eating by myself or that I'm humiliated, having all but proclaimed my love for him to my closest friends and imagined our wedding. I won't tell him how incredible it was to feel adored again that night, and how grateful I was that the pain Charlie inflicted on me might finally be repaired. So instead of telling him that, I say that I'm tired after a manic day at work and that I'm OK without a dessert.

* * *

Archie had worked out something was wrong by the time we came to say goodbye, of course he had; this morning, I woke up to another text and they've been coming through all day. I sent him a quick reply at lunch citing workload, which with the pitch coming up is relentless, but I can't use this excuse now I'm at home. The last text was his fourteenth. I take a deep breath and reach for my phone.

Rosy:
Archie, this all feels a bit
much for me. You seem
great and I enjoyed
meeting you but last night
it just wasn't really there
for me . . . I'm really sorry x

Within minutes, Archie replies in agreement:

Archie:
Yeah, it was a bit
weird last night . . .

Then with mild hostility:

Archie:
You've been quite
dishonest about things,
I think.

And then my phone is quiet for a moment before he texts again. He wishes last night had gone differently, he says, and he's sorry – maybe it was too much to see each other so quickly. There's a bit of exposition about how work has been stressing him out and after his ex, I'm the first girl he's really liked (I know the feeling), then makes one last-ditch attempt to salvage things by reminding me how I'd referred to Saturday as '*so amazing*' (at 1 a.m., when I was drunk) but whatever I had for Archie has gone. If your first date is thirty-one floors in the air, the only way left to go is down.

12.

HOW TO BE INVISIBLE

In the city, the phrase 'lunch break' is so misleading it should be legally, universally, changed, to something like 'speed ingestion' or 'food interlude'. As part of my induction at work, my then boss, Lindsey, told me that I'd be getting an hour for lunch. Lindsey didn't arrive for work one Thursday morning: she'd been fired for being very bad at her job and a passive-aggressive bitch. She was also a liar, because in the three years since I've been here I've taken my full lunch hour exactly thirteen times. Everything I needed to know about life in this office I learnt in my first three weeks: which loos were most likely to be empty when I needed to poo; which mugs were for general use and which belonged to Arlene, our OCD office manager; who got aggressive if you ate the last Malteser from the tub of Celebrations . . . these are but a few examples of the office essentials I had to grasp to avoid being hated and/or nicknamed. I also learnt the literal meaning of 'lunch hour', which translates as: a short, unspecified and inconsistent period in which to purchase and eat processed food and have a quick flick through *Mail* Online.

Back in those heady first weeks of work, way before 5:2/6:1 ruined the thrill of food, I used to dedicate a lot of my morning to deciding what I'd have for lunch; sushi? Sandwich? Soup? Salad? If none of the alliterative options appealed, I'd detour to Sainsbury's for a wild-card picnic that could consist of anything from a packet of Hobnobs to a selection of Italian meats, and often both. Pip walked past my desk as I was arranging my feast one Tuesday (sausage roll, packet of ham, a flapjack, can of Lilt) and gave my shoulder a squeeze, saying: 'Someone's having a tough day.' She was right: the bus had been late, I'd spent three hours researching a project that Helen then cancelled and I'd had a fight with Charlie the previous night. The time my shower leaked, the day after I had my bag stolen, whenever I was due on my period . . . any time I have something on my mind, something that niggles and I can't quite work out, I eat. I've had to ban myself from supermarket lunch shopping on all but high days and holidays. Ten days post-Archie and I'm starting to feel the pull. I've managed to resist today; instead I'm making the six-minute walk from our office to the road where all the chains are clustered. You'd think that Pret's chef salads were becoming rationed from the way grown men jostle for them, weaving and leaning in and out of each other and peering up on tip-toes, trying to secure the holy grail of the sandwich you want rather than the sandwich you can reach. The women are no less feral, just more organised. They will have planned *en route* so they can take a direct path to an old favourite and sling the right change at the cashier before dashing back to the office in time for the Ideation Cluster Fuck at 2 p.m. Girls my own age chatter in pairs as they buy small salads and water then furtively grab a brownie in the queue. I've never felt like I fit in with them. I'm not sure why.

I am weighing up a pot of edamame beans against a side salad (it's a fucking '1' day) when I hear her. 'Hello,' she whispers in my ear and I know instantly it's her from her voice alone; Kate once described it as 'the sound you'd get if you gave a monkey a double bass – and he turned out to be good'.

'Hello, Sal,' I say, spinning round. I wrap my arms around her slight frame and breathe in her expensive scent. Sally and I met at my first job, at the agency that had hired me fresh out of university. She'd been there for a year when I started and on my first day she gripped my elbow before briefing and whispered: 'You can still get out of here. I signed a contract, I'm dead weight, but you can make it, make it for both of us . . .' She took me out at the end of the day, got us both horrifically drunk and we ended up in a strip club. Sally left nine months later – I was promoted into her role – but we have achieved the miraculous and remained friends-who-used-to-work-together. She now works in publishing and has recently moved jobs – her new company must be around here.

'What else are you getting?' she asks.

'This is kind of it. I'm on the 5:2,' I reply, 'or a version of it.'

'Fuck that,' says Sally. She takes two salmon things from the shelf, barely looking, and two bottles of water then strides towards the tills. '*Get a table*,' she mouths from the queue. I have a feeling this might be the four-teenth time I take my hour.

*　　*　　*

'So you *are* on Tinder! I thought so,' Sally exclaims when I mention Archie. 'Sometimes I search for women so I can see which of my friends are on it. I haven't seen you, though. I would have Liked you.' She winks.

'You search through girls?'

'I've matched with a few!' Sal laughs. 'It's just fun . . . although I may have lined something up for Thursday . . .' She grins broadly. I'm aching to ask the first of the thousands of questions piling up in my head when she says, 'But I want to know about you.'

'I've hardly been on it recently,' I say. It is not far from the truth. I've been dipping in and out since Archie, but I've lost confidence in my ability to distinguish between the good eggs and the nut jobs. Matches lie abandoned in my inbox and questions hang unanswered in air that is fetid with stale jokes. I don't want to admit to Sal that I've left them to stagnate, neither acknowledged nor deleted, with some even unopened. In truth, I am ashamed of myself. My mother has always said: 'Say yes or no, but don't say nothing, it's cowardly.' If she suspects either Bru or I to be in the wrong her disappointment is palpable: she sets her jaw and won't talk. I'd never seen someone load a dishwasher passive aggressively until Bru revealed over dinner one night that he'd cheated in an exam.

I tell Sal: 'My dates have been train wrecks, except one, but he . . . disappeared.' I won't let myself think about Patrick any more; I tried to fantasise a different ending for us once but even in our imaginary relationship he still ended up leaving.

'Oh that's just Tinder.' Sally waves her hand, shooing away my dejection. There is a delicate tattoo on her wrist that reads 'Dubstep Unicorn' and was the result of too much rice wine and a lost bet somewhere/at some point in Malaysia (possibly). I laughed when I first saw it and asked if she regretted it; she looked me in the eye and told me that regret is for 'murderers and people who cheat'. 'You should get one,' she had said as I ran my finger over the bumpy, swirling text. It made me laugh more: I was the only child in my primary school that fainted *before* the MMR jab. I don't submit myself to needles voluntarily.

'Unfortunately,' she goes on, 'there's no vetting process for who is allowed on Tinder. Some people want to hook up, other people want to get married; there's no way of telling who wants what.'

'And some people don't know,' I add, thinking mostly of myself.

Sally does not suffer this affliction. 'Tinder is fucking brilliant!' she cries when I ask for her thoughts. People turn and stare. 'I take a cast-your-net-wide approach and

Like pretty much everyone . . .' She gets up, puts our
empty food boxes in the bin and takes a swig of coffee
as she sits back down. '. . . Because everyone thinks they
have a "type", but they don't. The more people you Like,
the more likely you are to find someone.'

'It sounds exhausting. Also, I really do have a type:
dark hair, not too tall . . .'

'Rosy, hush.' Sally plants her palms flat on the table.
'Your type, just like everyone else's, is a man who loves
you, who is nice to you and who doesn't fuck you around.
Or a woman.' The grin is back. I make a mental note to
ring her on Friday morning.

'Have you met anyone . . . special, Sal?' *Special* . . . it
sounds so saccharine but I can't think how else to put it.

'God, too many. I can't remember what conversation
I've had with whom – one guy blocked me after I asked
him about his job three times. People are just blank faces
and you have to add the detail. Joseph: plays drums,
banker. Simon: wears a hat.'

I know I should go back to the office, but I cannot leave
until Sally has finished recounting her latest Tinder dates,
including one with forty-year-old Toby, who she met after
widening her age parameters as an 'experiment'. I am
listening wordlessly as she concludes: '. . . and it was only
as I was scrabbling round for my pants in the morning that
I noticed the hearing aids on the side and suddenly I was
like, ooohhh, he's *deaf*. Then everything made sense.' She
giggles to herself whilst I close my mouth. The lunchtime
swarm of office workers has dissipated and been replaced
by mummies and babies, students and young guys with

laptops, working on their 'screenplay'. I want to spend the rest of the afternoon here, drinking coffee and marvelling at Sally, but as she points out, this would involve quitting my job. I weigh this up for several minutes.

We hug goodbye, set a date for dinner and I scurry back to the office, bracing myself for Helen's wrath, but when I get there Pip says she's in a meeting. In gratitude for my good karma, I work through my to-do list and don't stop until I get to the bottom. When I look up at the clock, it's almost six o'clock.

*   *   *

On the bus, I keep thinking of the zeal in Sally's voice as she extolled the virtues of Tinder and it's made me think that perhaps Tinder isn't the problem – I am. Of the six dates I've had so far, only one has progressed to a second and none to a third – admittedly, a second date with Doug would be unwise, but I can't keep blaming the men (OK, yes, apart from Doug, again . . .). If Sally can make Tinder work for her then so can I. I simply need to make some changes.

First step: new profile photos. The current pictures of myself . . . I don't feel they say 'me'. I've been considering one photo in particular; I'd previously discounted it because it's from Sophie's birthday last year and I look drunk, but hopefully this will translate as *I have fun and friends* rather than *I have vodka in the water bottle on my desk*. BF is standing beside me looking five times hotter, but I can crop her out.

Second step: tackle my messages. The most recent, from Will, 32, reads: *'Where have you gone?!!!!!'* I block Mum's disapproving frown from my mind as I scroll up to the start of the conversation . . . I remember feeling uninspired but then he'd mentioned his interest in photography and I got caught up in his passion. He used words in the same way I imagined he used a camera: his messages were brief but always thoughtfully worded and he was quite funny with it. Then he passed all my covert tests: yes, he liked PJ Harvey; no, he'd never had chocolate-coated pretzels but he was eager to try. It's not until I get further down the thread that I see why we never progressed: I'd been at work without my charger and my battery died; when I plugged my phone in at home, I saw that Will had sent ten messages in a row. I texted back to explain and he joked that I'd end up calling the police on him, which could have been funny if it wasn't so prescient. His final, plaintive plea – *Don't leave me Rosy!!!!!!* – sealed his fate (the exclamation marks alone were enough) and I took the coward's way out and stopped replying.

My next message is from Ian.

> Ian:
> Your tits look amazing in the 2nd pic! Cheeky I know, but you can handle it ☺

Evidently, I could not. I don't feel so bad about Ian. Delete.

As I'm reading, I am starting to see the same anecdotes, the same jokes and the same go-to schtick running through almost all my conversations like a motif – and unfortunately it's all coming from me. Reading the threads one after another like this, I can see I've referenced my ex-cheerleading captaincy with at least seven different men – it's not funny in six of them and irrelevant in one. Apparently this is the most exciting thing I have to say for myself. At some point I evidently decided that typing was too much effort, because I started copying and pasting comments:

Rosy:
Hey Jamie, how's
work going today?

Stuart:
Who's Jamie?

Yet I wonder why I'm still single.

When I open my messages with Max, I can barely remember him; our initial texts are so nondescript that there's nothing to differentiate him from anyone else. He looks handsome in his photos, though. Men tend to look rugged, or cool, or sexy or cute (a description I hear men just *love*); they are rarely described as handsome any more, but Max is. He has a straight nose, a square jaw and thick hair set into a side parting with dark eyebrows to match. He looks to be the tallest of his friends and they are an attractive bunch themselves. I bet Max smells nice. I was the last one to send a message, three weeks ago; he didn't reply but I was talking to Archie at the same time and wasn't fazed by ending up in Max's reject pile. Maybe he had an 'Archie' of his own; maybe he too had been on the verge of deserting Tinder after one too many weird, expensive cocktails, average evenings and girls who felt him up. I'll send him a message and if he doesn't reply, that's what I'll put it down to. But perhaps there's a chance we can restore each other's faith in the Tindersphere.

Rosy:
Hi Max, I know it's been a while . . .
you'll either think I'm endearingly
tardy or emotionally unstable (the
former, I promise) but just thought
I'd say hi . . .

Two days pass with no reply. Then, on the third:

Max:
Nice to hear from
you Rosy – yes it's
been a while!
How are you?

We chat for three more days, after which he suggests
a drink. I'm going to find out what Max smells like.

*   *   *

BF has lent me the dress she wore for her first date with
Ed: it's elegant, sexy in a subtle, refined way, rather than
the overt, slutty way I'm likely to opt for out of panic.
Wearing it feels like stepping into role: I become a confident, sensual woman, a far cry from my usual persona
of Girl Who Spends an Hour Getting Ready and Still
Ends Up Dishevelled; BF, having popped round to drop
it off, was only too happy to agree after being subjected
to forty minutes of me preening in front of the mirror.
If the dress managed to impress Ed, I told her, I was
confident it would work for Max. I noticed the smallest
of twitches in the corner of BF's mouth at the mention of
Ed's name.

'He's been a bit down,' she said. 'I thought I'd take him out whilst you're on your date, make a fuss of him.'

'Is it like last time?' I sat down next to her, watching her face for hints of evasiveness; if she was having doubts about Ed, she was working hard to disguise it.

'No, not as bad . . . he's just quiet.' And then she fell quiet too.

I held her tight as we hugged goodbye at the door. I didn't want to let her go but I was at risk of being late and BF wanted to get home to change. I have an unspecific fidgety feeling that's making me smudge my eyeliner. The dress is starting to feel all wrong, too tight, too fancy; never have I been so desperate to put on my jeans and hi-tops and blur the comfortable/unkempt dichotomy.

I can't see Max when I walk in, but according to my watch I'm five minutes early for our 8 p.m. date. I know he's on his way, but to the rest of the punters in here I'm a dolled-up female ordering a solitary drink; I feel so conspicuous I might as well be wearing a fruit hat. I pay for a vodka and soda and tug at my skirt whilst I'm waiting for my change. There is a high table free opposite the door, so I clamber up onto the stool, primed to spot Max when he comes in. I'm glad he suggested this place: it's close to my flat but we rarely come here and I would never have thought of it, but it's suited to a first date. The bar, the floor and the tables and chairs are all fashioned from the same dark wood and the room is lit with soft uplighting that is just bright enough to discern whether your date is good-looking or not. A girl comes out from the bar carrying tea lights for each table; stopping at the first, she lights the wick and nestles the tea light carefully into its jar. I watch the flames flicker gently against the glass and imagine Max and me coming here together, as a couple. It would become our local.

My eyes dart towards the door as it opens: a couple walk in. They are both dressed casually and neither is carrying a bag so I guess they live locally. It's Thursday, almost the end of the week; perhaps they want to wind down – maybe they were thinking of opening a bottle of red at home, a leftover, like from . . . when his sister came round for dinner last week. But, no: they've agreed to get out of the flat because they have no plans this weekend, although she wants to go to Ikea (she's holding off asking until Saturday morning – he swore he'd never go back, not after last time). They wait at the bar. She's changed her mind; she wants a bottle of white now she's here, whilst he still wants red – they'll compromise by ordering by the glass . . .

They order a pint apiece and find a table. I used to be able to read people.

I tap at the screen of my phone; it lights up and shows me it is 8.11 p.m. and there is no message from Max. He must be on the Tube – he said he'd be coming from work, but I don't know where that is or how long it could take him – plus it's rush hour. I feel the brisk draught as the door opens and I look up just in time to catch the back of a man in a denim jacket as he disappears outside, a cigarette dangling between his fingers.

Max will be here. I go to pull at my dress and am suddenly aware of the tension that is gripping my shoulders. I take a long breath in and force them down as I exhale. I open my messages with Max and scroll up to the one listing the details for tonight: unless there are two Fox and Hound pubs on Atherton Street, opposite a dry cleaners, I'm in the right place and on time – *8 p.m.* – just as he's written, and *on Thursday*. It's definitely Thursday . . . could Max have meant next Thursday? No. We arranged this on Tuesday. He's running late and he's on the Tube. He'll be here any minute. I browse the internet for a bit until I remember that the internet is quite shit and I really need to pee, so I finish off the rest of my drink and gather my bag and coat and hop down. Now I really need to pee.

The ladies is empty when I walk in; I go into a cubicle and sit down, sensing the moisture on the toilet seat as soon as my skin makes contact. How do grown women manage to urinate *on* the seat? This is an enduring and repulsive mystery to me. Do they stand up? Hover? If they find the idea of sitting on the seat so abhorrent, how do they justify flecking it with drops of their own urine? I may never know. At this specific moment, the relief of emptying my bladder is so rapturous that I'm barely fussed to be dabbing someone else's piss off the back of my legs. I go to the sink and wash my hands (three times) and catch my reflection in the mirror. The lighting in here is predictably bad: I am spotlit like I'm in Guantanamo, though poor lighting alone can't account for the face looking back at me. The painted, pouting Me I assessed as pretty enough to leave the house has been replaced by Me in thirty years' time – the version that took up smoking and sunbeds. The smoky eye shadow that I spent twenty minutes perfecting, that gave me a sultry allure at home, has smudged and streaked into the fold of my eyelids like grouting. My hair is a lost cause, the wind put paid to that. I might shave it off – Dad would be thrilled. I look so different from the Me in my profile pictures Max would do well to recognise me, let alone fancy me. I wash my hands one last time and am still shaking them dry as I head back out to the bar. The table is still empty: apparently nobody wants the prime position directly in front of the draughty door. I climb back up on my stool and scan the room in case Max has arrived, but I can't see him. I check my phone. It's 8.25 p.m.

I'm worried. What if something has happened? What if in his haste to get here Max ran into the path of a car? Or an articulated lorry? That would be worse; I wouldn't forgive myself. But if he is simply late I am going to have to dig deep to forgive *him:* ten minutes late is rude but twenty-five minutes, with no phone call or text, is balls-out offensive. Max better have the excuse of a lifetime prepared when he gets here: I've been sitting on this stool like a muppet for nigh on half an hour and I think the other drinkers are starting to think I'm a hooker. Maybe I should call him? I could call him. But he might be three minutes from walking through the door in which case he'll think I'm desperate and pedantic. There has to be a way of phrasing it to show that I'm totally chilled.

Hey Max, where are you?

Hey buddy, are you nearby?

Just checking, it's definitely tonight yeah?

Have you lost the use of your legs?

I hate talking on the phone at the best of times; I do whatever I can to avoid it at work (this can be problematic, working in PR: talking to people on the phone constitutes a large part of my job) so the chances of me ringing a date I've neither met nor spoken to via anything other than text is slim. I'm not going to ring Max. But I can't just sit here.

I tug the *Evening Standard* from my bag and lay it out on the table. What if Max has . . . no, he'll be here. I try to focus on the newsprint but can't and end up reading the same sentence four times. *What if Max has stood me up?* What if he looked at my pictures again and decided against it? Maybe he reread my messages and concluded I was boring and that our date would be long, uncomfortable and pointless . . . maybe he saw me through the window and turned around. I concentrate on the paper, trying to fill my head with new ideas that will force the bad ones out but the words are starting to swim as my eyes fill with tears. *What if Max has stood me up?* I would be unbearably humiliated, so ashamed. The sense of rejection alone would be crushing.

At 8.37 p.m., I ring Max. His phone goes straight to voicemail.

I hang up and text BF:

Rosy:
Max is 40 minutes
late.

BF:
What a dick . . . any
explanation?

Rosy:
No – can't get
through to his
phone.

BF:
Maybe he's mixed
up the date? Or
time? Or place?

Rosy:
Nope. Checked
already.

BF:
Oh.

I slide down from my stool and hit the wooden floor hard. It feels like every set of eyes in the pub is watching as I bundle up my coat and bag and push the door – as a small mercy, the tears don't start falling until I'm standing out on the pavement. I totter down the road to a bench and swap my prostitute heels for the flat pumps of a loser. I put on my coat and pull it tight, wrapping my arms around me and I stay like this for a while, I don't know how long. Max stood me up and I hate him for it, not as much as I hate myself, but still . . . I bet he came. He came and saw the same Me that I saw in the mirror, the bedraggled, ugly version; he saw my true self rather than a carefully selected profile picture designed to flatter. I can't blame Max. The blame is mine for being so desperate to find a boyfriend – as if I can make relationships work anyway. It's no wonder Charlie left me.

I get up to start walking home and pull out my phone to text BF.

> Rosy:
> He didn't get mixed up. Going home now. Hope you've had a nice night with Ed x

13.

PI

My phone is ringing but I can't be bothered to pick it up – as in, I literally cannot be bothered to get it from off the floor. I am lying on the sofa, I don't know how long I've been here. I was here when Oona left this morning for a work trip to Prague and I was here when Harriet came back from James's; I was still here when she left again to meet her parents for lunch – that must have been a couple of hours ago. As far as I am aware, apart from getting up to pee and to answer the door for the pizza delivery guy, I haven't moved. The TV is keeping me company; I don't need real people for that. Real people hurt you. *Millionaire Matchmaker* would never stand me up.

My phone had stopped but now it's ringing again and the noise is starting to grate. I look down and see it's BF, so I answer. 'Hi.'

'Are you OK?' she asks, though the concern in her voice suggests she knows otherwise.

'Yeah.'

'After Thursday, I mean.'

'I'm good.'

'What are you doing?'

'Just watching TV.' I feel something wet on my cheek and realise I'm crying. I've cried so often over the last two days I've lost the power to tell when I'm crying and when I'm not.

'He's a fucking bell end. I hope you know that.' She pauses. 'Do you want me to come round?'

I point the TV remote at the TV and bring up the guide to find the only things on are shit films and reruns of shows I've seen a hundred times. Then I smell something awful and realise it's my breath. 'I'm not really dressed or anything . . .'

BF laughs. 'Like that's ever bothered me before! Why don't I jump on the Tube now? I could be with you in half an hour.'

I sit up and brush crumbs off my onesie. 'What about tonight? I could make myself a bit more presentable then we could get a takeaway or something and watch a movie?'

'Shit, I'm sorry – I've got plans with Ed.'

'Oh, OK.'

'I'm really sorry . . .'

'Don't worry about it.'

'What are your plans tomorrow night?'

'Honestly, don't worry.'

'Sorry.'

'It's fine.'

I hang up and lie back on the sofa, staring at the TV screen. I feel . . . nothing. Not angry, not lonely, not particularly sad. I just feel . . . empty. I can't rouse the energy to hate Max any more, or pity him or even feel jealous of the other Tinder girls he'll actually show up for. I've tried replaying my rejection from Patrick, my disappointment from Archie, even the potentially slanderous accusations from Doug to spark an emotion . . . nothing. I'm done with Tinder. It is full of horrible men whose sole desire is to pull your heart from your chest with their big man fists and do keepy-uppys with it until it shrivels into a ball and you're left with a small, withered, rubbery lump of useless muscle. I pick up my phone, open the app and select 'delete'. *Are you sure?* Tinder asks. I was one of those kids who needed three goes to blow out my birthday cake candles but extinguishing the Tinder flame takes seconds. I am sure.

* * *

I look at my clothes hanging in my wardrobe. All of them are horrible. I have no clothes.

In my kitchen, Sally is making 'cocktails'. I hear her call to Harriet, asking if she'd like one, then everything is muffled until I hear Sally say '. . . vodka mixed with WKD Blue . . .' and Harriet replies, 'Is that safe?' I smile to myself. Sally created this brutal concoction years ago, having decided that combining spirits with a non-alcoholic mixer was an inefficient way of getting drunk – the excess liquid just slowed you down. She discovered that by mixing alcohol with more alcohol, and an alarming amount of sugar, we could be drunk, queasy and blue of tongue within roughly twenty minutes. I turn back to my clothes and my smile wanes; sometimes I want to take them all to Oxfam and start again.

Harriet and Sally appear at my door together. Sally clambers onto my bed, being careful not to spill blue liquid onto my bed sheets whilst Harriet hovers in the doorway. 'I have no clothes,' I say.

'Objectively, that isn't true,' says Sally.

'I hate them all,' I whine, 'I have nothing to wear tonight.'

Harriet says: 'Why don't you wear that green top? I think you wore it on Sophie's birthday, that looked so nice.'

I harrumph. I am one denied biscuit away from a full-on tantrum. 'The straps kept falling off my shoulders. It would be too irritating.'

'What about the dress you wore to my birthday?' asks Harriet. 'You looked gorgeous.'

Sally asks. 'You did look gorgeous, Ro, I've seen photographic proof.'

I look from one to the other, bewildered. 'Haz, your birthday was black tie! We're going to The Frog!' I did feel good in that dress though; I got more compliments in one night than I had from Charlie in three years as his girlfriend but it is in no way appropriate for drinks with Sal at my local. When I told Sally about Maxgate she insisted on taking me out, reserved this Saturday night and now she's here, looking incredible herself. I look over at Harriet, who looks deflated.

'I could try it on,' I suggest.

The dress is black, knee-length and fitted – very fitted. There is a deep V at the front and thick straps that pull my breasts up and stop the whole thing falling down. 'You have to wear that,' says Sally.

'I look overdressed.'

'Then put your Converse on and make your hair look shit, but you're not changing.'

I pull my sneakers on and my denim jacket over the top then look at my reflection: the dress still looks good, but I can now wear it out without looking like a dick. I take another sip of my drink. Once I've finished the glass, I doubt I'll care what I'm wearing.

The Frog is good-busy when we walk in: there are enough people milling around to create atmosphere but we can get to the bar without having to pretend one of us has a terminal illness. I'm not sure I need much more to drink after the final drinks Sally made before we left, but she buys a round and institutes a rule that we must order something different every time we go to the bar. By spiced rum and coke, we are sprawled across a sofa discussing our weird moles.

'I am in a Tinder rut,' Sally announces (she calls it a 'Tindrut'). 'Either I don't fancy the guy and I never see him again, or he doesn't fancy *me* and I never see him again *or* . . .' Sally slips off the elbow on which she is propped, spilling her drink '. . . or we date for a bit then both realise we don't fancy each other and I never see him again. Always the same.'

I say, 'I don't think that's Tinder,' but Sally can't hear me and shouts, 'What?' in my face.

'I don't think it's because of Tinder!' I yell back and then shuffle towards her, landing in the damp spot where her spillage has pooled. 'I think that's dating in general. That could happen if you dated anyone off anywhere.'

'You mean, date off Tinder?' Sally leans back against the sofa, looking aghast. 'Impossible. I've forgotten how to talk to people in real life.' When I think about it, my last 'organic' date was with Charlie. We met through work – it seems antiquated now. I look back at Sally and see she has become transfixed by something across the bar. I prod her arm. 'What are you looking at?'

She nods her head in the same direction and says, 'Them.' I follow her eye line to where three guys are stood, chatting and laughing amongst themselves. Sally jumps up saying it's her round, though it's not. I watch as she plants herself beside them at the bar; I must have blinked or fallen temporarily unconscious, as in the next moment she is chatting away to them. She points over at me and they all turn to look, at which point my phone takes on a hitherto undiscovered level of interest.

*   *   *

Sally and I are trying to play a stupid drinking game but it's not working properly with just two of us so I down my drink (that was pretty much the game anyway) and get up to go to the loo. When I come back, Sally is gone so I sit (fall) down and check my phone. I am still checking it when he sits down.

'Hello.'

'Hello.'

'How's your night so far?'

'Good, thank you. I'm here with my friend Sally but . . . I don't know where she is.' I look around and finally spot her at the bar where she has taken his place amongst his friends. 'What about you? Why are you out?'

'My friends won their football league this afternoon.'

'Well done your friends, then.' I lean back, going for that Gallic, nonchalant cool thing but the backrest is further than I think and I end up in a semi-recline. 'Do you play? Or are you in charge of oranges at half time?'

His smile is as wide as it is high, broadened by drink. 'I got injured in our last match so I can't play for a while. But *usually* I'm the captain.' It's all I need to hear: the word 'captain' is the shibboleth I need to launch into a potted history of my cheerleading captaincy, which ends, as always, with a discussion about the outfits. We segue back to football; I impress him with my accurate recitation of the offside rule and the nuggets of information I've gleaned from Bru through the years.

I remember him buying shots. Then I remember reuniting with Sally and getting introduced to his friends and there being some form of dance-off – I think I might have recreated a cheerleading routine for his benefit. After that, I don't remember much at all.

* * *

I open my eyes. Oh God, I've gone half blin— No, it's OK, I've only opened one eye, the left is glued shut. With my finger, I prize the top lid free and wipe away a cluster of mascara gunk and sleep dust. My limbs, though I can see they are attached to my body, feel inert so there is a chance I'm paralysed. I wiggle my toes: nope, fine. Although why is it so hard to lift my head off the pillow? I try and regret it instantly: my head feels like it's been filled with rocks and someone is pounding a bass drum in there. A glass of water sits on the moss-coloured carpet beside the bed; I've no idea who put it there or when but I reach down and slurp from it anyway. It tastes like hairspray. I lay back and survey the room. A yellow curtain hangs at the window that it is neither wide nor thick enough to be effective as a curtain and daylight is peeking around the edges. There is a bike propped against the far wall and a canvas wardrobe that's haemorrhaging clothes. So far, the only familiar things I've seen are my bra and dress that are splayed on the floor, just out of my reach. I personally am wearing nothing at all.

From behind my left shoulder, I hear the muffled grunts of another person and the duvet rustles and tugs against me as they shift position. I presume it's a man; fuck me, I hope it's a man, and I really hope this is his bedroom . . . I crane my neck round (this hurts my head a lot) and, careful as I am, my movement causes him to stir. I am staring at him as he opens his eyes and we blink at each other. Then his entire body seems to relax and in one movement he strains his muscles lengthways in a lazy stretch so that they tense against his skin. He reaches towards me as he strokes my arm with his forefinger. 'Good morning, Rosy.' Suddenly, I am wide awake.

'Did you sleep OK?' he asks. I sit up and gather duvet around me.

'Yes,' adding 'Thank you', a beat too late.

'I'm glad you stayed.'

'He' is the injured football captain from last night. I think. I am in his bed, naked, as is he, but he is no more familiar to me now than he was last night as a total stranger. He shuffles up the bed so that he is leaning back against a pillow, which allows my eyes to glide across his broad shoulders and down over his chest to the defined muscles in his torso: a swimmer's physique. His hair, a shade of dusty brown, is ruffled from sleep. I have cocooned myself in the duvet but I am increasingly aware that underneath there is nothing separating my flesh from his and I would like very much not to be quite so fleshy right now. With one hand clasping the duvet at my back, I teeter over the edge of the bed and make a grab for my dress, only just regaining my balance at the last second before I topple to the floor. I need a new strategy. On my second attempt, I stretch out my leg and am able to grasp my bra between my toes; my dress, however, is too heavy for a toe pincer movement and I have to use my foot to flip it towards me. I don't know where my pants are but I'm willing to sacrifice them as long as they're not too soiled with sex muck when he finds them. Although – have we *had* sex? I can't feel anything of note in my . . . vaginal locale.

The bed starts to shake. I turn back to see him hop off the end, then he turns round and stands before me, utterly, shamelessly, but not unimpressively, naked. 'Would you like a cup of tea?'

'I'm OK.' My voice appears to have transposed up an octave. He comes round the bed so his penis is roughly three feet away but it's very large so it's difficult to be accurate about the range; it's just . . . well, there it is. Surely I'd know if I'd had sex with . . . that. He turns to grab a dressing gown, revealing the most exceptional arse: high and taut, it's perfect but for a deep red mark on the left buttock. As if he can feel my gaze upon it, he reaches down and rubs it, then turns back to me with an impish grin on his face. 'I can't believe you did that,' he says. Oh holy fuck – I bit his arse? Does he think that's my thing? That I'm some sort of sex cannibal? The room feels like it is getting smaller; it's incredibly warm and the smell of alcohol and sweat has made the air fetid. He wraps himself in the dressing gown that was hung on the back of the door and walks out, I presume to go to the toilet, which means I have the time it takes him to empty his bladder to get dressed and do whatever I can to make my face non-repulsive. I put on my bra but in my haste, I fumble over the clasp (it's the gym all over again) and pull my dress on inside out; it's the right way round though, which is good enough. I see my jacket poking out from under the bed; it takes me a while to locate both sneakers but I am lacing them up as he comes back through the door.

'So what are your plans for the rest of the weekend?' he asks, sitting on the bed beside me.

'Sorry?'

'I was just wondering what you're doing this weekend?' Either he's making conversation or he's asking me out but I don't know which one it is. The one thing of which I am certain is that I won't be telling him the truth: sleeping off my hangover and ordering pizza is not a good enough reason to avoid meeting up if he suggests it, nor is it a good thing to admit in general. Unfortunately, just as I cannot bake, or not spend unexpected cash I find in my wallet, I cannot think under pressure and in the silence my mind is folding in on itself. I wish he would stop looking at me. The middle two of his lower front teeth are crooked in an almost identical fashion to my own. 'I don't have much planned,' I say, which isn't a lie.

'Would you fancy doing something, maybe tomorrow?'

Shit – he is asking me out. I should have lied after all – honesty is severely overrated. I say: 'That could be nice . . .' but it comes out in a croak.

'Cool,' he says, 'I've got your number so I'll text you.' When did I give him my number?

He goes to his gutted wardrobe and starts pulling out clothes. I take another pass at the room in search of my pants; I can't see them so I can only hope they spontaneously combusted in the night. I make a final sweep around my side of the bed and that's when I see it: one condom, used, crumpled on the floor. Either he fucks a different girl every night (and is an abhorrent slob) or one of us remembered to use protection; as I don't remember getting back here, it must have been him. I'm simply impressed I fit his penis inside me.

'Do you need to get going?' he asks and I nod with a touch too much enthusiasm.

The first thing I notice as we make our way downstairs is the wallpaper, though you'd be hard-pushed not to: brown flock with a floral design that's peeling in various places. I spy a pile of washing up through the doorway to the kitchen, sitting beside the sink in a perilous stack. As we come down to the front door, three shirts are hanging from a doorway into one of the rooms on the left, which is clearly a bedroom. Something about all of this is weird.

I ask him: 'How long have you lived here?'

He raises his eyes up as he thinks. 'Must have been . . . we moved in end of September, so, about nine months? We left it really late before term started so this place isn't the nicest.'

I wonder if I've misheard, or misunderstood. 'You're at university.'

'Yeah, almost at the end of my second year.'

I try to slow my mind down as it whirrs. If he were a postgrad student, he would have surely mentioned that. And none of my friends that have done postgraduate degrees have lived in what looks alarmingly like under-grad digs. I don't want to, but I force myself to ask anyway. 'How old are you?'

'Does it matter? It's just a number,' he laughs. I'm sure all the girls at the student union think his grin is like, super-duper cute but I want to smack it off his mouth. 'I'm twenty,' he reveals finally and everything goes quiet in my head. He opens the door and I stand for a second, letting the cold air rush over my skin and when I turn back, my barely pubescent mistake leans forward and kisses me full on the mouth until I feel the tip of his tongue warm and wet on my lips. I pull away. The inside of my mouth tastes like garlic and carpet.

He asks if I'll be all right getting home. I might have said yes, I might have said no; I might have told him I loved him or that I was the reincarnation of the Lord Our Saviour but I'll never know because the only words in my head are *twenty years old* and they're spinning round on a loop. This is why numbers matter, all of them: I have now had sexual relations with someone born in 1994. He wasn't alive when Clinton became the 42nd U.S. president, when Czechoslovakia divided in two, or when *Jurassic Park* was released – the *first* one. I hear the door close behind me and I start to walk; I don't know where I am so I head in a straight line and eventually I see an Underground sign glowing in the distance, calling me. I move gratefully towards it, doing my best to flatten down my bird's-nest hair as I walk past the knot of people near the entrance. I want to go home, sleep, shower and eat three days' worth of calories in one ham and mushroom pizza, and not necessarily in that order.

14.

DON'T GIVE UP

'OK – give me your honest opinion.'

'Should I cry?'

'I don't think you have to.'

I open my eyes. Kate is standing before me, wearing a wedding dress. I've never seen her in a wedding dress before and it's been a while since I've seen one up close, but it might be the most hideous wedding dress I have ever encountered. It's as if Weddings – any of them, all of them – have thrown up on her, with no cliché left unspewed: diamante, tulle, volume (*so* much volume, despite half the dress being corset), satin, lace and embroidery have all somehow, unbelievably, been combined in one dress.

'You look beautiful,' I say instead of laughing, or saying nothing at all.

Kate turns to look at herself in the mirror. 'It's awful. I look like I'm wearing a duvet.'

'A fancy duvet, though.'

'And an expensive one,' Kate adds, examining the price tag. 'I can't believe people pay so much money to look like . . . this.'

The store-owner lady glides into the room in her low, navy heels, holding a veil. I think I'll call her Barbara. She stands behind Kate with her hands lightly placed on Kate's shoulders and, one reflection to another, says, 'You look *lovely*,' all on the in-breath.

'It is a great dress,' Kate says, turning so that they can talk real person to real person. It occurs to me, not for the first time, how much lying is involved when it comes to getting married. Kate adds: 'I think, in my head, I had always imagined something a bit more fitted.' A shadow passes over Barbara's face and I am worried she might cry or do whatever it is the refined upper classes do to express anger, but her expression settles on something closer to concentration and she says, 'I think I know what you mean. Wait a tick,' before hurrying out of the room. Kate bustles back into the changing room as fast as the duvet allows her.

I've never been to a bridal boutique before. I was a flower girl for my godmother Liz, alongside Bru as pageboy who stomped down the aisle in protest at being dressed like a grown man in a mini-suit from John Lewis, but we were given our clothes three days before the ceremony and our responsibilities began and ended at each end of the aisle. When Kate asked Sophie and I to be her bridesmaids she made it clear that she wanted us involved with every aspect of the wedding, from dress picking to hen-do planning; reluctantly, yet gracefully, I have accepted that this does not include accompanying Kate and Bob on their two-week honeymoon to Sri Lanka. And I am not helping her try on dresses today – not officially, anyway. We met for lunch and were on our way back to the Tube when I spotted the bridal shop and suggested we go in.

'We can't, you have to book an appointment and pay a deposit,' Kate had said.

'You have to pay money to try on dresses?'

'In case you don't turn up.'

I peered through the shop window; it didn't look like anyone else was in there, so I argued that we had turned up even if no one else had and pushed through the door with Kate trailing in my wake. There was much hand fluttering as Barbara greeted us and explained that, being independent, she didn't require a deposit, adding that the shop was only empty now due to a cancellation. I gave Kate a look like, *problem solved*, and she gave one back that I thought was *thank you* but in retrospect might have been *I wish you weren't my bridesmaid*.

I have learnt more about getting married in the three months since Kate and Bob got engaged than I have in my twenty-seven years of life, mainly that weddings are astronomically, I-could-buy-three-cars-for-that expensive. I have also learnt that women don't promise to 'obey' their husbands in their vows nowadays; small bunches of flowers are called posies (and not 'small bunches of flowers' as I/other rational people had thought) and that pre-meal canapés are an increasingly acceptable alternative to a starter. Exploring this alien world of weddings has, for the most part, been entertaining but this is because I'm doing it vicariously through Kate. The thought of getting married myself makes me feel hot, then cold, then hot again. The whole thing was fun, anyway, until we got onto table plans and usher-to-bridesmaids ratios and for the first time I saw myself on the day itself – it ran like movie frames in my head. First, I am with Sophie and Kate's sister Mia, squeezed into the 'monstrosity' of a bridesmaid's dress Kate assures me she'll choose; next, I am squeezing Kate's hand and trying not to cry before following her down the aisle. Then we are at the reception and I'm with our friends (although sometimes there's a cut-away to me dry-humping an usher in the toilets) and everyone is dancing. But mostly when I picture myself at Kate's wedding, I'm alone. And then weddings don't feel like entertainment any more.

Barbara dashes back in holding a long white dress that to my eye looks essentially the same as all the other long white dresses I've seen hanging up. She taps lightly on the changing room door and squeezes herself through a crack when Kate says 'come in'. There isn't much to do in a bridal boutique if you are not trying on wedding dresses/cooing over somebody wearing a wedding dress, though Kate mentioned that you are given free champagne in the swanky ones – we should go to one of those soon. Barbara has made me a cup of instant coffee, which was kind. I stand up and stretch, then wander over to the accessories display. On the top shelf of the glass stand, a selection of tiaras sparkle as they catch the light. I pick up the most extravagant of the bunch and go to the mirror to place it on my head. I think I look like a princess; I angle my head this way and that to make it catch the light. However, the longer I wear it, and in the absence of the Cinderella costume I got for my fifth birthday, the tiara is starting to look increasingly ridiculous. I try to tug it free, except it has entangled itself in my hair and now I'm panicking because I want it off before Barbara sees. With one final yank it comes free, ripping out a clump of my hair along with it. I need to warn Kate about this. I pull the strands of my hair from the prongs and put it back with its friends. I'm experimenting with a veil when the changing room door opens and Barbara emerges, followed by Kate who turns to look at me face-on. I stop what I'm doing and stare at her. I forget the veil is in my hand and it drops to the floor – I can't take my eyes off her. Barbara nods her head just so and quietly clasps her hands. 'Well?' Kate asks me. 'What do you think?'

If anything, this dress is worse than the one before, so much worse, just a totally different kind of awful. Instead of big and puffy, this one is tight and shiny, apart from at the bottom where it looks like a swan has exploded, whilst a set of spindly spaghetti straps of the type last seen on *Top of the Pops* circa 1992 stop the whole ghastly creation from sliding to the floor.

'It's different from the other one,' I say as Kate manoeuvres herself in front of the mirror. I've just worked out that there are no mirrors in the changing room itself.

Kate is mesmerised. For a long time, she simply stares at her reflection, occasionally twisting to see another angle and as time ticks on I am growing increasingly concerned that she might actually like it. In the end, it is Barbara who breaks the silence.

'It's better with jewellery, I have a necklace that I think you'll . . . I'll just pop out to the . . .' With that she's gone, off in search of a necklace that may, but almost definitely will not, magically transform this dress into a nice one. Kate turns to me, her face impassive, and I'm about to say, 'Kate, no . . .' but then I see her mouth start to wobble at the corners and her lips curl into a smile and seconds later we are both laughing like cartoon characters, the kind of laugh that starts with a noise like 'BAAHHH!' and turns into the hiccupping gulps that make it hard to breathe.

'You have to get me out of this before she comes back,' Kate gasps and I help her back into the changing room. Kate locks the door.

'It's going to take me ages to undo all this corseting,' I say, tugging at random ribbons in hope of something coming loose.

'Imagine how long it would take us to do it up.' Kate sweeps her hair off her neck and looks at me in the mirror. 'We'd have to have an evening ceremony. Maybe I should get something with a zip.'

'You'd better wear an anorak, then.' Zips are not a common feature of wedding dresses: this season's fashion is for lace detailing and intricate fastenings. I've read a lot of magazines.

My fingers start to cramp after five minutes and I demand a break; I have unwound Kate just enough that she can bend so we sit on the floor and I halve a cereal bar I found in my bag.

'I just want to look amazing,' Kate says, wiping crumbs off the 'satin'. 'For one day, I want to look amazing.'

'Kate, you will. We're going to find you the perfect dress and you're going to look stunning.'

We share a look we've shared many times before – it's the look we use when we can't say it with words. Kate says, 'And you will too. I won't make you wear velour, I promise.'

'It doesn't matter what I look like.'

'Yes, it does, Ro. I don't want fugly bridesmaids ruining my photos.' She grins at me. 'How is the dating going?'

I scrunch up the wrapper and shove it in my pocket before standing up and helping Kate to her feet, then spinning her to face the mirror and resuming the undoing. 'Not great.'

'Is this because you slept with that child?'

'Hey,' I give her bare shoulder a slap and pull at the endless ream of ribbon. *That child* texted me the next day just as he said he would, asking if I wanted to go out for a drink. I was starting to write out a reply, a gentle thanks-but-no-thanks, when it occurred to me: I didn't know his name. I messaged Sally to see if she could remember; she replied saying she thought one of them had been called Harold . . .

'Dating is just . . . relentless. I'm tired of it.' I look at Kate in the mirror.

'But that's the point,' she says, 'I dated tons of morons before I met Bob. Remember Wide-eyed Jim?'

Of all the men Kate dated at university, I'll never forget Jim, whose eyes, set so alarmingly far apart on his face, instantly earned him his nickname. I'm glad Kate can laugh about it now because at the time it annoyed her the exact same amount it amused Sophie and me. None of us were laughing, however, when we discovered he'd been cheating on her – that was when Sophie and I developed some other names for him. But I get what Kate is saying: dating is inherently exhausting and if you don't work through the bad ones, you won't recognise the good ones when they come. But am I desperate enough for a boyfriend to bother?

I've finally made it down to the bottom of Kate's back. She shimmies the dress to the floor and steps out, leaving it in a harmless-looking heap, though I suspect it's a fire hazard.

'You have to keep going,' says Kate. 'How many dates have you actually had?'

The faces of my dating life flash before my eyes as I tot them up: Grinning Elliot, Scummy Jonathan, Perfect Patrick . . . I squeeze my eyes shut for a second until his face floats away. Then there was Über-cool Andrew, Doug the Toff, Archie the Disappointment, then Max the Invisible, so he doesn't count – nor does my John Doe teeny-bopper. 'Six,' I announce.

'*Six*? And you say you're tired? Give me your phone, I want to show you something.' I hand it over. Minutes pass with Kate deep in concentration.

'What do you want?' I ask.

'I'm just finding something . . .'

I pick at an errant crumb from the cereal bar off my jeans. I almost definitely should not eat this . . . another minute ticks by. 'Kate, what are you looking for?' I wait another thirty seconds then I can't wait any more. 'Kate, what are you doing?' I demand. She looks up at me: the look on her face reminds me of my cat when I caught her taking a shit in the washing hamper. 'Don't be mad,' Kate says and flips my phone around so that I can see the screen.

'You've restored my Tinder account.' I feel like I'm blinking a lot.

'Tinder. Is. Amazing,' Kate says, waggling my phone.

* * *

It took a while for me and Kate to extricate ourselves from Babs' shop (more dresses had been lined up) but we are in the relative safety of a Wi-Fi-enabled coffee shop and I have left Kate 'playing on Tinder' at the table ('God, I wish this had been around when I was single,' she said) whilst I collect our post-traumatic dress order of chai lattes and muffins. I carry them back, sit down and look over her shoulder. Kate is engrossed, swiping to the rhythm, 'No, no, no . . .'

Then she stops: 'What about him?' 'Him' is Guy, 29.

'He's not bad.' Kate brings up the rest of his pictures: Guy in a club with his friends, open-mouthed with fluorescent paint dotted on his face; Guy mid-speech at a wedding; Guy grinning madly from behind a sea-front cut-out of a mermaid whilst a pretty girl (who is obviously just his friend/cousin/long-lost biological sister) plays the part of the burly sailor. 'He is attractive,' I conclude.

'What do you do now?'

I explain to Kate the implications of Liking someone and I show her how. I let her swipe Guy right.

15

DEEPER UNDERSTANDING

Here is a list of things I hate:

1. Marmalade
2. Cobbles
3. My patronage of the *Daily Mail* website
4. Hypocrisy
5. Snow
6. *Top Gear*
7. Terracotta
8. First dates

To the marmalade-loving, hypocritical *Daily Mail* readers of Durham (there are lots of cobbles in Durham), some of my dislikes may seem arbitrary, but surely the resounding consensus is that nobody likes first dates; they are essentially an interview to assess how good you are at being yourself. Despite my experience in the field, I find first dates no more enjoyable now than I ever did. I want to skip the first one and jump ahead to the seventh when Guy and I will be conversant in each other's lives and able to chat without awkward pauses. He'll be here any minute; I might put it to him.

At work this afternoon, I volunteered to photocopy and file the recent press cuttings. This job must be carried out on a monthly basis and is universally loathed throughout the office; you can tell when it's coming up because people start sending pre-emptive emails about their egregiously heavy workload . . . *I'd SO do the cuttings round-up, guys, if it wasn't for this one client . . . bloody clients, eh? Who's with me?! You get it. Definitely sign me up for next month, though . . .* Usually, we just make Ella the Temp do it, but today I elected myself for two reasons:

1. I knew it would result in the plaudits and respect of my colleagues, plus maybe gifts of cookies.
2. It would force me to be away from my desk, thus away from my phone.

Having my mobile in sight only made the temptation to text Guy and cancel that much harder to resist. I had even come up with a list of possible excuses: I have food poisoning; I've mixed up my dates; my hair is dirty and/ or on fire . . . of all the first dates I've had, this is the one I'm most dreading. It feels like I'm on Tinder for the first time.

Guy and I matched whilst Kate and I were still having coffee. She demanded I message him immediately, confirming that people in relationships do not understand the mysterious, nuanced ways of Tinder; the man usually messages first, I told her. Kate said I was a pussy and if I didn't contact Guy, she would. So under her supervision, I wrote:

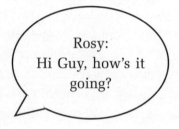

Rosy:
Hi Guy, how's it going?

To which he replied:

Guy:
Very well thanks, how are you?

I didn't text again until I got home; he messaged back a minute later (cue mild alarm: too keen?) and we waded through the Tinder classics: *how's your day been, where do you live, would you rather have toes for fingers or fingers for toes*, then he asked what I did.

Guy:
Based purely on
looks I'd say . . .
mechanic.

Rosy:
Is that what I give
off? Spanners and
oil?

Guy:
Well it was a joke at
first, but let's talk
more about this
oil . . .

Guy:
Fine, OK . . . not a
mechanic. Got it:
beekeeper.

Rosy:
Is that something
you can even do
professionally?

Guy:
Yes! You realise
you've just insulted
apiarists
everywhere . . .

Rosy:
Yeah . . . those guys
hate me.

> Guy:
> Not a mechanic, not a beekeeper – I don't know what else you could possibly do? Please don't say you're an accountant. I'm an accountant – we're very dull.

Guy is an attractive man who makes me laugh. He is dating best practice.

In a nod to my gallant photocopying efforts, Helen lets me leave ten minutes early so that I can buy a travel deodorant from Boots and use the testers to apply last-minute emergency make-up before sprinting through the Underground to get here. I'm five minutes early as a result so there is time for one final face check. When I watch other girls look in the mirror, they purse their lips and dip their chins as though they are affirming their beauty has remained intact; I check my reflection in case I have seeds stuck in my teeth. In the sea of dark suits swarming out of the Tube, Guy is easy to spot in a pair of pale chinos and a blue checked shirt that I recognise from his photos. He is wearing a pair of brown brogues (my mother would describe them as 'well-loved') that are tied with mismatched laces and have been polished to make them gleam. It is definitely him, it has to be, yet I can't shake the sense I'm looking at his twin brother because in place of the *brown* hair I saw in his photos is a crown of tousled, russet locks.

Guy is ginger. How, in the name of all I hold sacred (Kate Bush; Melissa Bank novels; hummus) did I not notice this? I conjure up his photos in my mind: the shot in a club – that was dimly lit. The pier-front tomfoolery – where his hair wasn't visible. The wedding – oh no. The wedding picture was in black and white. He looked so handsome in it, excessively so, and it was taken at a wedding . . . my ovaries must have scrambled my brain and made me forget the danger of monochrome. It is an inexcusable breach of the Tinder Rules and I've no one to blame but myself. Wait – yes I do: this is all Kate's fault. People in relationships shouldn't be allowed near Tinder, they simply don't know what they're doing.

Guy spots me and waves, flashing a crooked smile that makes me want to look after him and fuck him all at the same time. But I am fixated on his hair. It could almost, *almost*, pass for rusty brown; his brows are a little sandy but his eyelashes are dark and as long as a camel's and he has a warm complexion, not pale and insipid like mine. At a glance, at night, if you were squinting, you might not even notice he was ginger at all. However, as a fellow specimen it is *all* I can see. At best, two gingers together are mildly amusing; at worst, their ability to procreate is a threat to mankind.

'Rosy!' Guy calls out before he reaches me and kisses my cheek. 'Great to meet you.' His voice is deep but light, musical but measured.

'Hi Guy.' I cringe at the rhyme and intuitively he says, 'Everyone does that, don't worry.' He smiles and I relax, and for a second I forget his hair. He claps his hands. 'So, Rosy, what's the plan?'

The plan. Oh God. Guy was so funny and charming in our messages, and I was so excited at the prospect of a good Tinder date after all my recent disastrous sorties that when we came to arrange it I told him I would take charge of planning and assured him I'd think of something fun; it dawned on me about ten minutes later that I now had to plan an unusual, exhilarating date and that drinking our way through a happy-hour cocktail menu did not meet this criteria. Drinking was always going to play a crucial role – alcohol is to first dates what Lynx Africa is to adolescent boys – but I needed more, so I set about asking everyone I knew for their suggestions.

'The theatre,' said my rich boss, Helen.

'A trapeze class,' said Sophie.

'What's wrong with a regular date?' said Liam.

'There's this massage place next to a kebab shop in Holborn and if you ask to "meet Mr McPeake" . . .' said Sally, before I made her stop. When I asked Kate, she had to think. 'An exciting date? I'm just happy if Bob gets home in time for dinner and we can have sex before I fall asleep.' BF suggested we 'wear funny hats and go for a curry' and that when suitably drunk, I tell Guy I'm not wearing underwear. After three days of research, I was no further on.

On the fifth day, I phoned home, seeking Dad's advice on how to fix the hoover and (somehow) my dating dilemma came up.

'I once took your mother on a surprise trip to Paris,' he said. I told him that budget was a factor. He told me not to be snarky, and to try cleaning out the hoover's filter. But when we hung up, his suggestion must have stuck because when I woke up the next morning, I had it.

'Tonight, Guy, we are going around the world.' Guy regards me with what looks like a mixture of fear and pity. 'An around-the-world bar crawl,' I clarify, quietly.

'Where?'

'Down the high street.'

With grave sincerity, Guys says, 'That sounds brilliant.' It doesn't, it sounds lame and I know it, but Guy's enthusiasm sounds real and when he looks at me I feel a burgeoning warmth in all the good places.

'Where first?' he asks.

'Japan,' I say, gesturing down a side street, 'this way.' I've not been to Japan, but I doubt it bears much resemblance to Matsumi, an overpriced sushi restaurant that nevertheless serves good martinis.

Guy suggests I find a table whilst he goes to the bar. On his return, he hands me a lychee martini and says: 'Japan is nothing like how they describe it in the books.' He has an Aperol spritz for himself and before I can comment on the lychee that is bobbing on the surface like an eyeball, he adds: 'The barman says it's what makes the drink Japanese.'

'I thought lychees came from China, originally?'

'Our bartender comes from Dudley, originally.' Guy lifts his glass. 'Here's to travel.'

'And Dudley's fine education system,' I add, clinking our glasses. I'm annoyed that I forgot to say: 'Kanpai!' which is Japanese for 'cheers' – I spent fifteen minutes researching that this afternoon.

I had planned a strict itinerary for tonight that involved one drink per bar, but our date is turning out to be much the same as every other holiday I've taken: we are an hour in and the schedule is moot. Two drinks down (and four lychees apiece) we are still in Japan.

'OK,' says Guy, leaning towards me, 'if money was no object and success was guaranteed, what would you do with your life?'

'My dream job?'

As Guy nods I'm conscious that I'm already hesitating, not because I don't know the answer: apart from friends, boys and chip day on Friday, writing was the only thing I cared about at school, and I was good at it. I had an English teacher, Mr Austen, who was one of *those* teachers; he pushed me, urging me to pursue journalism as a career and for a time I was set to follow his advice, but when it came to applying, my UCAS form languished on my desk as I dissolved in panic. I was so scared of failing as a writer that I couldn't limit myself to its pursuit, and opted instead to read Politics in the belief that an academic-sounding degree would proffer more options later on. Left to my own devices, and without Mr Austen's enthusiasm to bolster me, I lost all confidence that I'd be good enough. When I got the offer from my first PR firm, that was it; I had the opportunity to follow my dream and I abandoned it, out of fear. Our first date doesn't seem the opportune moment to mention this to Guy. But as I look at him, waiting patiently for my answer, smiling his wonky smile, there is something about him, some sense of safety I feel in his company that makes lying seem faintly ridiculous.

There is no derisive sneer on Guy's face when I tell him, nor does he fall into fits of laughter. 'What sort of writer do you want to be?' he asks. 'As in, what would you like to write? Books?'

'That's the ideal. I like writing from my own experience, that first-person confessional type of thing.'

'Are we talking sex memoir here?' Guy arches his eyebrow. I'd have wanted to shower instantly if Scummy Jonathan had made that comment; when Guy says it, I want to touch him. 'Have you written stuff before?'

'Bits and bobs; I won some competitions when I was younger and I kept a diary for years. I used to write loads at university – my laptop is littered with the beginnings of novels.'

'So what's stopping you now?'

I sit back and swirl my remaining lychee around the glass. Lack of opportunity. Lack of motivation – it doesn't help that I spend most of my time at the office. If someone could just guarantee me immediate success and financial security for life, I'd be a writer tomorrow.

Guy looks at me dead on. 'Quit your job. Do something flexible, then you'd have time to write.'

For a moment I am swept up in Guy's insouciant enthusiasm. I picture myself in my perfect office: light and airy, photography on the walls and a vase of fresh flowers sitting atop my writing desk . . . it all seems so perfect and so utterly plausible – about as plausible as Guy and I being in 'Japan', in fact.

Our next destination is Mexico, a.k.a. a shabby restaurant further down the high street with yellow walls onto which faux brickwork and snaking vines have been painted to evoke, I'm guessing, long, balmy nights of tequila and *botanas* – I don't know, I've not been to Mexico either (I should really travel more), but Guy has. 'This is exactly what it's like,' he says as our Latvian waiter shows us to our table. The place is half full so that to our right, the space vibrates with noise and movement, some bold diners having ventured out onto the decking to eat sizzling dishes of *enchiladas* under heat lamps. It's late July but the evening air still has a bite.

Guy asks what I'd like to drink in the mistaken belief we'll be having anything other than frozen margaritas (I compromise by ordering a jug to share rather than one each, and a straw) and Guy fills our glasses to the top. Looking round, I notice that every other table has ordered food and then there's us, table for two, dining on booze. 'Should we eat?' I ask.

Guy flips the menu. 'Let's see . . . beef fajitas? Armadillo eggs? They're stuffed chillies.' He reads aloud: '"Super hot – only for the brave." Is that us?'

I say, 'The super hot bit, maybe,' and immediately regret it. Does Guy think I mean me? Does he think I mean him? *Do* I mean him? 'Nachos?' I say quickly.

'*Nacho*rally.' He grins. 'So what about these eggs, then? Would you describe yourself as brave?' His tone has changed – he's asking seriously. Instantly, I am back in the Japanese bar, or I'm back in Sixth Form writing my UCAS, it doesn't matter which; it's like Guy has worked out what happened and now he's testing me, trying to get me to admit it.

'Sometimes . . . maybe. What about you?'

Guy considers the question for a moment before answering. 'Not as brave as I'd like to be. I take calculated risks, I'd say.'

Then he looks at me in a way that makes me wonder . . . am I going to be one of them?

In the end, we order a second jug of margarita and nothing more than a large plate of nachos and toppings to eat so I'm wobbling as we head down the street for the Spanish leg of our tour. Spain involves drinking sangria in a small, hot tapas joint where everyone speaks English: the quintessential Spanish experience. I must be drunker than I'd thought because I detest sangria (it's the red wine element) yet I sup it down like it's juice. We get on to talking about our families. Guy's questions about mine are thoughtful, his curiosity genuine: what does my brother do? Are we close? How often do I visit my parents? I answer with equal sincerity but I want to hurry up and talk about his. I like to learn about people's family, it's like taking apart a watch: you study all the tiny parts so that when you put it back together you understand how the watch works. 'What about you?' I ask in turn. 'Family?'

'As in, do I have any?'

'I assume you do; or was *Oliver Twist* in fact a biopic of your life?'

'*Annie*, actually,' Guy says, patting his hair. I must have stopped noticing his hair around the second jug of margarita. Now it is back in my head and I can't push it out. Red for danger, red for stop . . . red for passion and lust. I am definitely sexually attracted to Guy, even if two gingers mating goes against nature. 'I'm one of five,' he says, 'well, four.' He rubs the side of his face. 'My sister died a few years ago. I still forget not to count her.'

'I'm so sorry.'

'She had cancer. She was ill for a long time, but then, you know, all of a sudden . . .' I'm shocked; Guy is such a positive person, I can't imagine him experiencing such sadness. In my mind's eye, I see my aunt Paula, Mum's sister, laughing whilst trying to fix the tap in our kitchen; in the next frame, she is hairless, virtually lifeless, taking up just a sliver of the bed – she died two weeks later. Her cancer came on so quickly it was almost overnight. I prompt Guy: '. . . the cancer got too aggressive.'

'No, Phoebe went into remission; she was hit by a truck on her way to the gym.'

My tongue seizes up, then my whole face so that I can do nothing but stare at Guy as I slowly submerge in guilt and shame. His eyes are wide and impassive.

I am opening my mouth to start my apology when his own mouth twitches, then his wonky smile spreads and he bursts out laughing. 'That was Phoebe's joke, she made me swear to say it when anyone asked how she died.' He starts laughing again and I let myself join in, primarily out of relief, but also because it's funny; his sister must have been just like him. 'She sounds incredible,' I say.

'She was.' The smile remains on Guy's face and he gazes just past my shoulder, partly here but somewhere else, too.

We both sip our drinks. Then Guy leans towards me on his stool and says: 'You're quite incredible.'

I feel my cheeks warming. 'That's the sangria talking.'

'And my dead sister.' Then he leans towards me and presses his lips against mine. We kiss for a long time. With tongue.

*   *   *

When I wake up, I am fully clothed. There is something stuck to my cheek; I feel for it and pull it off – a sachet of ketchup. Either everything hurts or I can't feel anything and the light is intolerably bright. I look around; my last recollection of last night involves Guy holding me up as we stumbled to our final destination: America (McDonald's). On my bedroom floor, a few chips and half a cheeseburger are poking out of a crumpled brown bag. I feel acutely ashamed of myself – who leaves half a burger? I remember being in Spain and . . . we kissed.

I scrabble around for my phone and find it in my shoe. There is a text from Guy, sent at 2.03 a.m:

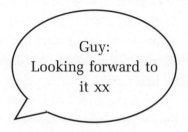

Guy:
Looking forward to
it xx

To what? I unlock my phone and scroll up the thread:

Rosy:
Than£ks for an
amassing night, let us
do itT again some
time xz

I didn't just kiss him – I asked him for a second date (I'm also spelling 'thanks' with a pound sign now, apparently) and Guy is looking forward to it.

Standing requires some effort but I force myself to shower and eat breakfast (NB: leftover McDonald's does not work the next day) before calling BF. She answers after three rings. 'How did it go?' she asks, dispensing with 'hello'.

'I asked him for a second date.'

'Did he reply?'

'Yeah – he said yes.'

'Isn't that good? You don't sound pleased.'

'I'm pretty hungover.'

'But are you looking forward to seeing Guy again?'

I tell BF about his hair. I feel shallow just saying the words but doing so brings some small sense of relief, too.

'He's ginger?' she says, and I can hear the confusion in her voice. 'Didn't you notice that in his pictures?'

'I don't know, maybe I didn't look properly. It wasn't easy to tell.'

'Well he can't be that bad, then. Not that being ginger is bad, I mean . . . you know what I mean.'

'I do.'

'Look,' says BF, her voice firm, 'you said he was funny in his messages, did he make you laugh last night?'

'Yes.' I smile in spite of myself. *Nacho*rally.

'And he wasn't racist, or a misogynist? He didn't pull his pants down in a bar or eat a bat?'

'No.'

'Then what the fuck is wrong with you?'

Later, Guy sends me a link to the '100 most important cats of all time'. I look through it twice and once I have stopped laughing I forward it to most of my friends. Then I send him a reply, asking if he's free on Wednesday.

16.

THIS WOMAN'S WORK

Wednesday, 8.52 a.m.
'How's Guy?' Pip asks when I arrive at my desk. This is everybody's new favourite question; it's the latest pop-up question in the office. Why is it that once you are with someone, your own welfare becomes secondary to your partner's? 'Off to his tonight?' Her eyes slide down to my travel bag as I sling it onto the floor by my desk.

'I am,' I say, 'we're having dinner.'

'Ooh, where are you going?' Pip waits breathlessly for an answer. I'm getting used to people having extreme reactions to mundane things like dinner plans – Kate almost cried when I told her I was due to meet Guy's friends. It's like this at the beginning; I had forgotten.

I try to push the bag under my desk with my toe but it merely tips so I brace myself with one foot and use the other to shove it forward. This is another thing I've failed to recall about serious dating: it is incredibly heavy. Within this bag lies the very essence of Me: make-up; perfume; hair straighteners; hair products; grips, clips and ties (to sort my hair when said straighteners/products won't work); clothes; underwear; toiletries and various chargers. These are the objects that transform the natural Me into recognisable, socially accepted Me, the one whose face doesn't make animals run for high ground. I explain to Pip that Guy won't tell me anything about tonight – he has insisted on keeping our dinner location a surprise.

Helen is not at her desk. I swivel back round to my computer and fire off an email that is designed to:

a) wish her good morning, and
b) alert her to the fact I'm not late.

I am reading through my to-do list when Helen's out-of-office response pings into my inbox.

This is perplexing. Her handbag – of approximately the same value as everything I have ever owned, currently own and shall likely ever own in the future – is propped up on her chair. I glance at Pip who tilts her head towards the meeting room, located at the far end of the office. The glass is frosted, but I can just make out the shapes of people moving around inside; whilst I watch, OCD Arlene backs through the door arse-first, carrying a tray laden with three of the good coffee cups usually reserved for clients (I learnt this the hard way after once using one to make a microwave muffin), and I glimpse what looks like Helen's ponytail before the door closes.

'Six-month appraisals,' says Pip, 'did you forget?' There is no definitive answer to this. Thanks to general office murmurings, I knew they were coming up and they have been listed in the online office calendar for months, but this is a document I check with an incompetent level of infrequency and I hit the cross on any and all pop-up reminders from muscle memory. What I have failed to realise is that they are happening today, a lapse not lost on Pip who reminds me to fill out a self-appraisal before swivelling back to her computer.

I delve into the shared document folder and bring up a fresh form. The questions are the same every time: in a variety of ways I am encouraged to rate myself in the blank box provided. My mind wanders back to my sodding dating profile – what a fucking waste of time that was. Thinking about it now, I was going through the motions, hoping that the end result (sex/boyfriend/ blissful, long-term marriage) would justify a process that held all the *joie de vivre* of setting my eyebrows on fire. I never wanted to internet date, I feel like I fell into it in a mixture of panic and ignorance. It is disarmingly similar to the way I ended up in PR.

Question 1: How do you feel the last six months has gone?
I feel the last six months has gone fine.

Too brief? I don't know what else to put; for a pseudo-writer I am struggling to find words. Mr Austen used to mark my text with 'don't over-write' in non-persecutory pencil whenever the spirit of Byron took me and I launched into overblown (and generally awful) flowery prose; it's a hard lesson to un-learn, but I suspect Helen will be looking for more. At least 'fine' is better than 'boring, monotonous and morally depleting'. I close the form and look over at Pip in the hope she's in the mood to play, but from her screen, I can see that she is taking advantage of Helen's absence and is mid-way through the latest installment of an email to her husband, Geoff, entitled 'New Bed'. Pip and Geoff have been deeply involved in this exchange for the past two weeks: from what I have gleaned, it is a comprehensive, in-depth discussion of the variables involved in the purchase of a new bed. And from what Pip has told me (also what I have accidentally on purpose read over her shoulder) the decision to go ahead and *buy* said bed has yet to be made; they are still at prep stage. Issues of size, storage and colour have all been debated though I understand significant progress was made at the end of last week in the king vs super-king debate. I open my email and elect to compose a new message, entitled: 'Simplifying the Process'.

Dear Pip, I type, *Step 1: Go into bed shop. Step 2: Buy a bed.*

Then I make myself delete it in case I lean on my keyboard and accidentally hit 'send'. For Pip and Geoff (and, frankly, having met and liked Geoff, I am disappointed he's let himself get sucked into this) the act of bed-buying seems to necessitate meticulous research and planning; granted, Pip once spent a week weighing up the benefits of almond milk over soya so maybe it's a quirk of their particular relationship. Yet if this is a portend of what happens to couples once they get married, I'd rather stay single forever, or die in my mid-thirties in some booze-fuelled, adrenaline soaked act of reckless awesomeness.

I turn back to the appraisal form. I have to focus.

12.43 p.m.
Lunch doesn't officially begin until 1 p.m. but in my head it started over an hour ago and I've been fantasising about what I might have. I won't last until one, I ate my emergency banana from home shortly after half past nine. My motivation to do work of any kind has gradually ebbed away; I've taken to adding items I've already achieved to my to-do list just so I can cross them off. My self-appraisal remains at large.

1.39 p.m.
I went to Sainsbury's. I have bought: olives, sausage rolls (x3), a yoghurt, some nuts, a can of Lilt and a packet of dark chocolate digestives to share with my colleagues for spirit-lifting purposes.

2.07 p.m.
I have eaten all but seven of the digestives.

3.19 p.m.
I am on my fifth draft of a release for one of our major clients, concerning the launch of a new app that I am assured is a 'fresh, innovative platform designed to give our viewers premium engagement'. Helen will hate that, mainly because it doesn't mean anything, but after twenty minutes I am no closer to making sense of it myself. I select my self-appraisal form and watch as it swooshes open. *Question 1 . . .*

I have nothing to say about my job. Somehow this seems worse than saying I don't like it.

4.45 p.m.
Suddenly, Helen is beside my desk. I jump when she says my name and instinctively close down whatever window is open on my screen before I remember it's an email to a client and quickly open it again.

'How's it been today?' she asks.

'Fine. Great. Pretty brilliant, yeah.' I make myself stop before things become unbelievable, incredible, stupendous. 'Filing is done; I sent out the round-up first thing, the Snapper release went out – Sabrina at *Media Week* is going to pick it up . . .' Some of these things are actually true. I've also ordered some new headphones off Amazon but I decide not to mention this, or the fact that the bulk of my to-do list remains untroubled and my evaluation is still blank.

'Can you make sure the post goes out today?'

'Absolutely.'

'And if you could get hold of Coralie Lavelle about

the thing before you go that would be great.' An email flashes up on Helen's phone and she is soon engrossed. Reviews must be over for today, meaning mine will be tomorrow. I feel like I should say something about it but I don't know what, or even why I have the urge to bring it up. I look at Helen, her lips occasionally mouthing the words as she reads; she looks up and locks her phone with the derisive snort she reserves for things she doesn't agree with. 'So that's great then,' she says, clearly having forgotten we were having a conversation. She starts to walk off, then she stops and turns, and I find myself catching my breath as she leans down towards me. 'Rosy, how's it going with Guy?'

* * *

I leave the office as soon as the clock hits six but I am thinking about work as I lug my bag down the road to the Tube. I am thinking about it when my bag gets stuck in the electronic barrier and it won't come loose despite my tugging and French tourists start to laugh at me. I am thinking about it whilst I drag it along the long passages and surprise staircases on the way down to the platform: I gave up carrying it in case my shoulder slid out of its socket. Work is still on my mind when an elderly lady offers to help me whilst everyone else wheels around, tutting just loud enough for me to hear. I get on the train and think about work whilst simultaneously thinking about how much I hate other people.

I am still thinking about work when Guy opens his

front door and says, 'Hello, you.' He gives me a kiss and hoists my bag onto his own shoulder as though it's filled with sunshine and jellybeans instead of a corpse as it has felt to me.

'I'm sweaty,' I say, stepping into the hallway, 'I wouldn't come too near me.'

'I'm so glad I invited you,' Guy smiles. Then he sniffs me and says that I smell fine but if I want I can take a shower, and goes off to get me a towel.

When I emerge, I can hear music. I can also smell something delicious and follow the drift of the scent into the kitchen. The table, which is usually bare and covered in the life detritus belonging to Guy and his housemates, has been hidden under a white tablecloth – a proper one, not just a bed sheet like I used when I hosted lunch for Mum's sixtieth birthday – and cotton napkins have been folded under cutlery, enough for three courses. At the centre of the table, candles are burning in coloured glass holders. Guy is standing at the hob with a tea towel slung over his shoulder, stirring the contents of a saucepan.

'This is where we're having dinner?' It's come out wrong; when I look at Guy, he looks remorseful. 'God, sorry, I didn't mean . . . I was just surprised. I can't believe how beautiful it is.' This I do mean. It's a relief to see Guy smile, though he replies: 'I hyped it too much.'

I press myself against his back, wrapping my arms around his waist. 'I don't think you hyped it enough.' He turns and kisses me, holding the wooden spoon over our heads, and he lets me cling on to him, even though

I can tell he's fretting about what's in the saucepan. I let him go and he gives me a quick final peck before turning back.

I take a seat at the table. 'What are we having?'

'Pan-fried scallops to start, and . . .' Guy crouches down to the oven and opens it a crack, examining whatever is inside, 'lamb for main. Does that sound OK?'

'That sounds great.'

Guy pours us both a glass of wine; he tells me about his day and though I understand very little of what he did, it's nice to sit and listen. By the time he serves the first course I am on to my second glass. He's cooked the scallops with crispy cubes of pancetta and served them on a swamp of green mush that Guy says is supposed to be pea puree.

'It still is, technically,' I say before I try it; it tastes wonderful and I say that, too. It is only when Guy asks about work that I realise, for ten blissful minutes, I haven't been thinking about it.

'It was fine. You know – good.'

Guy swallows. 'I'm so glad we had this chat.'

'Sorry.' I put down my fork, slide my hand over to his and give it a pat. 'I don't know . . . I've got my sixth-month review tomorrow.'

'Are you worried it will be negative?'

'No, I think it will be fine.' Unless Helen has discovered it *was* me who broke the binding machine. 'It was just watching my colleagues going in and out of their meetings, they all looked so . . .'

'What?'

'I don't know . . . content.'

'Because getting praised for your work is a bad thing?' He laughs, and leans over for a kiss. 'You're weird sometimes, you know that?'

'I do.'

When the lamb is ready, I have to move everything out of the way before Guy can set it down; he wants to carve at the table, just as my father would. I serve us both potatoes and veg then Guy sits and we say cheers for what may be the third time tonight. He asks what I think of the lamb before I've swallowed my first mouthful. I can hear the pride in his voice, as well as an edge of anxiety in anticipation of my response. I chew as quickly as I can but it is a well-known fact that it takes seven times longer to swallow after someone has asked you a question. *What do I think?* Guy is looking at me from across the table as I look back at him and chew. This is taking forever . . . Guy is patient, though; I know he'll wait. Guy is also kind: he's gone to a huge amount of effort tonight with the table and the meal (I spotted a cheesecake when he opened the fridge) and I think it's demonstrative of his feelings for me. I think Guy is warm, and caring, and funny . . . he has a great sense of humour, the holy grail of characteristics. And I think the time we've spent together over the past few weeks has been nice. But right now, he just wants to know about the lamb.

Finally, I swallow. 'Really nice.'

We were not allowed to write the word 'nice' at school; Mr Austen placed a blanket ban on its use, saying it was too bland to be effective as a descriptor, that it doesn't mean anything. But it is a convenient word; there will always be a place in this world for 'nice'. 'Nice' is fine. It is satisfactory, not too much, but just enough; it is good, manageable . . . pleasant. I remember clutching at it when BF asked me about Ed (but in that context, I used it merely to stop myself telling her he was a knob). Now, here, in the soft light of the candles, as Guy digs in with a contented smile on his lips, I think: he may be the nicest man I've ever met.

17.

THE DREAMING

As a child of about ten I discovered what I thought at the time to be the most incredible trick: that if you say the same word over and over and over, it appears to lose its meaning. I used to pick a word at random – 'sofa', 'loosely', 'eleven' – and repeat it incessantly to myself until it lost all symbolic sense and dissolved into a jumble of sounds and syllables. As an adolescent at the zenith of my Tori Amos phase, I tried it with the question: 'Who am I?' and promptly had my first existential crisis, which at the time I thought was low blood sugar (I had some orange squash and felt better). It was such a powerful experience that I've not tried it since, not consciously; perhaps it is always lodged in the back of my mind somewhere. It's a hard question that may not have an answer because none of us are just one thing; we are a muddle of our biology, our experiences, our own valencies and values and culture and resources. I am my parents' daughter; I am a Politics graduate; I am a resident of London and the sort-of almost girlfriend of Guy Bartlett. I am also a PR executive . . . but I wish I wasn't.

*   *   *

I was there in the room, and, as far as I know, not having a stroke, yet when I said, 'I think I might want to leave,' the words sounded like they were coming from someone else, perhaps Helen, who was seated across from me at the table, or Joanne from HR, whose chipper Geordie tones did not infuse me with chipper-ness but convinced me bad things should happen to her. Yet their shocked expressions indicated they were in receipt of the news, rather than the ones giving it – that was definitely me. Helen said, 'Oh. Right,' and I probably should have said something back but I didn't know what, so I tried to look apologetic but I think I went cross-eyed. Helen looked at me directly and asked me why. Why did I want to leave an established, well-paid job in a firm that supported and valued me?

Going. That was the word. Helen had used it, right at the beginning of my appraisal; when I sat down, she had asked me, 'How's it all going?' I doubt she thought twice about her wording, and why would she – it was a normal, generic query to which I could have replied *fine, great, normal*, just like I always do. But as the word came out of her mouth, something flickered in my head, and the word 'going' travelled up my ear canals and exploded in my brain, causing synonyms to burst forth like fragments of a bomb.

Going: it equates to forward motion, to travel and progression. It suggests the future and hints at development; it is bound up with action and determined intent – when Helen said it, I realised that these are all the things missing from my life. I have been in my job for three years, in PR for six, and six years is a long time to spend doing something you don't want to do, especially when it stops you pursuing something you do.

At some point Joanne must have started talking; in my recollection she went: 'Blah blah blah blah snap decision blah blah blah further discussion blah blah vodka and ice-cream.' In hindsight, I might have been hearing what I wanted towards the end. The three of us agreed that I would take some time to think about it, and that Helen and I would meet next week to discuss how things were . . . going.

*   *   *

The mood in the pub is jubilant. Short Martin offers to buy a round, causing a cheer to ripple through the group (were it not for his short stature, Miserly Martin would suit him just as well). We are crowded round two tables someone pulled together and my colleagues are chatting, laughing and ploughing through wine and Mini Cheddars in celebration of the end of another round of appraisals. Amelie is getting a promotion and nobody was fired, so we've chalked it up to a success. I haven't told anyone about my meeting; Pip asked, but I told her it was fine. Great. Normal. Yet I know now what I couldn't articulate to Guy at dinner: as I sit in amongst my colleagues, all buzzing from cheap booze and cheese-flavoured biscuits, I feel left out. Their contentment makes me feel unsettled, different; they are so happy to know their jobs are safe but I can't bring myself to share their joy. I hadn't intended to walk into my appraisal and tell Helen I wanted to leave, but it popped out regardless, as though my subconscious shoved it out of my mouth.

My phone rings – it's Guy. I take it and walk to the other side of the bar where it's quiet, away from my colleagues. *Ex-colleagues*: I try out the phrase silently on my tongue.

'Hey.'

'Hi,' says Guy, 'how are you? How's your day?' I tell him I'm fine, my day's been OK, I had my six-month appraisal and am thinking of quitting my job.

'Quit? Why?' He leaves no time to answer before his questions begin. What did I say? What did Helen say? How long have I been thinking about this? There is a shade of anger in his voice that takes me by surprise. The muscles in my shoulder are starting to throb; I knead them with my free hand whilst I listen.

Finally, Guy says: 'What would you do about money?'

Money. In the end, it usually comes down to money. It's not like I haven't thought about it. I have a few hundred pounds of savings and roughly the same in my current account; beyond that, I could sell a kidney but once *that's* gone, yes, I'd be broke. I am not indifferent to this issue but I don't want to think about it right now. This is unfortunate for Guy, who doesn't want to talk about anything else.

'I reckon your savings would get you through the next month or so. My friend Grace works in PR, she might know of other jobs that are going, do you want me to talk to her?'

'But I don't think I want to work in PR any more.'

'Then what?'

I don't say 'writing' straight away. I consider lying (marketing, advertising, something in a related field; anything that will make Guy's questions stop) or joking (stripper) but the deal between Guy and me is that we're supposed to tell each other the truth. I explain that writing has crossed my mind, but at this stage it's just an idea.

There is a long pause, and then Guy says, 'Oh.' Just that, which is odd, because he had plenty to say before. Before . . . on our first date, it was he who suggested I leave my job and try to make it as a writer. What happened to that?

'It's just . . .' he says, hesitating, faltering for the right words, 'we were just talking. I thought you knew that wasn't real.'

18

THE MAN WITH THE CHILD IN HIS EYES

I have decided, as a thrilling change, to order a flat white from Coops at Caffè Nero – I've been coming here so much recently, Coops and I have progressed from first name to nickname terms. I place it on the table, leaving a good distance between cup and laptop (I've watched too many novice drink-typers put their beverage too close to their computer to know how disastrous the conse-quences can be) and open up a website I've been looking at. I've chosen the table at the back by the wall so nobody can see. I'm not back on Guardian Soulmates, it's not that bad. I just happen to be casually looking at job search sites, as any regular person might do on a regular Saturday afternoon.

I'm allowed to look; everyone is allowed to *look*, it doesn't mean I'll actually *do* anything. I could, maybe, if I went to the gym more, make it as a stripper, but the hours are tremendously anti-social and leaving one profession I dislike for another sort of ruins the point. However, as I am coming to realise, the problem with job hunting is that there are too many jobs. This might not sound like a problem, but then everyone thought Communism sounded pretty rad at the beginning and look how that's turned out. There are hundreds of jobs, thousands, on every site I look at . . . and I don't want any of them. I don't want to be a secretary. I don't want to be a PA. I don't want to be in banking as an executive, a manager or a director (fortunate, as I'm not qualified to work in banking). I don't want to have a career in social work or healthcare. I don't want to work in the charity sector or IT. Or hospitality, or horticulture, and being able to cook would presumably be key if I want a job in catering. Yes, I want to work close to where I live and yes, I'd like to earn more than £10,000 a year (as would my landlord) but otherwise, no. No – in general. No, no, no, no, no. I'm certain I don't want to be a PR executive, but that's all I know; beyond that, I haven't a clue what job would make me happy. Being a writer might, but there's a reason they call it a *dream job*: like Guy said, it isn't real.

I'm scrolling through link after link of unsuitable dross when I spot something: 'Marketing and Social Media Manager'. The link is still active so I click through and read the job spec. It looks like the job involves less Facebooking than I'd hope, but it describes the offices as 'funky', which makes me think I absolutely definitely want this job. My office could not in good conscience ever be described as 'funky': 'inappropriately heated' would be nearer the mark, or 'of questionable structural integrity'. I don't want to work with a hot-water bottle on my lap any more – I want a funky future. The spec uses words like 'brand values' and 'implementation', which sound like things I may have experience in. I've never managed anyone, however, let alone a social media department, although I did sometimes tell Ella the Temp which trade mags to buy. This job isn't as well paid as my last one and it isn't really part-time either – the hours are referred to as 'flexible' – and OK, *technically* it's in Essex, but overall it sounds so much better than anything I've been doing for the last six years. After one final read through, I click 'apply now'. It's just for fun, to see how I get on. I'm not really applying. Not technically.

Right, here we go: Name – easy. Email address – fine. Covering letter . . . OK. It can't be more than 3,500 characters, which is a mere 800 words or thereabouts: in my second year I wrote a 2,000-word essay in three hours so I know I can do it (although the essay was laughably bad). Once I've talked about my experience and the fact I have sent 128 tweets in my lifetime – one of which was favourited by Tim Dowling from the *Guardian* – I should be up to 400 words at least. The rest can be bumpf about why I should get the job – and I *should*: I am a dynamic, motivated and organised individual; I can take initiative and work independently, yet I also perform exceptionally as part of a team. I am used to working to and meeting deadlines; I have experience in leading projects and delegating whilst being supportive and encouraging of my colleagues. Similarly, yet a bit differently, I can anticipate the needs of my seniors and provide consistent and efficient support of a high standard, though I can also do sub-standard work when required . . . I am fun yet reserved, quiet yet loud and I will basically do whatever you tell me because I want a new job and I've read the job spec twice and I've decided it must be this one.

I rest my head in my hands. I should come back to this; for the moment, I could do with sorting out my CV. I haven't updated it for years and it still has a section concerning my two years as a waitress at The George when I was in Sixth Form. Translated onto my CV, laying the tables became 'taking a proactive role in the design and maintenance of the workplace' and taking orders was 'liaising professionally with clients to meet their specific needs'. I'll have to create a new section to cover the last three years. The whole document needs a makeover really, to reflect the dynamic-organised-focused-multi-tasking member of the proletariat I have turned out to be. I close the screen and go on Facebook.

* * *

Guy suggested we watch TV. Initially, I was keen, but I think I've had too much coffee as I feel restless and I'm struggling to relax. The news is on; he trails his fingers up and down my leg as we watch reports detailing the unbearable sadness happening the world over, followed by a story about a donkey sanctuary. I turn to look at him. 'Do you want to go out for a drink?'

'Not really.'

Against all odds, the newest jenny in the sanctuary has given birth to a foal; it has been cause for a three-day celebration and the foal has been named 'Happy', which to me seems a lot to live up to. 'We could go out and have a walk? It's a nice evening,' I suggest.

Guy squeezes my leg. 'I've had a long week, honey.' ('Honey' is new – when did 'honey' start?) 'We could order food if you're hungry,' he suggests. 'How about Indian?' I'm not hungry, and I think I might scream if I have to stay in the flat much longer, but I tell him sure, yeah, Indian sounds good and Guy reaches for my laptop to find a place. 'Shall I go out and collect it?' I ask, my pitch high with optimism.

Guy leans over and pinches my waist. 'Someone's a fidget tonight.' He gives me a quick kiss and turns back to the screen. In my stale, tense and restless mind, it registers as an insult.

*   *   *

We are lying in bed and my stomach hurts. I ate until I was full, then I continued eating until all my food was finished and now my body feels so heavy and sluggish it's as though korma sauce is chugging through my arteries. Guy rolls towards me and kisses my neck: the international male sign for Let's Have Sex. I try to let my muscles relax and ease into him but the touch of his hand on my breast actively turns me off. 'Could we wait until the morning?' I say, giving his thigh a rub.

Guy gives an elaborate, woeful comedy moan, like: *Foiled again!* I can hear the frustration behind it though, and it makes me feel guilty. Equally, I feel like a wedge of human and utterly unsexy. In a phoney Germanic accent, Guy says, 'You Brits, you are not keen on ze sex, ja?' It's our own little shtick: it's what one of us says whenever the other seems reluctant for sex; I can't remember how it started. It makes me smile, but in the darkness Guy can't see. I feel his body relax and assume he is falling asleep, but then he rolls back to face me. 'Do you want kids?' After the joke, the question takes me by surprise.

I prop myself up on my elbows. 'Why? Is this because I'm not in the mood? It's just because I ate too much, I'm really full . . .'

'Rosy.' He reaches out to me but in the darkness his fingers poke my face. 'Sorry,' he laughs. Then he tells me to stop being dumb: his colleague came back from maternity leave and brought her baby to visit the office; he'd meant to tell me, then we saw the thing about Happy the donkey. He was just curious about my thoughts.

I lie back down. 'I do, I think. Not for a while though.'

'Boys or girls? Hannah's is a little boy, Noah. He's very sweet.'

'Girls, definitely, I don't want boys with ginger hair.' It takes a second for the impact of what I've just said to hit me. Fuck. Fuckity, fuck, fuck fuck. It doesn't matter that I can't see Guy, I can feel his reaction: his muscles tense up and he rolls away from me, not totally – just enough. He's not projecting out anger, though; it's like he's donned armour.

'I guessed my hair was an issue for you,' he says.

I sense this is not the time to ask him how. Instead I say, 'It's not,' but it comes out too quickly.

'I can't change it . . .'

'I know, I wouldn't want you . . .'

'You saw me on our first date. You Liked me on Tinder.'

I can't believe I said that; I'm such a fucking idiot. Shit. And I can't bear feeling Guy pull away – it's like Charlie all over again. I need him back. I shuffle after him and rest my arm across his chest and he lets me. I didn't think he would. 'I wouldn't change one thing about you,' I say. 'I like you exactly as you are.'

Guy places his hand on mine. He says: 'That's how I feel about you,' except he is telling the truth.

19.

IN THE WARM ROOM

Just write anything. It doesn't need to be good, it just has to be written, it just has to be words on a page. This isn't the best strategy for applying for a job, I know, but the midnight deadline for the social media role is in twenty minutes so I don't have time for strategy. I've jotted down a few sentences about how I am suited to the media industry and that I revel in the fast-paced, professional environment of an office but now I'm not sure whether I should put that because at the end of the form I have to declare that everything I've written is true. I take a slug of my second cup of coffee, which I only remember is freshly made as the liquid scalds my tongue. I spew it back and place the cup back on my bedside table, then push my fingers into my hair.

I hear the keys turn in the lock. I assume it must be Harriet because Oona is away in Paris, but when I turn

round I realise Oona is not in Paris: she is standing in the
doorway to my bedroom. She doesn't need to use words
in order to communicate what she's thinking; I already
know what that is for one thing and if I didn't I could
guess from the look on her face. Because it's Oona, however,
she uses words too. 'Rosy, your room is disgusting.'

This is objectively a fair assessment. There are piles
of washing everywhere; empty food wrappers are scat-
tered randomly and my dresser is littered with dirty
mugs and glasses. A ramshackle stack of DVDs by my
bed threatens to topple at any moment. My chair is
covered with books and magazines and a towel is hanging
from the lampshade.

'You need to clean up.' She weaves her way through
a trail of discarded clothing, paperwork and charger
cables, and that's when she spots it. My eyes dart across
in pursuit but it's already too late. I meant to throw it
away. Shit. 'Have you been eating that?' asks Oona.

I train my eyes on my laptop. I can't look at her. 'Yes.'

She inches closer and peers inside the container. 'You
know it's melted.'

'I know.'

'It's right by the radiator.'

'Yeah.'

'Rosy, it's ice-cream: you can't eat it if it's been sitting
around, you'll get ill. Have you even left the house
today?'

'I went to Sainsbury's.'

'Did you go to get the ice-cream?'

I hide my face in my hands. I can feel the prickle of

tears in my eyes but I dig my fingernails into my palms to force their retreat. I do not want to cry in front of Oona, it would be a horrendous experience for both of us. She shifts the clutter from my chair onto the floor and sits down. 'It looked like you're doing a job application.' She gestures to my laptop and I nod back. 'Are you leaving your current job?'

I tell Oona about everything: the monotony, day in, day out, and how I've started to feel like I'm stagnating by just being in the office. I explain how I started in PR, a story she's never heard; that I took the first job I was offered without any thought as to what else might be out there. I get to my appraisal and describe the way I blurted out my reticence to Helen (she's barely speaking to me now and giving all the most interesting jobs to Pip). Oona sits listening and nods reassuringly when I hesitate. It's unnerving when she's being kind.

When I'm finished, she says: 'It doesn't sound like you're committed to PR.' I reply that I'm not, and the sheer relief I feel saying it out loud takes me by surprise.

'Rosy, I know I'm not really an "out-there" kind of person,' she continues, and I force myself not to laugh because I can't tell whether or not she's joking. 'I don't make a big hoopla about stuff, but one thing I'm really passionate about is my job. It's tough, don't get me wrong, but I love it, and I think it's crucial to enjoy what you do because most people spend more time at work than anywhere else. You clearly don't enjoy what you're doing, so the logical next step is to get out and find something that you do.'

This may be the longest time Oona has ever spent talking to me. It had never occurred to me that despite the long hours, the constant travelling and weight of responsibility on her shoulders, Oona might relish the life she's chosen. Very little has ever occurred to me about Oona, in fact; I've always thought of her as cold, but I can count on one hand the times I've shown a real interest in her life. As I cast my eyes over the detritus in my room, it's like I'm seeing for the first time how it looks through someone else's eyes: the mess and dirt look like a physical manifestation of the muddle my life has become.

'You could do with getting away,' she says, her tone back to brisk and I fear my quota of Nice Oona has been filled for today, possibly forever. 'Why don't you go back home for the weekend?' It takes me a good ten seconds to understand that Oona is referring to my parents' house. To me, this flat *is* home but seemingly for Oona, this flat is but a dingy bolthole, sufficient for only as long as it takes her to save up a deposit and escape to Parsons Green.

'I would love to,' I reply, 'but I don't think I can, not with all these applications and . . .'

'Rosy,' she says, cutting me off, 'I can help you with job applications. But until you can relax you'll be no good for anything.'

'I would really appreciate that, Oona . . . thank you.'

She stands up and starts to move towards the door, so I get up too in order to give her a hug. She turns to me and I am just going to stretch out my arms when she stops and says, 'But please make sure you tidy your room.' I freeze and assure her I will. Oona won't like it if I hug her, I should have thought of that.

When she is gone, I sit back on my bed and go over what Oona was saying. In my mind, the idea of developing yourself, moving forward in life, is bound up with a sense of being happy and fulfilled. I think of my appraisal, Helen saying 'going', and just how loaded the word has become. To give it its full definition:

going, *noun:* a departure or farewell.

20

MOTHER STANDS FOR COMFORT

The train to my parents' house is always crowded, no matter what time of day you go. It is also always delayed and several of my fellow travellers, apparently unaware of this, are starting to shuffle on the spot and exhale aggressively. The man to my right is fidgeting in a seriously un-Zen manner that is starting to stress me out too; when the train pulls in, I make sure I choose any carriage other than the one he steps into and stuff my travel bag into the overhead compartment. BF came round to help me pack, by which I mean she made me sit on my bed whilst she packed for me because my method involves surveying an empty bag for three hours then throwing in anything that might prove vaguely useful in the ten minutes before I leave. In Corfu three years ago, I opened my suitcase to find I'd included a sewing kit and a lint roller but forgotten to bring any underwear.

There is no elegant way of manoeuvring into a (standard-class) train seat so I do an ungainly half-crouching side step and tip myself into position, glad of the empty seat beside me, and lean my forehead against the window, watching the tower blocks and factories as they stream past. They will peter out as the train moves further out of London and be replaced by row upon row of terraced houses; then, as I get closer to home, the terraces will give way to detached homes and eventually these will cede to the open fields of the countryside. Ollie, an urbanite since birth, still marvels at the sight of roaming cattle; to travel with him is to experience a grown man yelling, 'Cows!' like a child seeing them outside of a picture book for the first time.

Yesterday evening, before I left the office, I made sure my filing was done, marked up everything that needed posting and emailed Helen my resignation.

If you want to blame anyone, blame Oona. She just had to fucking go and start being kind and reasonable, just at the pivotal moment when I was thinking of leaving my job. She has since affirmed that she thinks it's the right decision, although she also had concerns about how I'd pay the rent, it being *her* rent too, and she had no qualms about sharing these with me. At length. Everyone else I texted last night was broadly supportive: BF was pleased and not at all surprised, The Couples likewise; my parents were a little more alarmed, but I'm surprised at just how understanding they've been.

I meant to ring Guy but it got too late. I'll ring him from Mum and Dad's – or maybe a text would be better. It could probably wait until I get back.

I'm not sure how I feel about it myself; a little bit thrilled at my daring, a lot terrified and concerned at my stupidity and I suspect I'm still in shock. I sat at my desk for at least an hour yesterday pretending to proof-read a release, whilst all the time debating whether to press 'send' or not. I was too scared to resign face to face and having requested this Friday as a last-minute holiday, the thought of handing Helen a letter made me feel dizzy with nerves. So, like the coward that I am, I wrote the email and sent it at 7 p.m. on the dot, then I grabbed my coat and bag and ran. I haven't heard from Helen yet; I feel like I'm in trouble, although (the binding machine excepted) I've done nothing wrong.

*   *   *

My mother is waiting for me when the train pulls in. I spot her from the footbridge, hanging out of the car behind her driver's door and waving up at me, just in case I have forgotten what she looks like and our genetic similarities aren't enough of a clue. She envelops me in a tight hug and I wallow in the primitive glee of being held in my mother's arms, breathing in her scent: Guerlain and wood polish, the smell of my childhood.

When we turn into the gate, Dad is already on the drive, waiting to relieve me of my bag. 'I'll take this up to your room, love,' he says, throwing his free arm round my shoulders. Technically, 'my' room is now the Guest Room; there was a six-month grace period during which it lay in state, but once Mum was satisfied my job and flat in London were stable she got out the paint rollers and took my soft animal menagerie to Oxfam. The room is now reserved exclusively for the guests that are yet to come, and me. Hector, our aged beagle, comes trotting down the hallway towards me and I crouch down to receive him, scratching behind his ears and nuzzling my face into his flank. Beagles are hunters by nature and as a young dog Hector was no exception: no frog, rabbit or (as demonstrated on one horrifying Sunday afternoon) fox was safe in his presence (Dad was deployed with a shovel for the fox). However, once he turned twelve he started getting a bit slow and shuffly, and at fourteen years old he is long into his twilight years. He seems perfectly content, even with the spectre of death looming over him: he eats his dry kibble as and when he wants, he takes his daily walk and he sleeps a lot. Sometimes he chews a slipper. It's the sort of retirement I dream of for myself. We go into the kitchen and Hector pads off to curl up in his bed whilst I head straight for the spot in front of the Aga where I plan to stand for the majority of my stay.

'Cup of tea?' Mum asks.

'Yes, please.'

'Do you want a sandwich? I bought some ham from the butcher's.'

'I'm OK.'

'What about some soup?'

240

'No thanks, Mum.'

'A scone? I've got scones.' She looks fretful. My mother won't be content until I'm ready for the foie gras factory. If it's an unconscious attempt to feed me to amend some imagined shortfall in her love, she is woefully misguided. Though for her coffee cake I'd play along.

Dad comes in having dispatched my bag. 'Would you like a cup of tea, love?'

'I've already put the kettle on, Arthur. We were just talking about having some scones.'

'Actually Mum, I'm . . .'

'Scones, yes – that sounds good, Susan,' says Dad. 'We could have the jam Next-Door Stella made us.'

'Choir Stella made the jam; Next-Door Stella lent us the sander.'

'That's it. We've had that sander a while now, I'm surprised Rod hasn't been round asking for it.'

We sit around the table to eat (scones with Choir Stella's jam, as well as butter and clotted cream, and a round of last-minute ham sandwiches, plus the last bits of shortbread in the tin) and I listen as debate breaks out between my parents about whether Rod actually *uses* the sander because (as Mum confides, *sotto voce*) Stella is always moaning that their house is a wreck. This leads on to a discussion about whether Dad should invest in a sander of his own, despite my interjection that with free rein on Rod's their sanding needs have essentially been taken care of. I drink a second cup of tea and eat two scones, four triangle sandwiches and a bit of the shortbread that 'needs to be finished', and once Dad jiggles the tin it's no longer a request. Mum refuses my offer of help to clear the table. Instead she tells me dinner will be in a few hours, and sends me to the sitting room to relax.

Oona had a point. I love being at home.

* * *

The darkness in the countryside is truly dark. I forget until I go to bed and I'm lying in it; it feels like I'm underwater (add in a menacing shark and Ian Hislop in the role of an austere lifeguard and I could be in my recurring nightmare). The silence is truly silent, too: gone is the growl and rumble of traffic; there is no drunken tomfoolery happening outside my window and no doors slamming upstairs where the two lads I suspect to be drug dealers live. There are no sirens, because nobody gets ill in the countryside. In fact there are only two modes of existence around here: hardy and hearty, or dead. If you do happen to ail, you are expected to power through but if it's really nasty you'll have to visit the fancy hospital up in town, because the best you can hope for from the local surgery is some aspirin and the heartfelt good wishes of Dr Reed, who is also the postman. Crime is virtually non-existent, apart from the odd occasion teenagers drink cider on the village hall roof, in which case Mr Taylor (school groundsman/local policeman) rides up on his bike, changes his hat and tells them to come down. They usually do. The peace is in such stark contrast to the constant commotion of

London that I am struggling to sleep – though I'll want to chain myself to the Aga when it's time to go back and London will seem inordinately noisy when I do.

I had intended to sleep late into the morning but when I wake up it is 8.05 a.m. The early start could be down to any number of things: the sounds of Mum pottering in the kitchen, Dad's twenty-minute shower, the smell of bacon or the occasional bark it elicits from Hector. Years ago, I asked my mother why she rises so early (6.30 on a week day; 7.00 as a weekend treat) and she replied: 'I have so much to do.' She couldn't expand upon exactly what these things were but Dad says that the house would fall down if it weren't for Mum. Maybe she spends a lot of time grouting.

She is depressing the plunger on a cafetière when I wander into the kitchen in the pyjamas BF packed and a dressing gown I found in what was formerly Bru's bedroom, now the place where Mum irons.

'Morning!' My mother is like a kids' TV presenter in the morning. I am more like my old driving instructor, Nigel, who hated anything that wasn't trout fishing and smoking (that included teaching teenagers how to drive). 'Would you like coffee? Tea? Hot chocolate?'

I sit at the table and rub my face. 'Give me a minute, Mum.' I pick some sleep dust from my eyes. 'Could I have hot chocolate with little marshmallows?'

'Oh, the bake sale!' Mum exclaims, coming to a dead stop. Her face looks sad and it's making me feel sad too, but overall I am confused. I don't know what she is talking about or how a bake sale is relevant to my getting marshmallows in my drink. 'They went in the rocky road I made for the charity thing at Canbrook,' she explains. 'I'm so sorry.'

Canbrook C of E: I haven't heard the name of my primary school said aloud for years. It takes me back, instantly; the place had such a distinctive smell, bleach mixed with chip fat – I can smell it now, which at 8.15 a.m. is unpleasant. I remember my peg, stuck to the wall with my laminated name and the ubiquitous drawing of a rose above. I remember a fight I had with my friend Andrea after I hid her pencil case. I remember taking ballet in the assembly hall; it was subsequently 'recommended' that I leave for 'galumphing'. 'Mum, why are you still baking for Canbrook?' I do quick figures in my head: I left sixteen years ago.

'I'm a governor there.'

'I didn't know that.'

'Well, there you go. They need a new piano.' Again, I'm stumped.

'Would you like tea instead?' she continues, stirring baked beans on the hob.

'Tea would be great.'

Mum goes to fill the kettle. 'Breakfast won't be long, but you've got time for a quick shower if you want.'

'I'll wait.'

'No problem.'

Nothing is a problem at home. It's no problem to take a shower; it would be no problem to then eat breakfast wrapped in one of the large, soft bath towels Mum laid out on my bed last night; it would be no problem to stay in my pyjamas, watch TV and eat Pringles for the rest of the day. It wouldn't be a problem if I wore nothing but pyjamas until I leave, merely an excuse for Mum to go into town to buy me more pairs. I can't remember the last time I woke up in London and had no problems.

Dad appears in the doorway. 'Are you making tea?' He can sense a boiling kettle the same way Hector can hear his dog whistle. He sits at the table opposite me. 'You look like you've slept in the barn!'

'Oh she's fine, Arthur.'

'You're lucky you scrub up,' Dad says to me, glancing at me over the top of the paper, 'then you'll have the boys fighting over you.'

'Or just one, maybe.' I feel my cheeks heat up.

'Did you get a boyfriend?'

I can't help but smile at my father's phrasing – he makes it sound like when you want a boyfriend you get one, just as you might pop out to pick up milk. The answer in my head is no, although Guy called me his girlfriend. He took a work call when I was last at his and though he walked into the other room to speak I heard it: *'I'm just with my girlfriend now but I'll make sure it's with you first thing . . .'*

'We're seeing each other,' I tell Dad.

'I don't understand that,' says Mum, placing four flavours of jam on the table (despite the fact I only ever eat raspberry), '"seeing each other". What does that mean? You're either together or you're not, aren't you? Is this man "seeing" other girls too?'

'I should hope not,' says Dad, 'unless it's a two-way

street.' He throws me a wink. I try to imagine Guy cheating on me: taking his phone to the bathroom, asking his friends to confirm his stories, ignoring my call when he's with 'her'. It seems improbable. Impossible. Guy is safe, reliable. Like a second-hand car.

*   *   *

It is a depressing moment in any girl's life when she finds out her middle-aged mother is fitter than her. When Mum suggested I join her and Hector for his walk, I pictured us ambling along footpaths with the sun on our faces, stopping occasionally to pick wild blackberries and admire buttercups. Unfortunately, we are not walking Hector in 1928 and my mother does not amble.

There is no sun on my face, only tears from the wind that whips at it, making my eyes water; I'm partially protected by my fetching ensemble of wellies, Mum's fleece and a blue beanie from Bru's brief spell as a Millwall fan/thug but it's uncomfortable nonetheless. Mum strides ahead as we make our way up the hill, leaving Hector and me puffing in her wake. I don't know which is worse: that I am not as agile as a 61-year-old or that my fitness level is on a par with an aged, arthritic beagle. I have to get back to the gym. It's easier to keep pace once we reach the flat; Hector trots along amiably at Mum's feet and I take time to drink in our surroundings: green fields stretch into green fields beyond with some delineated by neat rows of crops; all lie under the vast expanse of blue-grey sky that yawns into the horizon.

It is beautiful. In the space, in the air, I feel like I can finally breathe which makes me worry about what I'm inhaling in London. Cities have landmarks, at least; out here, there is nothing by which I can orientate myself – one crop looks like another crop, this hedgerow is identical to that one and without Mum here to navigate I'd be lost after seven minutes and I'd have to cobble together a shelter and hope a dray of squirrels accepts me as one of their own.

'So, your boyfriend,' Mum says, apropos of nothing, 'what's his name?'

I don't want to get into a debate so I let her pointed 'boyfriend' go. Guy, I tell her. His name is Guy.

'And what's he like?'

'He's nice,' I say. He made me dinner and he said he wouldn't want to change me – nice. 'He's an accountant.' *Oh, and he has ginger hair.*

'Is he good-looking?' asks Mum.

'Yep.' *Although, you know, the hair . . .*

'How did you two meet?'

The wind picks up again and it is so strong that Mum and I have to lean into it to stay upright. It ruffles Hector's ears, but he is so low to the ground he can plod along unaffected. 'We met through a dating app,' I shout above the gale.

'A what?' Mum shouts back. I wait until the wind dies down again to explain. 'You download it onto your phone, it's called Tinder. It shows you all the single people in your area who are on it too and matches you if you both say you Like each other's picture. We got talking and now we're . . .' I say, 'together', but one final gust of wind spirits the word away.

'I think I read an article about it . . .' Mum says, letting her words trail off, which means she's thinking carefully about what to say next. 'Wouldn't you rather meet someone in a more . . . normal way?'

We reach the viewing spot that looks down into the valley. A few picnic tables have been erected for those who believe eating sandwiches on the side of a blustery, desolate hillside to be time well spent. Maybe it's the anomalous tables, but this is the sole part of the route I recognise; I look down into the dell, search out the little bridge that runs over the stream then shift my gaze slowly to the right until I spot the glint of a red post box and a small coppice of trees above – our house is nestled just behind. Years ago, I saw Bru having a surreptitious cigarette by Dad's shed and had to feign a chance hawk sighting to stop Mum spotting him too.

Mum is a way ahead as Hector and I meander down the hill. I suspect her urgency correlates to her having 'so much to do' though it's never easy to discern what Mum is thinking – harder still when she's thirty metres away with her back to me. Clean sheets; fluffy towels; breakfast served and food on tap: I've felt like I've been on holiday since I've been back. There's something freeing about the lush, open countryside. I feel like I could expand endlessly into the space without worrying I'll bash into a Nando's or a car park, or another person. It's only as I speed up to catch Mum that I realise: this landscape that I have vaulted to utopian heights is simply the backdrop to Mum's everyday existence. Walking the dog is a daily chore, not a luxury; my holiday home is her office, my breakfast just another item to be crossed off her to-do list. And I bet she always reaches the end of hers.

When Hector wanders off to sniff some twigs, I fall into step with Mum. 'When did you know you were ready to get married?'

'That's out of the blue,' she says. 'Why are you thinking about that?'

I tell her, 'I'm curious,' which seems as good a reason as any to pose a question, though in truth I'm not sure. Maybe's it to do with Guy; I also have a sudden sense that I don't know enough about her life. Mum is silent in thought. 'I suppose you don't *know*, not for certain.' She looks around for Hector and when she can't spot him she calls his name and he bounds out of a bush, as much as Hector can bound anywhere. 'I don't think it's black and white,' she adds.

I know it's better to wait and let my mother organise her thoughts than to push her for clarity – I'm more like Dad in this respect: restless, impatient, impulsive – but we are getting closer to home and I want to prompt her before the moment is lost. At the rate she's going you'd think I'd asked her to calculate infinity. Finally, she says: 'I was in love with your dad, and I knew if he asked me to marry him I'd say yes. It took another five years but he did.' She leans down and gives Hector a pat. 'You take it as read that there will be ups and downs and you hope it will last forever, but you say yes knowing it might not be . . .' Her pace slows a little (I notice because it is suddenly easier to breathe). 'No, that's not quite right. That sounds like I thought a lot about it but I didn't – I was happy and I wanted to marry your dad. It was just the right decision. So maybe that's why, because I didn't have to think about it.'

On the basis that Mum hasn't actually answered my question, I change tack. 'When did you know you were in love with Dad?'

'Does it work like that?' She laughs. 'There wasn't a precise moment. It wasn't as if I was doing the washing up and thought, oh, I'm in love with Arthur. It was a gradual thing.' Her voice sounds different as she says this – softer, slightly higher – she is talking in role as her younger self, remembering how it felt to be caught up in that first rush of love, knowing as she does, as I do, even at half her age, that once it fades, it's gone for good. She sounds odd – not bad, just odd. I'm being inducted into time before I existed.

'What attracted you to him?'

'Well, he was very good-looking,' she begins, and I'm sure I see her cheeks flush, though it could be the wind, 'that was a good start. He was very charismatic and very funny. And when we met he had just started at Tyler Shoot, so that impressed Gran and Gramps.'

'It sounds like he was a catch.'

'I'm not saying he was perfect,' she says. 'Nobody's perfect.'

The back door comes into sight up ahead. Hector is lagging and I'm glad he'll be able to rest; he'll likely collapse into bed when we get home. There's a strong chance I'll do the same. 'There was a moment,' Mum goes on, 'when I remember thinking: "He doesn't annoy me."'

I squint at her, uncomprehending. 'What do you mean?'

'I mean with other boyfriends there was always something – he drives too fast, or, you know, I don't like his friend so-and-so, but with your dad, I remember thinking, I'm not bothered by anything much.' We walk up the path. 'I think that's what initially attracted me, all the good things about him, you know.' Mum opens the door letting Hector toddle through first. 'The longer you're with someone, you start to see all the bad things about them. Of course you like their good bits, that's what attracts you in the first place. But when you get to know their bad parts . . .' My mother pulls her boots off one by one and tosses them on the mat; she pads towards the kettle to make tea, her thick walking socks still tucked over her jeans. She turns over her shoulder and looks at me. 'When you accept someone's bad parts,' she says, 'that's when you decide to stay.'

*   *   *

Later, I find all the parts of my father on the sofa where he is watching football, because he enjoys football and because it is Sunday afternoon, and because this is the order of things in my family and has been for as far back as I can remember. Bru would join him when we were

251

kids, drinking ginger beer in imitation of Dad's harder stuff and goading him into arguments over the quality of players and other football-related . . . things. Mum and I (happily) left them to it: she would make a start on dinner then take coffee and papers into the garden room, or else she'd ring my godmother Liz, thus preventing me from surfing the web (these were the dark days of yore when we still had a dial-up connection and people still said 'surfing the web'). When that happened, I'd go to my room and make up dance routines.

I hover on the threshold of the living room. 'Hey, Dad.'

'Hello, love. You look . . . relaxed.' I look down at my post-walk, post-shower outfit: ancient joggers, my pyjama top and Mum's cashmere cardigan – I couldn't be more comfortable if I were dead. I move towards the armchair; Dad doesn't order me out in spite of my vagina so I slide down over the arm and curl up. 'What's the score?' I can see the score on the screen but this is my in.

'2–1 to United,' he replies, concentrating on the match. 'Bit undeserved, though, they haven't been playing that well.'

Dad supported Man United in the womb, as did his dad and *his* dad before him and now Bru does too. Sketchy reports from the birthing suite suggest Dad *may* have welled up when I was born, but he's been known to openly weep after particularly significant Man United losses. As I understand it, the quality of United's play holds no less importance for him than the result. I could never grasp why Dad was disappointed if his team hadn't performed well to earn their victory; to my surly, adolescent mind, a win was a win and you're lucky to get one (because I was always a loser and the world was against me and I was fat and no boys liked me and SHUT UP YOU CAN'T TELL ME WHAT TO DO). As I've grown up, I've come to understand that the means can be just as important as the ends; the outcome might not be what you'd hoped but the way you purport yourself *en route* is what will be remembered. I love my father for his magnanimity – however, I still contend that if a team wins it's because they're the *best team.*

The whistle blows for half time. 'How are you doing?' Dad asks me.

'I'm good. It's nice to be here.' We're both drawn back to the TV as the adverts start: a man is shaving with the newest, sharpest, most bestest razor whilst the green screen backdrop swirls around him. To my taste, his conventional good looks render him asexual, but then I'm not the target market: men presumably look in awe at his hairless body and shockingly square jaw.

'Have you thought about when you'll head back to London?' Dad asks.

'I guess I'm trying not to think about it.'

'That bad, eh?'

'No, it's fine . . . just not much to hurry back for, that's all.'

'Well, you've got this new man.'

'Mm.'

Dad chuckles and turns his attention back to the TV. 'He sounds like a keeper.' I suspect he's said all he's going to on the matter; I'm single or I'm not, it's much

the same to him and he won't get involved until somebody wants to marry me and even then it will only be
to try and scare the guy off. I don't know if Guy is a
keeper or not. I turn his name over in my head: *Guy.*
Just a guy I'm seeing.

'Dad,' I say, when a trailer appears for upcoming
games, 'when did you know Mum was "the one"?'

'No such thing as the one, is there?'

'When you wanted to marry her, then.'

He chuckles to himself. 'Still going back and forth on
that one.'

*   *   *

Over dinner, my mother asks what I'm going to do about
getting a job. Actually, she doesn't ask, not directly; what
she does do is tell me that Izzy, the 21-year-old daughter
of Philippa from church, is just about to move to London
and is looking for her first job; Philippa is worried, but
then Philippa is a worrier . . . Mum trails off, which is
my cue to talk.

'I sent off an application last week.' I pause, waiting
for my mother to congratulate me on my industry and
my possible future career as a Marketing and Social
Media Manager, but am met with silence. Eventually,
she finishes her mouthful and says, 'That's something.'

'Any ideas what you might do longer term?' asks my
father.

My parents are a tough crowd. I should go for a joke,
warm up my audience. 'I hear PR offers good prospects.'

Dad manages a limp 'ha'. Mum spoons spinach onto her plate. Then I add, 'Maybe I should ask Izzy for some advice,' and laugh, though the more I think about it, the less it seems like a joke.

'With all your experience you'll have no trouble getting something,' Dad offers kindly, though he doesn't specify what that 'something' might be.

My mother incises a sausage in one clean motion. 'You need to think about what you'd like to do. It was never PR, was it?' Then Dad says: 'What about writing?'

It takes a second for me to process what he's said – I didn't know Dad knew about my writing. And, what *about* writing? This debate, whenever I've held it with myself, has always ended the same way, with the sound of Guy's voice: *I thought you knew that wasn't real.* 'I don't know if I can make a career out of that.'

'If that's what you would like to do,' says my father, 'you just have to work out how to go about it. And if it's a question of money . . .' My mother purses her lips. I'm not looking at her as she does this, I just sense it.

'I can't ask you for that.'

'Well, we're not millionaires,' says my father, in case twenty-seven years' worth of pony-less birthdays aren't enough of a clue, 'but I'm sure we could work something out.'

* * *

In the morning, I open my eyes at precisely 7.46 to the strains of Mum making breakfast and Dad's shower

255

rendition of 'Makin' Whoopee'. I lie still, listening. The peace is disrupted by the beep of my phone.

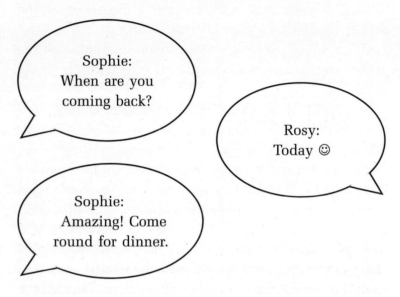

> Sophie:
> When are you coming back?

> Rosy:
> Today ☺

> Sophie:
> Amazing! Come round for dinner.

I could stay here for months, maybe years, hanging out by the Aga, going for walks, sleeping – essentially living the life of an elderly beagle. But I would always know that I'd run away and wonder how things could have been. I would also grow to become my mother's nemesis: she'd complain I was getting under her feet and disrupting her stringent timetable of choir, Pilates and unspecified busy-ness. I'd miss my friends, the silence would become intolerable and no shop in the countryside stays open past 5.30 p.m. This will always be home, but London is my life and it's time to get back, whatever is waiting.

21.

GET OUT OF MY HOUSE

When I wake up, my clock reads 8.18 a.m. It is my first day as an Unemployed Person. The flat is quiet so Harriet and Oona must have already left for work. I roll onto my front and go back to sleep.

The next time I wake, it is 9.42 and because I am neither hungover nor seventeen, I force myself to get out of bed. I pee, then study my reflection in the mirror as I wash my hands. Remnants of yesterday's mascara have dissolved into gluey strands and migrated to my lower eyelids so I take a cotton bud from the cupboard and fish them out, careful not to jab my eyeball and blind myself – I have enough going on right now. It is an immensely satisfying process. There is a blackhead on my cheek that is so large it could develop its own grav-itational pull; Harriet will be looking for the remote one day and it will turn out my blackhead has sucked it in.

I squeeze it gently until gunk starts to ooze out like a larva being born. There are more on my nose and a small constellation on my chin; this shit must have been clogging up my face for months. No more. This is a new day – the first of my shit-free life.

I go into the kitchen. I fix myself a bowl of Rice Krispies and run into the lounge so I can eat them in front of the TV before the milk turns them soggy. I should have turned on the TV first, damn – must remember that for tomorrow. Flicking between channels is a depressing business: I have a choice of people selling houses, people looking for antiques or people being admonished by Jeremy Kyle, so I watch people selling houses for a bit then wonder if there is any glass I could swallow as alternative entertainment.

I wash up my cereal bowl. I open the fridge and take a look: a pot of taramasalata has gone way past its use-by date so I take it out and go to throw it in the bin. Flipping the lid open, I notice that the milk carton is nestled inside when it should be in the recycling box beside my right foot. I look at the carton for a bit. I look at the box. I throw the taramasalata in the bin and close the lid. I should take a shower but I'm in my pyjamas, and they are very comfortable, and also, I can't be arsed. I open the food cupboard and inspect its contents in case there is something to eat that doesn't need cooking, but everything does. Stupid food. On my way to my bedroom, I stop off in the bathroom and stand there. I leave after a minute.

When I go into my bedroom, I see my laptop on the

floor where I left it last night; I grab it and lie down on my bed. I love the internet. The internet is brilliant: it is packed full of fun stuff that leads on to more fun stuff and sometimes *that* fun stuff is even better than the original fun stuff you've already found. My job has been eating into my fun-stuff search time so in a very real way my redundancy is a positive change as I'll have more time for internet stuff now. The internet will keep me entertained until I find a job, or until I get bored, or I die.

On the homepage of the *Guardian*, Angelina Jolie is sitting inside a white tent with a group of children – the caption below says they are in the Congo. She is wearing a baggy cream shirt-cum-nightdress and green khakis over desert boots, and her face is scrubbed clean of make-up, yet she still looks about one kerjillion times prettier than I ever shall, even if I too scraped my greasy hair into a tight chignon and highlighted the plight of children in African nations. I type 'angelina jokie' into Google – *did I mean 'angelina **jolie**'?* I did.

I convert the listings to Google Images and go through shot after shot of Angelina looking concurrently immaculate, kind and egregiously sexy. One of the pictures originates from a list entitled '50 most beautiful women in the world' so I click through and scroll down slowly, examining each woman in turn: actresses, models and musicians stare out at me with their perfectly set, symmetrical eyes. If I look back at them for too long their beauty serves to amplify the multitude of my own physical imperfections. *Your nose is too short*, say

Emma Stone's elbows. *You're fat*, says Keira Knightley's chin.

At the very bottom of the page, underneath the final picture of a beaming Scarlett Johansson, there is a list of suggested links for more '50 most . . .' sites: '50 most dangerous cities'; '50 most bizarre names'; '50 most disturbing movies'. Having been once made to sit through *LOL* (starring the inimitable duo of Miley Cyrus and Demi Moore) I am confident I have seen the most disturbing movie of all time so I plump for '50 most adorable animals' and I am not disappointed. A bunny in a tutu! A guinea pig in the bath! SOME KITTENS IN A BOWL! These creatures have serious cute capital. To my mind a piglet wearing tiny wellies is considerably more appealing than a picture of Margot Robbie looking hot. I am becoming aware of an odd popping noise in my head which is followed by a shrivelling noise, like a balloon deflating: I believe this is the sound of my brain cells dying off one by one. I close the window and shut my laptop. I get up and brush my hair. I go to the loo. I pull my pyjama top up to my ribs and examine my stomach sideways on in the hallway mirror.

Back in the kitchen, I take another pass at the food cupboard, shifting some soup tins just in case a chocolate Freddo is hiding behind – that happened once. Today there is nothing. I should text Guy but I've put my phone somewhere and looking for it seems excessively arduous.

Forty minutes later, I ring it from the landline and find it under my duvet. I pull up Guy's name.

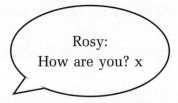

Rosy:
How are you? x

A further fifty minutes passes before my phone beeps, by which point I have moved on to painting my nails and have to jab at the screen with the pad of my finger to open the message:

Guy:
All good here, just in the middle of a client thing. Call you tonight? x

When my nails are dry I text back to say that I'm looking forward to his call and add some emojis (smiley face, telephone, egg timer) but I forgot to put a kiss, so I send one after. I'm worried that looks a bit desperate.

Rosy:
Forgot to put a kiss, sorry! xx

I throw my phone on my bed. This is turning into a long day.

* * *

It is 1 p.m., which means it's time to eat again. When Aunt Paula was in hospital, she used to talk about meal times being the highlight of the day – not the food itself, that was inedible – just the time at which it was served. I visited a lot during the last couple of months. I remember sitting with her on a Tuesday afternoon as she explained to me that hospital 'time' is unique, that it doesn't follow a linear structure like regular time; meal times were the only way to orientate oneself because 'days' were essentially a series of blank spaces that began upon admission and would only end 'when you die', Paula said, darkly. When you can smell toast and hear the rumble of the tea trolley, she told me, it means the day has started. The arrival of lunch means the day is half way through. When dinner comes, it won't be too much longer until the day is over. ('It's bedtime when you hear the last bit of the *EastEnders* theme tune,' she concluded.) On my next visit, I took oatcakes and gin, which were the only two things Paula could keep down by that point. I didn't know it then but the theme tune had already started playing for her and the end of her blank space was not far off.

I'm thinking of Paula as I set about creating my lunch, which is *very* much the highlight of my day. I am not constrained by a hospital menu or limited to something desk-friendly that must be purchased and eaten within a forty-minute window; I can cook anything I want, the only restriction is the limits of my imagination. My food cupboard appeared barren when I looked this morning, a mish-mash of useless, mundane foodstuffs, none of which looked edible, but on closer inspection it is an Aladdin's cave of delicacies. I am an alchemist who can turn these basic ingredients into gold. I am a food magician.

My props include:

- 5 x cans of lamb and potato soup
- 1 packet of spaghetti (open, half empty . . . or half full, depending on how you look at it)
- 1 bag of sugar
- 1 jar of mincement
- 3 x boxes of rice (in various states of depletion)
- 1 onion
- 1 box of Yorkshire tea
- 1 bottle of sushi seasoning
- 2 x disposable foil baking trays
- 1 large bag of sweet 'n' salty popcorn

I could sweat the onion, boil the spaghetti and add . . .

No – I could cook the rice and make a sauce from the . . . soup?

Tea, popcorn and mincemeat . . . pie? I'm being ridiculous – you can't make a pie without pastry. For my first trick, ladies and gentlemen, boys and girls, I shall need a volunteer from the fridge: there is milk, a courgette (origin: unknown, use-by date: unknown), a jar of mayonnaise and four bottles of nail varnish in assorted shades.

I fear the limits of my imagination are closing in on me.

*   *   *

Lunch was disappointing: in the end, I made spaghetti tossed in ketchup-and-mayonnaise sauce. By the time I had cooked, eaten and washed everything up, only forty-five minutes had passed. I am lying on my bed, staring at the ceiling, having planned to take a nap. When I came up with this plan, I felt good about it; at university, napping was as fundamental to my schedule as attending lectures until I stopped bothering with those and my daily nap took on an even more central role. This afternoon's nap was meant as an homage to the great naps of my halcyon university days (if I had a copy of *Heat*, a Kinder Bueno and a Chinese Nationalism lecture to go to, I could stage a total re-enactment) but I've been trying to drift off for the last twenty minutes without success. I think I've lost the ability to nap. It doesn't help that I'm not tired, having only woken up from a regular night's sleep five hours ago, and I suspect my body is simply not used to resting at this time of the day. It's used to being hunched over a computer, desperately trying to keep the pull of sleep at bay. I open my laptop and log into Facebook.

Scrolling down the newsfeed, the first pictures I come to are of Sophie and Ollie, posing at his parents' house during their visit last weekend, doing the things she's already described to me over text: Ollie holding his brand-new niece, Lily; here's Sophie, wearing the sweater I gave her for Christmas. I scroll further down. Amy Rathmell, an old friend from school, got married and here's the evidence – all 274 photos of it. I click through to look for photos of her dress but I get bored after photo fourteen. Back in the news feed, a guy named Alex Hodges has recently updated his status; his name is familiar and Bob is a mutual friend but beyond that, I can't place him. There are privacy restrictions on his photos but those I can see have a similar theme: kickboxing. Here's Alex in a ring, kicking an opponent and here he is standing next to a fellow kickboxer. There are various other shots of him receiving a belt at what appears to be a kickboxing tournament. I deduce that Alex Hodges is into kickboxing. Sadly, I am not, and as I cannot recall having ever met him, I un-friend him. It is an unfriendly thing to do, but I doubt he'll notice I'm gone.

All I can glean from various other status updates and photo uploads is that everyone else is living a life of unqualified joy and they are all prettier/happier/richer/more successful than me. A set of recently posted photos show Maisy Baker, a girl I used to work with, drinking champagne and wearing sunglasses. Inside. I allow myself a moment of pleasure at the sight of another uni friend, Richie – tanned and beaming – stood aboard a boat, dressed in a white polo shirt bearing the insignia of a scuba-diving school. He lost both his parents in the space of the three years we studied (yet still managed to get a First) and when we graduated he decided he had seen too much sadness to not prioritise happiness, so he spent part of his inheritance on a one-way ticket to Bali to train as a scuba-diving instructor. He was incredibly warm and funny when I knew him. He was also responsible for a portmanteau word that to my mind remains unsurpassed:

procrasturbation, noun:
a word Richie invented to describe the act of mastur-
bation when used as a procrastination activity

I used to procrasturbate a lot at university – eventually I had to force myself to work in the library rather than my bedroom. I found my Politics degree so profoundly dull that doing *anything* else was more appealing, whether it was cleaning the bathroom, doing washing or watching porn, and watching porn easily trumped bathroom/washing duties. I am lucky to have studied at a time when porn had become free and readily available – I remember the days when it wasn't. If you didn't catch *Eurotrash* or turn to Channel 5 at exactly the right moment you could only see porn by watching an encoded Sky channel (and hoping your parents didn't scrutinise the bill) or buying a magazine. At fifteen I would have rather had my fingernails pulled out than request an item from the top shelf in my local village shop. My parents wouldn't let Bru and me have Sky (and now I see why) so the only time I saw porn was when I went to Clare Frenton's house. Clare would ensure her mum was asleep, then type in the four-digit code and we'd look on as Mr Businessman returned from a long day working at his business, only to find Mrs Businessman nuzzling the vagina of Yewtree, their blonde, cheerleading next-door neighbour, even though Yewtree had only popped round to borrow sugar or a monkey wrench or something. Mr Businessman's outrage would lead to total acceptance of the situation and he'd swiftly become an eager participant. Clare and I would provide a sarcastic running commentary and laugh about how 'funny' it was even though I spent the whole time feeling awkward and massively aroused.

I close Facebook, type in the address of a trusted porn site and skim through the videos on the home page. There's a lot of men cumming in women's faces, far more than I remember there having been in the past. Is this something women like now? I missed it when all women started liking Jennifer Lawrence, I don't want to miss this too. Is my womanhood at risk if I don't get on board? Should I suggest to Guy that instead of ejaculating into my convenient, containing vagina, he indiscriminately spray his sperm in and around my nose? We'll discuss it when I see him. I select a video I've seen before: male masseur steps far beyond his professional remit to a surprisingly welcoming reception by blonde lady with huge tits. I know how it ends (I know how they all end, to be fair) but it's still good.

*　　*　　*

At around ten to five, I wander into the kitchen and open my food cupboard.

'Your life is pathetic,' says the onion.

'I know,' I say.

'And you could have brushed your teeth,' adds the sugar. I tell them to fuck off and close the door.

*   *   *

Having been in the flat all day by myself, it's almost a shock to see Harriet cooking in the kitchen; she looks exotic amidst the monotonous landscape of the flat and I have to keep glancing at her to make sure she is real. She is keen to know the details of my day but I adamantly do not want to admit that all I've done is eat, wank and take a panic shower when she texted to say she was on her way home from work. I distract her by asking about her day instead; it is such a relief to hear noise emanating from another human being instead of the TV, which refuses to respond no matter how much I shout at it. It reassures me that I'm not the sole survivor of a nuclear holocaust after all, a genuine fear circa quarter past six.

She asks how my job hunt is going. I pull a face. 'That well, hey?'

I sigh. 'I have to figure something out, I'll go crazy if I'm cooped up here every day.'

Harriet turns and takes a bowl from the drying rack. From the saucepan she's been stirring, she tips out a green sludge that makes me grateful for the out-of-date microwave meal I found in the freezer. 'It's probably not what you had in mind but we're looking for some LSAs at the moment . . . Learning Support Assistants,' she adds, in response to my helpless expression. 'They help the teacher with the class; supporting activities, preparing resources, running small reading groups, stuff like that.'

'I've never worked with children before.'

'I know,' says Harriet, spooning some sludge into her mouth and, unbelievably, not retching, 'but you're smart and switched on, and you're so good at English – you wouldn't believe some of our statistics on literacy levels. It's a big problem.'

I hop off the kitchen counter where I've been perching and follow Harriet into the lounge. 'You think I'd be good at it?'

She nods and I wait for her to finish her (gross) mouthful. 'If you're interested, I could talk to our head-master? He's so nice, I'm sure he'll give you a job.' I suppose a pity job is better than no job at all. Although those times I've pity Liked anyone on Tinder, it's always come back to haunt me: the guy unfailingly gets in touch and then you have to phase, which is mean, or take the hit of guilt that comes with being weirdly busy on every day he moots to meet up. I've never even considered working with children. I used to babysit for some of our neighbours when I lived with my parents, and to my knowledge none of those children swallowed bleach whilst in my care but it's a world away from PR. Although . . . that's sort of the point.

22.

NEVER BE MINE

I am sitting on my bed, watching a pigeon that has landed in the small patch of grass outside the flat that I sometimes refer to as our 'garden' when I want to have a laugh. The pigeon pecks at one of the many sprouting weeds and pulls it up, shaking it in his beak before dropping it down, only to repeat the process for a second time. My phone is clasped in my hand. I open the text that came through from Guy a couple of minutes ago and read it again:

> Guy:
> Hey you, did you get my text
> yesterday? I sent it quite late,
> thought you might be asleep.
> How are you? Let me know if
> you're free tonight, I could come
> round xx

I meant to reply last night but I must have fallen asleep just as Guy surmised. I should definitely reply to this message. I have no plans tonight, so he could come over; it might be . . . nice. Outside, the pigeon ruffles his feathers and hops about a bit before taking flight up to the wall where he perches with a flutter of his wings. I didn't actually know pigeons ate plants.

What is wrong with you? . . . that's what BF asked me after my first date with Guy. I couldn't tell her then and I still can't – I'm wondering myself. It's not about his hair, not really; it's more than that. Something inside me has gone, or wasn't there to start with, not fully. None of it seems to matter any more.

*   *   *

True to her word, Harriet has arranged for me to have a trial day at Joan Scott Primary. Before this could happen, however, she informed me that I first needed to complete a 'DBS check' which sounded scary and official and immediately made me panic: I have three points on my driving licence; I attended a party that the police shut down; I once took a fried egg sweet from the pick 'n' mix at the cinema . . . was any of this going to make a difference? Harriet assured me it wouldn't, but I didn't relax until I received the official confirmation that I am definitely not a criminal.

This news apparently hadn't reached Betty, the school's receptionist: on arrival it took me ten minutes to convince her that, no, I wasn't lost, from the LEA or 'trying to thieve' (her words) but that I was here for a trial as an LSA. Eventually, she leads me down the corridor to the headmaster's office where my first appointment of the day is with the head, Mr Hand, before I go to class. My stomach is in knots as I sit here; suddenly I am nine again, waiting outside Mrs Coaley's office because Fiona Evans and Siobhan Chapman, a.k.a. the 'cool girls' (Fiona had a pony and Siobhan had kissed a boy) convinced me to skive music. Inside her office I was so contrite (i.e. I couldn't stop crying) that Mrs Coaley let me off with a one lunch-break ban as it had been my first offence. Meanwhile, Fiona and Siobhan were charged with masterminding the whole thing and sentenced to a week of solitary (*both* breaks in the class-room and they had to eat with a teacher at lunch). The only reason I'd agreed to skive in the first place was so that they would like me; they fucking hated me after that. The door opens and Mr Hand comes out. 'Is it Rosy?' he asks, extending his hand, inviting me inside.

Mr Hand reminds me of uncles from TV. He insists I call him Thomas, but fairies die if you call teachers by their first names so I stick to Mr Hand. Firstly, he wants to know why I'm interested in becoming an LSA. I tell him that I love children and that I'm looking for a new challenge – I've recently left my job and would like to do something other than eat, wank and watch shit TV whilst I figure out what to do next . . . words to that effect, anyway, and better ones than, 'Harriet thought I'd manage.' Next, he asks about my experience with chil-dren and because watching repeats of *Outnumbered* probably doesn't count I have to admit that I have very little, at which point I suspect I've blown it because a pre-requisite when interviewing for anything is, surely, some knowledge and experience in the job. Yet he appears undeterred. He wants to know about my back-ground: he asks about my degree, where I studied and my work in PR. As I remember it, the essential rule of job interviews – and, as it happens, of dating – is: don't tell the truth. I mean, you can, some of it, but never all of it. And always embellish what remains. I loved my degree! Kids are the best! There were elements of PR I enjoyed but overall I found it unfulfilling and concluded it was the wrong field for me! It's all kind of a truth/lie hybrid but it seems to work; after half an hour, Mr Hand says, 'Rosy, you seem great, you're overqualified if anything. I just had to check you weren't planning on stealing a child. We frown upon that here.'

The sense of movement and vibrancy is tangible as I walk along corridors *en route* to 2K: the walls seem almost alive, covered in displays of colourful artwork, and each classroom I look into buzzes with chatter and activity as afternoon lessons begin. The scene that confronts me when I look through the door of 2K's class-room is similar, but multiplied by ten, as though the kids have been doused with E numbers: children, lots of them, are doing lots and lots of things. I count four in the home area, hosting a meal for an assortment of dolls and plush animals. Others are seated around a square table, using Lego to build . . . something; two are working together to construct – what? A spaceship? A garage? A flying, space-bound garage? Elsewhere there are children drawing, children reading, children arguing over Connect 4 and one child who appears to be spinning in concentric circles around a fixed point on the floor. Betty told me that Miss Khanom, the class teacher, is expecting me so I open the door and slip inside. The noise takes me back to the experience of walking into Letters Bar with Jonathan except these sounds are happier ones. I spot Miss Khanom seated on a low, comfy, teacher chair unknotting a length of ribbon for the small girl at her side. She looks up as I approach. I feel like Gulliver amongst the Lilliputians.

'You must be Rosy,' she says, standing and wiping unexplained glitter from her skirt, offering me her hand. 'I'm Seema, lovely to meet you.' Had I been wondering, the strength of Seema's handshake tells me all I need to know about her ability to control a large group of excitable children. 'It's a bit crazy, we're having free play – Henry, put that down.' I follow her gaze to where Henry has frozen, wide-eyed, with what I take to be an illicit broom in hand. 'Sorry, I was saying . . . the kids start with free play on Wednesdays so I thought you might take some of them out to read. Have you done much work with children before?'

'This is my first time.'

Seema laughs loudly and says, 'You'll be fine!' which is alarming – it hadn't occurred to me I wouldn't. 'Right, now, let's see . . .' She picks up a file from her table and flicks through it, giving me a chance to take in the room. The children's work is displayed on every surface; their depictions of The Owl and/or The Pussycat take up an entire section of wall on their own and a project on healthy eating features paper plates decorated with 2K's Favourite Healthy Meals and teacher-typed, child-friendly posters of nutritional information:

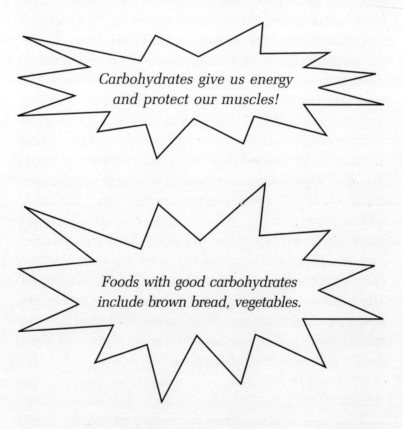

Seeing this makes me feel a lot better about the large Veggie Feast I demolished last week. At the far end of the room, the alphabet is displayed in huge, glittery letters, along with numbers and basic rules for grammar. This classroom would feel busy even if the children weren't in it. I love it: there is such a sense of creativity in the air, I feel inspired just standing here.

'Here we are,' says Seema, 'why don't you start with Dax and Billy. Let's see . . . Dax is over there at the water station and Billy, where is he . . .' I watch her eyes dart around the classroom; these children are seriously small, Billy could be anywhere – I'm impressed when Seema locates him within seconds and calls him over. He wanders up; I recognise him as one of the Lego-builders. 'Billy this is Rosy – she's going to be reading with you today.' Billy's expression is unflinching as he turns to me and studies my face with blank intensity. For such a small human, he is weirdly unnerving. I say: 'Hello, Billy.' I can't remember the last time I addressed a young child, other than to tut when they get in my way on the Tube. I'm worried my voice sounds creepy. Billy holds me in his gaze a moment longer then turns back to Seema. 'Can we get the Play-Doh?' Her tone is warm but unequivocal as she explains that he can but he must put down newspaper first and that when she says it's time to stop he must *stop* – I sense this is a conversation they have had before. For Billy's sake, I really hope he remembers the newspaper. I would.

'Well, that was short and probably a bit weird,' Seema laughs. 'He's a great boy, give him a bit of time to get to know you. Dax, however, is a total sweetheart, you should start with him.' Help the children, but don't tell them, Seema says; be patient but firm, let them work it out but pull them up on their mistakes. She hands me a pile of feedback forms on which I am to note their progress and shows me to the reading table just outside the classroom, all the time saying something about one of them; I hope it's not important, life-saving, this-is-how-you-inject-the-epi-pen kind of information because I've stopped listening – suddenly, this all seems like quite a big deal. These children are learning to *read*, a skill that's up there in the hierarchy of life lessons; I learnt to read at about their age and I've been doing it pretty much ever since. What if a child asks me what a word means and I tell them the wrong thing? Like if I tell them that 'banana' means 'submarine'? Will they even know what a submarine is? And what if I accidentally elbow them in the face?

'Does that all sound OK?' Seema asks, looking at me.

'Yes. Absolutely.'

'Great. I'll send Dax through – there are pens in the drawer for your notes.'

The moment Dax comes through the door, I know why Seema wanted me to start with him: Dax is the anti-Billy. He is small with blond hair and lashes to match and he barely looks at me as he comes to sit down. Neither does he speak, so I launch into a soliloquy.

'Hi, Dax! We're going to read together today! My name is Rosy, but don't worry if you forget that. Do you like reading? I like reading . . . this looks like a good book you've got, what's it called?'

Dax looks at his book, saying nothing.

'*Mum's New Shoes*!' I prompt, 'Wow, that sounds brilliant! Hm, I wonder what it's about . . .?' Dax does look at me then, with what I sense might be derision.

I suggest 'we' open the book and find out, though through my superior skills of deduction I've concluded it will be about a mother who has obtained new footwear. In a soft voice, Dax begins to read, following the words with his finger. '*Mum's – shoes – did . . .*'

'Didn't,' I correct gently.

'*Didn't – fit. They – hut . . .*'

'Hurt.'

'*Hurt – her – feet.*'

'Oh no!' I cry, 'Poor Mum! What do you think she's going to do?'

'Get new shoes,' replies Dax.

'You might be right there – let's see, shall we?'

Dax reads slowly and haltingly, making so many mistakes it feels too mean to keep correcting him. Personally, I go on an emotional rollercoaster with Mum, her three children and their dog (who is allowed in the shoe shop for some reason) as she tries on shoes, discards one pair for another and eventually chooses sensible lace-ups but leaves them on the bus . . . I get so into it that I've forgotten to make any notes as we come to the end of our fifteen minutes. I am effusive in my oral praise, however: 'You read so well, Dax! You knew almost all of the words! Did you enjoy the story?' He nods. 'Wasn't it funny when Mum left her shoes on the bus! Although . . . it was quite scary too . . . did you think it was funny or scary?' Dax nods. 'Funny?' Dax nods. 'It *was* funny, wasn't it?' Dax may not be exactly chatty, but I've had worse Tinder dates.

I take Dax back to the classroom and wait in the doorway until I catch Seema's eye and she asks Billy to come and read with me. I watch as he collects his book from his tray, walks past me as I hold the door then sits down in my chair.

'Hello, Billy, do you remember my name?'

'Yes, it's Rosy,' he replies, holding my gaze.

'Well, that's great then! And we're going to be reading together on Wednesday afternoons!'

'Yes,' says Billy. 'Why do you have a spot on your face?'

*　　*　　*

We are five minutes into our session. I have spent much of this recalling Seema's advice about how Billy needs to get to know me and I really hope it works because right now he seems to regard me with nothing but contempt. Billy's book, called *Race!*, concerns two polar bears that do indeed decide to have a race (polar bears being renowned for their prowess in sporting events) and it is quickly clear to me that his book is more complex than Dax's – there are polysyllabic words going on here – and that Billy is a far more competent reader. He reads quickly and fluently, allowing no time for my questions ('Which bear do you think will win? Why do you think they want to race? Isn't that a natty scarf the first bear is wearing?') before he is onto the next page. When he misreads 'every' as 'very', I have to force him to stop.

'What's this word here?' I ask, pointing at it.

He hesitates. 'Very.'

'Shall we look at it again? It actually begins with an "eh" sound. Can you say that sound?'

Billy keeps his eyes on the page and I see his jaw tense. 'Every,' he says stiffly, 'I knew that.'

He carries on from where he left off but he keeps doing it: 'every' is 'very' and soon 'then' becomes 'when' so I stop Billy each time and let him correct himself as Seema instructed; each time, though, Billy gets a little bit more pissed off until finally, he sighs heavily and growls, 'I *know*!', rendering me silent. We get to the end of the book (the race, adjudicated by a penguin, is a draw) and I make myself tell Billy his reading was very good which, for the most part, is true.

'I don't like that book,' he snarls.

'Why? It had polar bears in it . . .' Even in my head this sounds lame.

'It's for babies.' I assure Billy it's not although I have nothing to back this up – I have little experience with babies, they might be reading a lot earlier these days. He crosses his arms and goes 'hmph', which makes me laugh because I've only ever seen children do that in cartoons. Unfortunately, this only exacerbates the situation and Billy stomps back into the classroom, forcing me to jump up and hurry after him in case Seema thinks I have no control over my ward, which I clearly don't. To my amazement, he skips over to the carpet where he settles into his space and turns his attention to Seema. It is like he is mocking me.

I sit back at the table. I am clearly not cut out for this; I don't have the skill to help Dax become a better reader, nor do I have the time, patience or basic humanity to make Billy like me. This whole thing was a bad idea. Admittedly, Billy had a point about his book, which he has left, pointedly, on the table: it's not quite *Animal Farm* – no wonder he's apathetic about reading. He needs a story that is engaging, that appeals to him . . . what do young boys like? Spies? Football? Political intrigue? Billy is spirited (amongst other things): spies could work, or detectives, young boys like him who are tasked with solving mysteries . . .

Seema appears at the door. 'Everything OK?'

'Yeah, great thanks.' I go to get up, tripping on the chair leg as I stand.

'How did it go?'

'All right, I think.' I am trying to look at anything that isn't Seema's face; there is no way I'm going to be offered a job here if she finds out what happened. 'Billy is . . . a character.' I think people say this because it's not kind to refer to a child as 'a bit of a dick'.

Seema gives me a knowing smile. 'He is, definitely. You'll grow to love them though, I promise. Now come and have a cup of tea.'

*   *   *

'Is everything OK?' This marks the fourth occasion of Guy's asking. Technically, on the third time he said: 'Are you OK?' but it's semantic.

'I'm fine.' I don't know if I'll get away with saying that a fifth time.

'Something's up,' Guy says. He is not stupid yet I am treating him as if he were; I've been in role as Girl Who Wants to Be With You since I opened the door, except I'm not very good at it. When he arrived, the novelty of seeing Guy made it easier to keep it up and as we got chatting, I started to wonder if my doubts weren't in fact baseless after all – we've seen so little of each other in the last couple of weeks, perhaps I'd grown used to being without him. But they're not.

I say: 'Nothing's up,' but immediately Guy says: 'Rosy,' and it is a command: *tell me.*

I turn to him face on and force myself not cry as to do so would be egregiously unfair. 'I don't think we should keep seeing each other.' I dart my eyes away but I can feel his gaze still on me. When I look up, his expression is vacant, though no emotion suggests so much emotion that he doesn't know where to start. He says, 'Right,' then stands up and walks around in a small circle.

Leaning on the kitchen doorway, he asks: 'Has something happened?'

'No.' Nothing has happened. Maybe that's the problem.

'Right.' He goes to sit in the green chair, thinks better of it then sits down after all and starts asking questions: how long have I been feeling like this? Has he done something wrong? Was there something he should have done differently – is there anything he could do now? I answer each question as fully and honestly as I can but I don't know if I'm just making things worse. I've never broken up with someone before, I don't know what I'm doing – I am one of life's dumpees. The sole fact of which I am sure, the one thing I've known for certain since I came back from my parents', is that if I split up with Guy, that will be it: if I am lonely, rueful or drunk at 3 a.m., that's hard luck on me. Charlie strung our break-up out for weeks and by the end of it I honestly thought I was losing my mind. He stopped talking to me, other than to yell that I was bringing him down, or to lie about where he'd been; this he alternated with bouts of grand contrition about what a bad person he was and he wouldn't relax until I assured him he was not. I swore that should I ever come to break up with someone, I would never do the same.

Guy's anger comes next, mild at first but slowly building. 'If you had doubts you should have said. You've been wasting my time and you've made me look like an idiot,' he fumes.

'No, Guy, I was never . . .'

'Have you met someone else?'

'*No.*' I say it with ardour because I need him to know it's true. The suspicion of shadowy third parties haunt every break-up and I need Guy to know that this is all me, that he hasn't been cuckolded for a bigger penis or funnier jokes. It is the one benevolent thing I have left to offer him.

'So . . . why?' asks Guy, just as he was always going to, despite my selfishly hoping he might (for some reason) not care about why. I felt confident I would know the answer when the time came; it turns out I was wrong.

'It isn't there for me any more,' I say.

'What isn't?'

'That . . . feeling. Of wanting to be with someone – in *that* way, I mean, after the initial . . . knowing for sure that you like someone, that you *really* like someone . . . I don't think that's there, any more. For me.'

Guy blinks at me and I think he might cry; then his face hardens into something closer to vivid, concentrated disgust. 'Well, that's nice and clear then, cheers.'

I feel awful, but I don't think I'm allowed to right now. All Guy wants to know is why I have suddenly reneged on the feelings I'm supposed to have for him and it's the one thing I can't quite explain. I dig my nails into my palms. 'I think I just stopped fancying you.'

Guy pushes air through his nose and gives a small, black laugh. Then he nods and looks down, leaning forward so that his forearms are resting on his legs, his hands tightly clasped. He says, 'I don't want to go,' and my heart breaks into a thousand pieces.

*   *   *

He did go, though, in the end; he had to. He went through to my room and collected his bag and then I heard the front door shut. Now I'm sitting on the sofa in my silent flat, wondering if I've made the right decision. That seems to be happening a lot these days.

23

THE SENSUAL WORLD

Mr Hand rang me to tell me I'd got the job. He exclaimed, 'Sooma told me wonderful things about you!' and I could picture his avuncular eyes creasing as he smiled. The money isn't great – the sum Mr Hand mentioned is not so much a step down from my PR salary as a cannonball off a ten-metre board into the swimming pool of paucity – but the hours are brilliant: the school day finishes at 3.15 p.m. At the very least, having a job will please my mother and I've found this is a good enough reason to do almost anything.

As I don't start until Monday, I have decided that today I shall play at being a writer. I have a laptop and a notebook and I am drinking chai latte in a coffee shop in the middle of the day, ergo I am a writer. So far, my plan is:

1. Write bestselling, enthralling, genre-busting book.
2. Sell book to an agent. (NB: must find out how to get an agent)

I have also conceived of an Auxiliary Plan if The Plan (the first one) doesn't work: I shall publish my bestselling, enthralling, genre-busting book myself because according to Google you can do that now. It will be a slow burn, word-of-mouth hit and I'll become an underground, folklore-hero-underdog, except rich. Then my book will probably get turned into a film and I'll be rich *forever* and I shall be able to tell people 'I am a writer' instead of explaining that I really *am* a writer but I'm also an LSA, relying on hand-outs from my parents to keep me afloat . . . I am still reticent to say it until something I've written gets published. I don't think NASA lets people call themselves astronauts if they haven't been into space.

*   *   *

Wow – being a writer is hard. And quite boring. Coming up with story ideas is proving tricky; the document I have optimistically entitled "Book" remains resolutely blank, a washout, a whiteout, a snowstorm in the Arctic. It also transpires that there are a lot of reasons *not* to write, including (but not limited to): social media, online news, cat videos on YouTube, listening to music and looking (at length) at what's going on around me, anything at all; if it moves or makes a noise, I'm interested.

So based on this recent discovery, I have decided to start a blog. Now, I can see how this might appear, on the face of it, extremely similar to a procrastination activity and possibly the exact opposite of, and detrimental to, writing a book, but let me explain why it's not. The blog, which I have called Ms Comic Sans, concerns the everyday trials of a twenty-something girl who has recently left a job in PR to become an LSA and nascent writer; it addresses a whole host of topics from dating and working in London to why Kate Bush is superior to every contemporary female pop star. I started it as a Twitter feed, but then that got a bit boring and hard, too, because 140 characters aren't enough to write anything useful – so I started a blog. See? And it is so *easy* to write; I don't have to come up with ideas, I just bash out whatever is in my head, no different from how I wrote my adolescent diary except with less self-loathing and yearning references about wanting to lose my virginity. By blogging, I can hone my writing craft, even though it is of a different genre, subject matter and style to the bestselling, enthralling, genre-busting book I am going to start writing any minute now. It took me half an hour to come up with the blog's name.

*   *   *

It is late on Saturday afternoon. BF and I are on her sofa, half-watching the TV whilst she gets ready for a night out with Ed. I am Tindering. I've been going back and forth on my re-entry into the Tindersphere: I felt like it would be disrespectful to Guy and that I should leave a suitable grace period, but days turned into weeks and I realised I couldn't hesitate indefinitely otherwise I'd never have sex again. In need of a male perspective, I rang my old work friend Liam. We still hadn't managed to get together since I found him on Tinder but that's the thing with Liam – he'll answer the phone and it will be as though we saw each other yesterday. His advice was unequivocal: 'Get back on it.'

'What if Guy sees me and thinks I don't care that we were together. Or that I was killing time before someone better came along?'

'If he sees you then he's on it too, you fucking idiot.'

'I don't want to hurt him.'

'Only a girl would think that. Ro, you dumped him. That ship sailed.'

'When did Tinder get rubbish?' I ask BF. She is curling her hair in front of a shaving mirror she has perched on her lap.

'I wasn't aware it had.'

'It has. Tinder is shit now.'

'Why?'

'Look.' I shuffle up beside her and proffer my phone. 'There. Is. No one. On. Here,' I say in time with each face I veto.

'You're going too fast,' she says, 'let me have a look.' BF flicks off the curler and puts it down then reaches for my phone. Within seventeen swipes, she has found three fit men and swiped them right: Sam, Ben and Matt.

'Ugh! How are you doing that?' I take the phone back. 'There used to be so many hot people on Tinder but now it's all men posing with doped tigers in Asia and pictures of cocks. Do men think that girls see a cock and think, "Yep, husband material"? Are there girls who really think that?'

BF gives a tight laugh. 'Probably.'

I study her reflection in the mirror. Her mouth is set in a flat line; she looks vacant, and bored – I can hear it in her voice.

When I ask if she's OK, she says: 'It's Ed stuff.'

'What's up?'

BF sighs and turns to face me. 'It's stupid. I feel like an idiot saying anything.'

'Say it anyway.'

'It's lots of little things together,' she begins. 'Dumb stuff, like he'll randomly stop replying to my texts and I won't hear from him for a few days, or he'll tell me he's doing one thing and then it turns out he did something else – he can change his plans, obviously, it's not that . . . it's just . . .'

'Go on.'

'You're going to think I'm paranoid.'

'I doubt that.'

'I was showing his picture to Adele at work and she went, "Oh, I've seen him on Tinder."'

'He's still on it?' I say it too abruptly, before I have time to modify the alarm in my voice.

'That's the thing; she *thought* she recognised him but she wasn't sure, then she couldn't remember when so it could have been ages ago, like right when we started seeing each other or even before we met.'

I try to listen objectively, but it's hard when my nerves spark at the very mention of Ed's name. 'You'd have to be pretty stupid to put yourself on Tinder when you've got a girlfriend,' I say; at this, BF tips forward with her face in her hands and makes a sort of angry animal noise.

'That's the other thing!' she cries. 'I'm not his girlfriend, we're not official. I brought it up and, honestly, he couldn't change the subject fast enough so now I'm too scared to ask again. Then the other night his best mate asked me what was going on with us so he obviously doesn't refer to me as his girlfriend to his friends.'

'How long have you two been seeing each other?'

'Almost seven months.' She stares at the floor. She looks utterly bereft.

I could tell BF that Ed is a massive weapon who is messing her around and that she needs to get as far away from him as fast as humanly possible, but it would be pointless; she is not ready to hear it. I suspect she already knows, deep down in her psyche. Instead, I go into the kitchen and return to the lounge with two spoons and the jar of Nutella I saw when I made tea. She gives me a smile, albeit a feeble one, as I unscrew the lid.

'I'm sitting here, about to go and meet him, making a massive effort like I do every time,' she says, her speech gummy with chocolate spread, 'and I know I'll get there and think, yep, I look nice – maybe this time he'll notice and tell me that. And he never does, so then I think I'm ugly.'

'I hate that he makes you feel that.'

'Me too,' she says, digging her spoon back in the jar.

I walk BF to the Tube and remind her she can still ring and cancel (Ed has done the same to her, several times) though I know she won't because I doubt I would either. Then I remind her she can always ring *me* and give her a hug before she disappears underground.

On the bus back home, my phone beeps with a Tinder notification to say that I've matched with Matt, one of the three Likes BF gifted me earlier. Straight away, he sends a message:

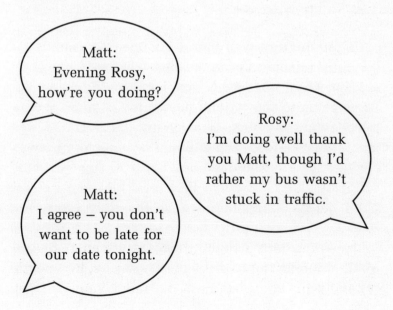

Matt:
Evening Rosy, how're you doing?

Rosy:
I'm doing well thank you Matt, though I'd rather my bus wasn't stuck in traffic.

Matt:
I agree – you don't want to be late for our date tonight.

I reread it. Have we chatted before? It's possible, though his name doesn't mean anything. It's possible we've arranged a date for tonight and that I've forgotten about it. It's possible 'Matt' is clinically insane.

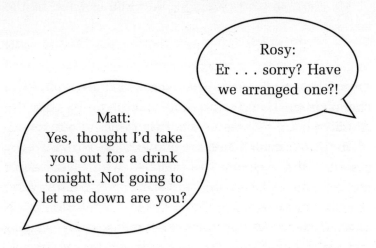

Rosy:
Er . . . sorry? Have we arranged one?!

Matt:
Yes, thought I'd take you out for a drink tonight. Not going to let me down are you?

I close the thread. If this is his opening gambit, it's certainly punchy; I'm undecided whether I like it or not. I'm seven stops away from home and I had a plan: I was going to shower and put on my pyjamas with a towel round my shoulders for my damp hair. I was going to make food, something nice using the prawns I bought as a Friday treat and eat it in front of some seriously shit TV. I might blog for a bit, then I could paint my nails and hop over to the shop across the road for a Crunchie if I fancied one . . . my un-rock 'n' roll but utterly delightful Saturday night. I reopen Matt's message and read it one last time before sending my reply:

Rosy:
I can't believe I'd forgotten. When and where?

*   *   *

I'm pissed, partly because I've eaten nothing more than chocolate spread since breakfast and partly because I've drunk two happy-hour cocktails in the last hour, on top of the three drinks Matt bought me in the pub. I am pissed – did I already say that? – so I'm hazy about certain things, like my ability to walk, and am desperately clinging on to objective truths to keep me afloat: Matt is a web designer. Matt is funny. Matt is smart and engaging and we've talked non-stop since we met four hours ago, except I feel like I've known Matt for four years. There are moments when I already feel like his girlfriend. I think I am going to be. Matt is fair, thin-lipped, tall and sturdy – not my usual type, but I am drawn to him for reasons that go beyond his looks; plus, my usual types haven't worked out so far. Love transcends the physical, anyway.

I think Matt is pissed too: from a polemic on cyclists, he swings wildly on to his thoughts on Shakespeare, slurring as he says, 'You should read *Othello*.'

'I did, at school.'

'It's brilliant; I loved it. There is this theme of opposites running through it, loads of references to light and dark, just like Othello and Iago. Shakespeare was way ahead of his time in the way he commented on racism.'

I nod. I can picture my A-level text, marked up with annotations on this very idea and I can still hear Mr Austen's voice as he delineated how Othello's essential goodness was ruined by Iago's dark, twisted mind. The play concerns race, of course, but I'd had this sense of it being not so much about opposites, but the way Othello and Iago represent the light and darkness that exists within all of us – together, they almost stand for one person. Talking about this now reminds me of Mum describing her feelings for Dad as we plodded back home after Hector's walk; she had talked about Dad in terms of good and bad, and how her love for him was only cemented when she could accept his bad parts. I think that's what she was saying. It's hard to remember, I'm pretty drunk.

'And then I've been reading this stuff about neuro-linguistic programming recently,' Matt says. 'It's really interesting. It makes you really think about what's going on in your head. You should check it out.'

'I will,' I say. I probably won't. Although they do say you should show an interest in your boyfriend's interests . . . they definitely say that. 'So, what is going on in your head?'

'Oh, I'm basically nuts. Everyone is.'

'Yes, *but* . . .' I counter, pointing at Matt, 'nuts are awesome.'

'Nuts ARE awesome!' he cries. 'OK: favourite nut.'

'Ooh, tough, I like so many . . .'

'I'll have to rush you . . .'

'OK, er – cashew.'

'That's a good choice,' Matt nods approvingly.

'Pistachios would have made it but they have fiddly shells. That lost them marks.'

'Harsh but fair; nuts need to be accessible. Good thinking, Rosy. I like that.' I choose to hear this as: I like *you*. I would like to kiss Matt, I think it would be good. I had no expectations when I walked into the pub this afternoon and very little make-up on, but this is turning out to be one of the best first dates I've ever had.

He says, 'What are you thinking about?' I usually loathe this question, but on this occasion my answer is simple: kissing aside, I'm thinking how much I need to pee. Matt thanks me for my honesty and says he will order more drinks whilst I go to the loo. Then, as I get up, he pulls me in towards him until his lips meet mine. He cups his hand under my chin and bites my lip; he slides his hand to the back of my head and gently licks my tongue until I think my clitoris is going to explode.

* * *

We are on the dance floor in a club and I am pulling out my A-game moves, which involve a lot of arse wiggling and body rubbing (my own). They are having the desired effect: I appear indistinguishable from Beyoncé, just a bit unsteady; occasionally I stumble and have to style it out as a kick-ball-change. Matt moves well for a guy, although we are intermittently foregoing the dancing for some serious tongue-kissing in the middle of the crowd.

He pulls back and leans in to my ear. 'Do you want some charlie?'

Amidst the mix of alcohol, music and hot sensations in my underwear, I think Matt means my ex-boyfriend Charlie, that he must be here, and in a muddle I look around to try and spot him. Matt is not talking about my ex, though the substance he's alluding to is equally toxic. I feel his hand reach for mine and press something small and smooth into my palm and I stand still, clutching it. I've done coke before but never like this, in a club, with a man I've known for six hours; despite this, all I can think is: don't let him think you're boring. The crowd pulsates around me as I push my way through to the toilets; I go into a cubicle and pull down the toilet lid, locking the door behind me.

Drugs! Illegal drugs! I'm living outside the law! I love that Matt is so exciting, if not exactly original; I don't think coke use can be classed as edgy any more, not since it got cheap and rubbish and boy bands started doing it, but it was a thrill to have Matt slip the baggie into my hand in the middle of the swell of people – perhaps more so after Guy, whose drug-taking, as he once told me, began and ended with the passing of a spliff one time. The bag is tiny, like a hamster's handbag; I hold it up and give it a gentle shake, expecting the granules will fly about but compressed in the baggie, the powder looks almost solid. I need something to snort it with but there's no cash in my wallet – I don't know why I'm surprised by this – so I resort to fishing out a receipt and spend several minutes rolling and re-rolling it into a tight tube before crouching over the toilet seat. How much to do? I've had more fun with Matt in the last six hours than I've had in the last six months and I don't want to ruin it with a vicious charge, or else a half-hearted high.

Although . . . do I really want to do it at all?

Matt is a blast: interesting, witty, cultured . . . but to reaffirm: I have known him for *six hours.* I am suddenly very conscious I am in a toilet, alone, with a bag of cocaine that could be cut with glass and rat poo for all I know, and that's assuming it definitely is cocaine and not crack, or flour, or flour laced with Rohypnol. I twiddle the receipt between my fingers. I want Matt to think I'm fun and adventurous, cool and exciting – Matt will like me if I'm like him. But I also want to not die, and inhaling a chemical substance of unknown origin seems like it might increase the risk of that happening, and I have a hair appointment tomorrow. If I grind my teeth, widen my eyes a bit and chat excessive amounts of shit to Matt in rapid, quick-fire succession, he might think I've done it anyway. I chuck my rolled receipt into the sanitary bin and stow the un-opened baggie inside my knickers – my hands are sweating and in my palm I fear the coke might . . . melt? Does it do that? Matt can retrieve the baggie and fondle me at the same time, it's a win-win situation. At the sink, I look at myself in the mirror and assume what I imagine is a suitably drugged-up expression before heading back out into the noise and heat, back out to Matt.

*   *   *

I am lying on Matt's bed, in my underwear, whilst Matt gets us both a glass of water. His bedroom is sparse in the way men's bedrooms are: flat-screen TV; cupboard housing approximately thirty-two items of clothing (including shoes); Xbox; pot of hair gel set beside an alarm clock and a lot of grey and blue. There's a framed picture from an obscure French film hanging on the wall but that's it for decoration. He comes carrying water and places the glasses on his bedside table and climbs onto the bed, sliding himself on top of me. He's heavy but I like the sensation of his weight. We kiss, softly at first but it becomes something more urgent; there's lots of writhing going on and hands, his and mine, are over and under his clothes until they become too inconvenient. Matt sits up on his knees and tries to pull his T-shirt over his head but it gets stuck and all I can see is the imprint of his face outlined in the fabric like Han Solo, frozen in carbonite. With one final tug, he is free (Matt, not Han) and he throws it to the floor. Matt kisses my mouth, my cheeks, my earlobes; he turns his attention to my neck, licking and biting which feels a bit gross but also madly erotic. He reaches behind me and unhooks my bra one-handed and now my breasts are free they are very much in play. He cups and fondles them, making me gasp with pleasure, and follows up with a period of less successful nipple twisting that he presumably thinks all women enjoy, probably because his ex did. With this happening up top, I do my super-erotic hand-slide down his torso until I feel the top of his jeans . . . shit, belt buckle: the horny girl's nemesis. My stronger right hand is in a sex-trap above my head and I need to keep my head still for all the kissing and sex-moans so my leftie must fend for itself and work by touch alone. My fingers fumble with the buckle; I move my hand down the length of the leather to suss out what's where and chance upon the end just as Matt shifts his weight; leftie is stuck under his right hip. I would try and pull it out, but Matt's tongue has moved into some . . . new areas.

Finally, we are naked, the light is off and Matt's hand is roving round between my legs. There's some prodding, then some rubbing that builds gradually and increases in speed and vigour . . . it's a promising start but getting gradually closer to the feeling of being sanded. I tough it out but when I can take no more I put my lips to his ear and say, 'Fuck me,' in a breathy sex-whisper I learnt from porn. There is a brief condom interlude during which I wriggle a bit and do some erotic panting then Matt lowers himself on top of me. Sex commences. It starts fast and stays fast, not traditionally my preference but I try to stay with it. Matt is thorough and certainly ambitious: he grabs me and manoeuvres me all over the shop and suddenly, I have a vision of my parents in the newly decorated lounge: Dad is hauling the armchair into different locations in accordance with Mum's instructions. Oh God, why am I thinking about that? Don't think about your parents: it's one of the fundamental rules of sex. I squeeze my eyes shut tight and dig my nails into Matt's back, and his solidity brings me back to the matter at hand.

Matt flips me over like a sandbag and hoists me up by my waist so that I'm presenting myself, then starts rutting away whilst squeezing my right breast. He trails his fingers up and down my spine, then moves his hand up to stroke my neck and the side of my face before running his fingers through my hair. Then he balls his hand up into a fist and yanks it. Hard. I had been getting a bit sleepy but in an instant my eyes flick open and are watering with pain as my moans of faux-ecstasy dwindle to a saucy whimper. His fingers are still tangled in my hair so I can't relax in case he does it again, yet Matt seems nothing if not encouraged: he starts going harder and faster and just as I'm edging over the wrong side of the pleasure/pain boundary, his body tenses and his muscles tremble and he comes with a heroic yodel and some meagre last thrusts before collapsing on the bed and rolling onto his back. After a minute, he opens his eyes and reaches towards me, skimming his fingertips along my arm. 'How was that?'

'Great.' This is my stock answer. For the most part it was fine, but I had to deduct marks for the near-scalping. Matt pulls me down so I'm lying next to him and pushes against me so that our bodies tessellate. I probably shouldn't bring the hair thing up, not now, anyway;

maybe it's part and parcel of Matt's wild, impulsive side. Given the past few months, being with someone exuberant like Matt could be good for me. Besides, he evidently has a softer, affectionate side, too; he mutters, 'Goodnight, gorgeous,' into my ear as he hugs me close, holding me tight in his arms – and this is how we fall asleep.

24.

LOVE AND ANGER

I so rarely get to see Liam any more. Negotiations lasted for three weeks as we tried to find a night we were both free and our original arrangement of dinner in town was substituted at the last minute for dinner at Liam's flat. There is no proverb to warn you that amongst its various tidings, age brings scheduling conflict: it used to be that you could ring a friend on Wednesday and be out together on Saturday night; at twenty-seven it is increasingly rare that I can organise anything less than a month in advance. Your commitments suddenly double when you get into a relationship, leaving you half the time you'd like to spend with your friends. Matt and I have been socialising a lot with his friends; he'll meet mine in due course, but he always says he's more comfortable when it's just the two of us, which is sweet. We have plenty of time. He has a work thing tonight so it was lucky that Liam was free.

Liam is also a superlative cook; we are half way through what may be the best red Thai curry I've ever eaten and he made it from scratch.

'It's so good! It's really, really good.'

'For the fifth time,' says Liam, 'thank you, I'm glad you like it. I can show you how to make it, Ro, it's not hard. Even you could follow a recipe,' he adds, emphasis on *even you*. This has not been the case in the past and I'd tell Liam so if my mouth weren't full of curry.

'How's the world of PR?' Liam asks.

'I wouldn't know. I left my job.'

'Why?'

I shrug. 'It wasn't what I wanted to do.'

'Are you going to write?' Liam is one of the few people in whom I've confided my literary ambitions; along with my parents, BF and The Couples – and not to mention Guy – Liam takes the grand total of people who know up to nine. He says: 'If you want to make a go of it you have to be proactive.'

'You sound like my father.' I'm aware of the note of irritation in my voice. Liam thinks that everyone should be living out their dreams, seemingly unaware that he only gets to play at restoring cars on account of his rich daddy. It is hard to imagine two people more dissimilar than Liam and his father: Henry Vaughn Richards PhD is an ex-Marine shipping broker for whom a day off means working from home. On the few occasions I've met him, he was unfailingly polite and extremely well dressed (and not unattractive for an older gentleman, though I thought it best not to share that with Liam); it made me wonder how he felt

having a clever son who is inherently lazy and takes sartorial inspiration from Huckleberry Finn. Liam says that he's
doing some of the company's bookkeeping from time to
time. 'It means I have time for other stuff.'

'There's no money in refurbishing old cars.'

'There's some, particularly if I spend a while on something.' He glances up at me, fork mid-air. 'That's not why
I do it.' We sit in silence as he finishes his mouthful.
Liam has no sense of urgency; he speaks only when he
has something to say. He is the opposite of me. Finally,
he says, 'Doing the thing that makes you happy isn't
always the thing that makes you rich.'

I don't want to talk about writing any more. Liam will
ask questions and talk about it constructively as though
it could be a reality but this would only get my hopes
up, and I could do with keeping them realistically low
for the time being. To distract him, I tell him about my
new job at Joan Scott Primary.

'You and children,' he mutters and I wait for the joke;
instead, he says: 'I can see that, you know,' and gives
me his full-beam smile.

When we've cleared out plates (and Liam has shown
me the pan as proof that there is no curry left), he grabs
us both a beer from the fridge and suggests we go out
on to the balcony so he can smoke. He takes us out a
blanket each and we sit in the garden chairs, huddled
up against the cold night air.

'How's Tinder?' Liam asks, taking a swig of his beer.

'Very well.' Heat flushes my cheeks. 'I'm with someone.
He's called Matt.' My face relaxes into a dreamy smile – I

can't help it. Saying Matt's name conjures him in my mind and I can smell his aftershave; I can feel the weight of his arms wrapped around my shoulders, keeping me warm.

'When you say "with him",' queries Liam, 'you mean he's your boyfriend?'

'I think it's heading that way.'

'Good-looking?'

I examine Matt's face in my mind's eye. 'He's not my usual type, but he's . . . beautiful.'

'*Beautiful* – the adjective to which all men aspire,' Liam says darkly.

'Looks stop being important when . . . you know.'

'When what? When you're falling in love?' Liam tilts his head, looking at me closely. 'How long have you been together?'

'Just over two weeks.'

'After two weeks you're falling in love with him? No wonder it's been so hard to get hold of you.'

'What are you talking about?'

'I called you what, three times? And you didn't respond to my texts for ages.'

'Things have been really busy.' I can feel it again, that itch of irritation, except it is blooming into anger. I pick at the label on my beer.

'I'm not falling in love with him,' I say.

'What then?'

'I don't know. God.' I sip my beer and force myself to calm down. 'Maybe it's nice to have someone really want you for once.' Liam is oblivious to what I've suffered at the hands of the Patricks and the Archies of this world – though he knows all about Charlie so I'm amazed he's being so insensitive. He has no idea what a relief it is to be with Matt, especially after getting pushed into a corner with Guy.

'What about you, then?' I ask by way of an attack. 'Girls falling at your feet?'

'No,' Liam replies, his voice calm and measured, 'I'm not on Tinder any more.'

'Why?'

'I don't get it.' He shuffles in his seat and pulls his blanket tight around him. 'Scrolling through endless blank faces, it's all a bit . . . soulless. And after I'd signed up I looked back at my profile and thought: *I look like an idiot.* I didn't recognise myself by the end. You can't sum yourself up in five photos, yet that's how people judge you.'

I've never felt timid around Liam before, but the strength in his voice is making me cautious to speak. 'I begged my parents to get cable TV when I was about nine,' he says, by way of nothing, 'and finally, they said I could have it and for about a month I thought it was the best thing ever. *Ever.* But after another couple of weeks I'd turn on the TV and there would be, like, a thousand channels and I'd be going through them all . . .' I don't know what Liam is talking about or why, but he is mid-flow so I judge it better to sit and wait until he's done. 'Eventually, I realised: there's nothing on. I'd watch something for five minutes but then I'd get bored and switch over to see if there was something better and there never was. And that's what it's like on Tinder.'

I think I get it: Liam is saying that Tinder is at risk of

imploding under the volume of all its users, that the magnitude of choice means that no one gets a shot and that we're always thinking ahead to the next swipe instead of the face on the screen; equally, he might also be saying that he misses the mighty Saturday night triptych that was *Baywatch, Gladiators* and *Blind Date* from back when TV was great. I know I do.

'It's still a good way to meet people,' I pout.

'There's other ways to meet people than through Tinder,' he counters. 'Go to a bar, join a club . . . there are about seven billion people in the world. Want to guess how many of them are on Tinder?' He downs the last of his beer then stands up, looking at his watch. 'You've missed the last Tube. Do you want to crash here?'

I pout for a bit longer then mutter, 'Thanks,' just loud enough for him to hear.

'Good. Bring your bottle and blanket in.'

When I know Liam is inside, I take my phone out of my pocket and select Matt's name:

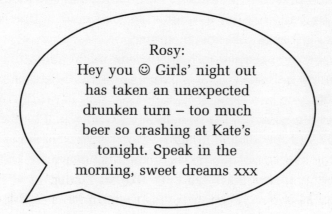

Rosy:
Hey you ☺ Girls' night out has taken an unexpected drunken turn – too much beer so crashing at Kate's tonight. Speak in the morning, sweet dreams xxx

I'm not sure why I lied; it seemed easier than telling the truth, even though nothing would ever happen between Liam and me . . . not again, anyway. We did have sex, just once, years ago: Friday drinks in the office turned into Friday drinks in the pub, then Friday drinks in a grimy karaoke bar, before we eventually stumbled back to mine. To this day, neither of us know how it happened; it wasn't that we wanted to sleep with each other so much as we were too drunk to stop ourselves. In the morning, he woke me up by farting on my leg and we laughed it off as an accident, yet if I tell Matt where I am he'll have questions: Liam who? How did we meet? And why did I stay with Liam instead of taking a cab to his? To Matt, the truth would sound like a lie. Matt and I are new, we're precious – I don't want him to think I'm being opaque. Besides, sometimes a lie is as good as the truth. Sometimes it's better.

*   *   *

Make-up; face-wipes; deodorant; toothbrush and clothes for tomorrow: I am a wandering girlfriend again. Not quite girlfriend. Almost girlfriend.

When I suggested to Matt that he might come round to mine he reminded me it was easier to be at his and on balance he's right; it's simpler for him to get to work from his, plus his flat is also better than mine: he has a cupboard specifically for the hoover so it doesn't languish in the hallway like ours has to and his housemate Lizzie is often absent, having a better-flatted boyfriend of her own. Matt has yet to visit my place, in fact – I should mention it. I'll make sure Oona is out then cook us dinner. Matt suggested making food for us this evening, then we'd check out the new cocktail bar that's opened at the end of his road. I should pack heels.

My phone starts to ring as I close the front door. I go to answer it – it might be Matt – but it must be at the bottom of my bag so I scrabble around until I see the light and grab it. BF's name is on the screen. 'Hey, how's it going?'

The noise that greets me is part human, part wounded animal and the phone only serves to amplify BF's wail, though I just make out the words: 'Not good.'

'What's happened?' BF rarely cries – I can think of three occasions in the nine years I've known her. She says what sounds like *he's eaten on me* but after a moment's reflection I realise it's: *he's cheated on me.* Fucking Ed. Fucking, fucking Ed; the swell of rage that surges through me is so all-consuming it's making me dizzy – I have to force my mind back to BF who is sobbing down the phone. We won't make progress until she calms down so I make her breathe in time with me, long, slow breaths, until she regains the use of speech. I set off towards the bus stop. 'Tell me what's happened.'

'He's been cheating on me.' She's stopped crying, and this comes out flat, detached – just a statement of fact.

'Are you sure? How do you know?'

She gives a short laugh; it would have been incongruous had it not been so dark. 'His phone. Some girl sent him a message and I saw the preview on his lock screen.'

I frown – I'm glad BF can't see. 'Just half a message,

though? That could mean anything, he might have been . . .'

'"*LOL, after last night you can fuck me any time anywhere you want.*"' She's memorised it.

'You saw all that in the preview?'

'The last two letters were cut off from "want" but I got the gist.'

'Is there any chance,' I say, trying to keep my voice neutral, uncritical, 'that it could be anything else? Could it have been a joke with a mate or something?'

'He'd saved the name as "Rebecca – Boujis".'

'Like the club?'

'He goes there with work.'

I pause; from here, there is nothing left but damage control. 'What are you going to do?'

'I don't have much choice.' BF starts to cry again; it's not the same primal anguish as before but a resigned weeping that denotes all the sadness and longing that is left once the shock wears off. 'Where are you?' she sniffs.

I feel the hairs on my neck stand on end. I know what she's going to ask and, selfishly, I wish she wouldn't. I know that's awful. 'Why?'

'Just wondering if you wanted to meet up. I could do with a drink.'

'Oh babe, any other night, but I . . . promised I'd see Kate, there's bridesmaid stuff that has to be done by tomorrow or she'll lose money, I'm not sure . . .' I hear my voice, syrupy, sugary, as I pour out the lie.

'Yeah, no, that's fine, you have to go.'

'. . . I'm so sorry. How about tomorrow? I could come round?'

'Don't worry about it.'

I reached the bus stop as we said goodbye.

According to the display the bus is due, yet it has been due for the last three minutes. My foot is tapping away, almost involuntarily – a sublimation activity for my frustration. When it eventually arrives, I go upstairs and find a seat at the back where I slump down and quietly fume. BF can't expect me to drop everything at the last second and come running; if she stays with this cheating bastard then she'll have to live with the consequences. I had to lie about seeing Matt so she won't feel shit, and now I feel guilty so I won't be able to enjoy it – and I'm going to be late too, which is fucking brilliant. I take my phone out of my bag. She hasn't even texted.

Through the bus window, I watch as late-night London rolls past, a landscape of artificial light and shadow. It's better that BF has time by herself, to sort her head out because when I see her next I'm not going to hold back about Ed. I reach for my phone; nothing. I put it back in my bag, then almost as quickly retrieve it again and bring up her name.

Rosy:
Hope you're OK.
x

*   *   *

By the time I get to Matt's BF still hasn't replied. He opens the door, wearing sweats and a hoodie. 'Hello gorgeous,' he says, pulling me in for a kiss. I follow him through to the sitting room and we collapse on the sofa as one.

'So,' I say, giving his knee a jovial slap, 'what's the plan?'

Matt stifles a yawn. 'I'm shattered, babe – shall we just hang out?' He switches on the TV and wraps his arm round my shoulder so I am pulled along with him as he leans back. Apparently my question was rhetorical. On the screen, I watch on as one girder is welded to another, before the scene cuts to a man in a hard hat who is poring over blueprints of said girders whilst the voiceover explains how they will be included in the bridge. We are watching a documentary about building a bridge. I glance over at Matt, who is gripped. 'Did you want to eat?' I ask.

'I'm not that hungry – but if you want to, go ahead.'

'Oh. OK.' Matt's arm is awkwardly placed and it's getting uncomfortable behind my back – I wriggle, and reflexively he tightens his grip. 'Easy, Matt.'

'What?' He gives my whole arm a squeeze. Then: 'What's wrong?' he asks in a faux-sulk, meant to ape me.

'Nothing.' I smile, forcing myself to relax. 'I don't know, my best friend called and it looks like her "boyfriend" is cheating on her . . . I feel a bit guilty not being with her, that's all.'

'Oh.' Matt says it like he's puzzled. He lets me go and angles himself, not so he's facing away, but he's certainly not gazing lovingly into my eyes. 'No, it's just I thought we were spending tonight together, like, I left it free for you, but if you'd rather . . .'

'No! That's not what I meant.' I scooch back towards him. 'She was just upset and I thought you mentioned something about dinner but maybe . . .'

'Oh right, so because I haven't cooked you a three-course meal you're going to fuck off?' He's smiling, but not joking. 'Look, babe,' he says, his tone flat, 'I'm knackered, I just want to relax and watch TV.'

'Yeah, sure – no, that's fine.'

He hooks his arm round my waist and jerks me towards him. 'Don't be in a mood,' he smooches into my ear.

'I'm not!' The injustice makes me screechy, making me sound like I'm in a mood, which I'm fucking not. Or I wasn't. I pull my bag towards me and take out my phone (the programme has moved on to the logistics of cantilevering – I'm not missing out) but there is still nothing from BF. I hope she's OK. I wish I knew what Ed said when she dumped him – better, I wish I had been there when BF dumped him, to witness his pathetic, foiled expression. I wish I were with BF now.

25.

HEADS WE'RE DANCING

I hadn't forgotten about Kate and Bob's engagement party: the date has been in my calendar but between school and Matt it slipped my mind that it was *tonight*. Matt is coming; Kate invited him last week and when I mentioned it to him he said it would be his pleasure, which was the perfect response. For the first time in years, for the first time since Charlie, I'm going to be with my couple friends, as part of a couple. I've given myself two hours to get ready and am half way through my make-up – or I was, until I sneezed whilst putting on mascara so I'll need extra time to wipe off the black flecks under my eyes. Harriet is looking in the mirror behind me, dithering between two dresses. Her boyfriend James is watching TV next door, having taken ten minutes to get ready.

'This one is too slutty,' Harriet says, smoothing a red dress against her frame, 'but the other one is too boring.'

'I like that grey one. I don't think it's boring.'

'Mm.' Harriet tosses the red one onto her bed. 'How smart is it going to be? What's Kate wearing?'

I describe the dress from the picture Kate sent me: white, frilly bits, beading around the shoulders. Harriet looks dubious. 'It's less *Dynasty* than I'm making it sound.'

'It sounds very formal.' She is fretting; I can hear it in her voice. She picks up the grey dress again and studies it in her reflection. 'What are you wearing?'

I smile. 'I'll put it on in a moment.'

It's another twenty minutes before I'm dressed and ready to leave, by which time Harriet and James are next door, drinking wine.

'Wow,' says Harriet.

'Blimey,' says James.

'What do you think?' I ask, posing on the spot.

'You look . . .' begins Harriet.

Wonderful.

'. . . So different.' Which is not 'wonderful'.

'I mean, God, sorry – you look great. Is that a new dress?'

'It is.' I hadn't meant to buy it; I had planned on wearing my black dress with different shoes but I stopped off to get tights after work yesterday and I saw this one in the window of a shop I'd never normally go into. The dress is navy and strapless, with sheer panels on the sides and it sucks me in all the way down to my knees. I tried it on, paid for it and was back outside within ten minutes, breathy with exhilaration

– I've never bought an in-the-window dress before. I've put my hair up and finished the look off with fuck-me heels. I can't wait for Matt to see me.

Kate and Bob have booked a private room at a swanky restaurant in a swanky part of town where we are greeted at the entrance by a *maître d'* in an immaculately cut suit who knows instantly where we should be and leads us up the staircase to what my father would refer to as a 'function room' despite there not being a sausage roll in sight. It boasts original period features, like the ornate cornicing that runs around the ceiling, and heavy drapes in pale blue hang at the tall windows; it is a lovely space by itself but Kate has improved it ten-fold with jam jars of peonies and cut-glass hearts that dangle in the windows and glisten in the light of candles that are burning in delicate glass holders. On the table, there must be at least forty bottles of Prosecco in uniform rows: they aren't decoration per se but they enhance the room all the same. We are right on time but already people are here; I don't recognise most and guess they must be Bob's high-flying colleagues when Harriet asks. Kate spots us and runs over. 'You're here!' she cries. From the timbre of her voice and intensity of her embrace, I'd imagine she's had two, maybe three, glasses of Prosecco so far. She insists we all get a drink ourselves and leads the three of us to the table, then pulls me aside. 'You look stunning. Wow.' Coming from Kate, who looks gorgeous herself and is also the focus of the night, I suddenly feel self-conscious. 'Didn't Matt come with you?' she asks.

'He had to go to a thing first so he's meeting us here.'
Matt was sketchy on the details, but he's sworn he'll be
here by 8.30.

'How's it going with you guys?'

'Really great,' I reply. 'Really, really great.'

'I'm so happy for you!' Kate cries, throwing her arms
round me.

'I'm so happy for *you*,' I say into her shoulder. I am;
I can feel my joy and Kate's radiate through me as I say
it and I hug her tighter.

When Sophie and Ollie arrive, Ollie says: 'You're
looking very nice,' which means, *your tits look good in
that dress.*

'You do,' says Soph, kissing me hello. 'You're really
dressed up.'

'I thought I'd make an effort. Also, you know, Matt's
coming, so . . .' Harriet and James wander over and we
stand as a group, drinking and chatting as the room
grows gradually warmer and noisier as more guests
arrive. Music starts to play over the speaker system – the
jazz-lite so beloved by coffee chains to make you forget
that paying £3.20 for a hot drink is indecent. I watch
Bob move slowly through the crowd, stopping every
half-metre to chat and top up glasses; nearer to us, Kate
looks like she's being tossed from one group to the next
and I notice she has to keep lending her hand for inspection of the ring. I hear the same questions on a loop:
what's the venue like? How many guests? Band or DJ?
Will Bob's grandfather be able to make it, does she think?
She catches my eye and though she's still talking, I know

that the creases round her eyes mean 'help me'; you learn these things when you've loved someone for a long time. I weave towards her and, as I get there, she is being collared by a girl I don't know.

Kate grabs my elbow and pulls me to her side. 'Rosy, this is Lisa, from work.'

'Hello Lisa from work,' I say. I notice Lisa's eyes flick to my shoes and back up before she greets me in a tone I would charitably describe as tepid.

'Is your lovely husband Terry here?' Kate asks.

'He's over there somewhere,' says Lisa, motioning vaguely towards the drinks table, 'I think he's talking to Oliver about rugby.' *Who's Oliver?* I'm just about to ask when I get it: she's not talking about Sophie's Ollie, but Bob – this is a couples' thing. Lisa and Terry, Kate and *Oliver*; I don't get invited to that stuff. I really hope Matt gets here soon. On cue, Kate asks me when he's due.

'Matt? Is that your boyfriend?' Lisa sounds bored even asking the question.

'*Yes*,' giggles Kate, and I don't correct her.

I excuse myself and move off towards the toilets, stopping in the hallway to write a text; I send it twice, to BF and to Matt, then I loiter, waiting for replies. After a couple of minutes with none forthcoming, I stash my phone and follow a pair of girls into the loos. At the far end, I examine myself in the mirror. Shit. I spent an hour on my make-up and after just forty minutes here it's started sliding off. I find my mascara and brush an extra layer on my lashes, watching in dismay as they clump and flake. Wiping it off seems to be making it worse. Fuckity fuck fuck.

The door opens and BF walks in, stops dead and stares at me with wide eyes. I'm baffled; we've sorted things since the night I abandoned her for Matt (I called her the next morning and said, 'Sorry for being a dick.' BF contended that she had been the dick for making a fuss, then we had a small fight about who was a bigger dick) so she can't be angry, although technically it's not anger displaying on her face – she looks both surprised and anxious, as though she's seeing me for the first time having recently been told I was dead.

'Hello,' I say. Then, 'Are you OK?'

'Yeah, great!' In a head-spinning U-turn back to normality, BF sounds so jolly I know there's something she's not telling me, but when I ask again she assures me everything is fine with a look that says: *drop it*, and adds, 'You look nice.'

'Really?'

'You know you do. Is this because Matt is here, perchance?'

'Actually – he isn't. Not yet.'

Together we head back into the heat and bustle of the main room. My friends are gathered at the bar where young, harried-looking girls in white shirts and black ties are trying to keep up with the demand for beers and spirits now the Prosecco supply is waning. I spot Harriet further down and James, hovering behind; I wave to get her attention, but she is preoccupied by what looks like a shot of Sambuca: with a pinched look, Harriet picks it up and sinks it. It seems unlike her. I survey the crowd for Matt and when I turn back, they've both disappeared. BF has gone over to chat to Sophie and Ollie; I watch Ollie's eyes adhere themselves to her cleavage when she leans forward to hear and Sophie must have seen, too, because she gives Ollie's waist a 'playful' pinch and his eyes snap back to her as a knowing smile spreads across her face. Ollie leans down and whispers something in her ear, then kisses it and her smile widens. Sometimes, being in love is incredible. I take another pass at the crowd for Matt.

When I turn around, he's there: Matt, my Matt, walking towards me, clad in a slim-fitting black jacket and jeans that make him look as handsome as I've ever seen him, and he is looking around for me. His mouth slides into a huge, exuberant grin when he finds me and he picks me up, swinging me round and kissing me hard.

'You're here,' I say.

'Of course.'

I tell him, 'You look great,' and he replies, 'I wanted to make a good impression on your friends.' Then he says: '*You look absolutely stunning, Rosy, I am so proud and lucky to be with you*,' but only in my head.

For the next half hour, Matt is charm personified. As he chats to my friends, he exudes the type of wit and confidence people go to seminars to learn; he asks questions and shows genuine interest in the answers, and he nudges Bob and Ollie, joking that they are both punching well above their weight with Kate and Sophie. He is the right amount of flirty with BF, knowing that she is here on her own, then he buys us all a round of Jägerbombs before he, Bob and Ollie fall into natural conversation about sport or raw meat or whatever it is men talk about. I lean in towards Sophie, Kate and BF. 'What do you think?' I whisper.

'Fun,' says Kate.

'Funny,' offers Sophie. The music changes from Muzak to something more upbeat, the pop and dance chart hits that make us all think we can dance.

'He seems nice,' replies BF. She sounds vague and I watch as her eyes dart around the room. I announce that I need the loo and glare at BF until she gets that I want her to join me. Away from the heat and noise, I draw her aside.

'What's going on?'

'Nothing!' she insists. I arch my eyebrows and keep them raised until her hard expression softens to one of reluctance. 'I've been texting Ed.'

'You're joking.'

'Oh God . . .' She covers her face with her hands then slides them down her face, pulling the skin into a grotesque, despairing mask. 'I'm an idiot. I cracked and sent him a message on Monday and, honestly, I didn't think he'd reply but he did and we got chatting. And then . . .'

'Please don't tell me you're meeting him.' BF squeezes her eyes shut and grimaces. And that's when it finally clicks. 'He's coming here, isn't he?'

BF nods, avoiding my gaze. 'It's an engagement party, I knew it would be full of couples and I didn't want to be the only pathetic single in the room and be forced to hang out with . . .'

'Oona isn't here,' I pre-empt her, 'she's at a conference in Leeds.'

Deadpan, BF says: 'See – even Oona didn't want to hang out with me.'

We look at each other without speaking; I'm struggling to think of something more empathetic to say to BF beyond, 'You're a fucking idiot,' but before I say anything, BF shakes her head and mutters, 'I know,' as if she's read my thoughts. 'I don't know why I don't just walk away.'

'Because, for some unfathomable reason, you like him.'

I take her into the toilets and we pee before performing checks and balances on each other's make-up and head outside. Matt is walking towards us having been in the men's himself. With a wink, BF disappears back into the main room.

He says, 'Hello you,' and kisses me again, this time tipping me backwards and pushing his tongue far into my mouth. He pulls me up so fast that I'm dizzy as I come back to standing.

'You're a hit,' I tell him as I regain my balance.

'And you're *fit*.' It comes out a little slurred; I wonder how much he's drunk. He grins at me and I grin back and we stand there grinning together, and for a moment or two I feel blissfully, ecstatically happy. Then I see it and as soon as I do, I don't know why it hasn't occurred to me before. It's no more than a trace but the coke is stark white against the inside of his nostril. I open my mouth to speak – but I am not the only one. From inside the room, Bob's voice, amplified by a microphone, is asking the room for quiet.

Matt pulls me after him and we edge into the crowd, then he swings me round so that I am wrapped in his arms with my back against his chest. It feels nice; I allow myself to relax into him. We can talk afterwards.

'Good evening, everyone,' says Bob. A voice shouts out that they can't see him so Bob climbs on a chair to whoops and applause. 'Good evening,' he starts over, 'I'm not a great public speaker so I'll keep this brief. So, in conclusion . . .' He gives a goofy smile and has to wait until the groans die down before he can speak again. 'On behalf of Kate and myself, I'd like to thank you all for coming out to celebrate our engagement; there's a few bottles of Prosecco left over so please help yourselves . . .' He pauses, searching through the crowd until his eyes alight on what they were looking for and come to rest. Kate.

Bob starts by saying how lucky and grateful he is to be with Kate, citing the time he made soup and almost burnt down their flat as an example of her unconditional love (he should be grateful – Kate was furious) and promising to try and be more for her, to be better, to be the husband of her dreams (technically impossible – for Kate that would be Ryan Philippe circa *Cruel Intentions*). He talks about how far they've come and all the good things ahead of them, but I miss a lot of it due to the whoops and cheers of the crowd. He says something about his love for Kate and his joy at their engagement then ends by imploring us all to get drunk. The room explodes into applause and Bob jumps down and goes to Kate. The way he looks at her just then . . . it doesn't matter that I lost his words because seeing him with her in that moment, there is no doubt in my mind about the way he loves her. It was like he saw all of her: every fault, every secret, every bad joke she's ever told and every poor decision made, and loved her in spite of them. Because of them. Now I understand what my mother was saying, about accepting the good and bad. I see Bob mouth the words, 'I love you,' just as Matt spins me round and pulls me towards the bar.

The end of Bob's speech also signals the end of the dignified, polite stage of the evening; the music is turned up, the lights dimmed and the space becomes a dance floor thanks to the bravest (drunkest) few who throw some 'comedy' moves to make it acceptable for the rest of us to dance. I feel light-headed and giddy from the alcohol and the heat and when I look around at my friends I am overwhelmed by love; at this precise moment, the feelings I have for Matt are not dissimilar. So he's done a couple of lines of coke, fuck it – he's enjoying himself, I am too and we're great together. He clutches me to him and pushes me back out in time to the music; he spins me and catches me in an embrace and kisses me. A trash song I remember from uni comes on and we jump around like idiots; by the time it's over, I feel like I'm boiling in my own sweat.

'I'm going to get a glass of water!' I yell over the music, but Matt can't hear so I mime drinking and push off into the crowd. A hand grabs my arm – I look up to see Terry, Lisa's husband, his tie hanging loose around his sweaty neck: he is clearly smashed. I can't see Lisa. Terry flings me this way and that in a drunken attempt at a jive and it's fun for about seven seconds until I'm bashing into people and I feel like I want to throw up. Terry pulls me into him and moves me in a tight hold; I can feel his sweat moistening my dress, which does little to relieve my nausea but is marginally preferable to my stint as a human rag-doll.

I am extracting myself when a hand grips my shoulder from behind and there is a jolt as a second hand pushes Terry back. I turn and see Matt: his face is contorted and there is a steely look in his eyes I've never seen before. He is shouting but I can't make out the words beyond several permutations of 'fuck'. Whatever he is saying, he's aiming it at Terry who is standing inert with a look of bewilderment on his face – his passive resistance just seems to incense Matt who takes a step forward and pulls his arm back, with his fist a tightly clenched ball. If Matt is going to punch Terry I should probably do something, but I am frozen, seemingly incapable of rational intervention. Maybe I don't want to get in the way, which isn't unreasonable – I don't want to get punched; also, I have never seen someone get punched up close before and I kind of want to see what it's like. Before Matt can act, however, a group over his left shoulder starts up an over-enthusiastic dance-off and he is shunted forward, into Terry.

It is your classic climactic event: the room seems to

fall silent and still as Terry, now in slow motion, stumbles, loses his footing and crumples into a posse of girls behind him. I look on as their wine glasses launch into the air, raining down warm Sancerre on the unsuspecting crowd below. Someone, somewhere, screams . . . finally, the room bursts back into life with colour and movement and the sound of glass smashing to the floor. There follows a stunned silence as everyone takes in the scene – even Matt looks shocked, but also really, really angry. Mainly angry. James, who has left a very drunk Harriet drinking water on a chair by the window, is the first to react: he steps in front of Matt and grabs him in a clinch whilst the rest of the men get their shit together and pile in (to prove they are Men); Lisa rushes over, finding time to shoot me a filthy look before helping her husband to his feet. People have stopped dancing to peer over shoulders and under arms, trying to see what's happening whilst the music plays on and I see Matt being led out of the room by James and Ollie. A guy whom I don't recognise turns to me. 'Your boyfriend is a twat.'

'He's not my boyfriend,' I say as I walk away.

The boys are not in the hallway when I get there, so I head downstairs to the outdoor smoking area, partly because the boys might have brought Matt here to cool off, but mainly to see if I can scam a cigarette. I get one off a guy sitting with his friend, largely thanks to the dress, light it with one of his matches and thank him, then find a lone table as far away from other people as I can get. It's almost the end of November and freezing, but the chill in the air is refreshing after the heat, noise and violence upstairs. I take a long drag on the cigarette and look out into the darkness as a piece of ash falls onto my dress and I swipe it away – I wore this dress to impress Matt and there's no reason it should be soiled any further. Matt. He was supposed to be my big reveal, my funny, exciting soon-to-be-boyfriend who my friends would love and he'd love in return; my spontaneous, fun-loving, perma-Plus One. No more end-of-the-table dinners for me; with Matt, I'd get my share of the lamb. He is the one I thought might be The One; it would be Sophie typing *You'll be next* on my wall, her finger weighed down with a rock of her own. I thought I was falling in love with him. Suddenly, everything feels wrong.

I wonder whether Sophie or BF are looking for me, or Kate . . . crap, Kate: I'll have to make it up to her. I'll be the best bridesmaid ever: I'll wear whatever pink satin monstrosity she gives me and smile about it; I'll get her a stripper for her hen-do, a really fit one . . . No, I'll get her *ten* strippers, each fitter than the last.

I'm going in as a man is coming out so we bump into each other like we're in a farce and both mumble, 'Sorry!' at the same time. I look up, and see that it is Ed. Before I can stop myself, the words, 'Oh, it's you,' have slipped out of my mouth. I gather myself and could quite easily stop myself adding, 'Why are you here?' though I've chosen not to.

'Why am I here?' He repeats it as though the answer is self-explanatory so I say 'yes', as in, *I want an answer.*

'Because she fucking invited me, that's why.' I swear

on Hector's tail that at the end of the sentence he snarls at me.

'You need to leave her alone. She can't get over you otherwise and she needs to.'

'She doesn't need you making decisions for her.' He tries to push past me but I put my hand up and the shock as he thumps into it makes him stop.

'Yes, at the moment, she does because you're clouding her judgement. You'll screw her over – *again* – because you are a cunt and she can't see it, but everyone else can. Nobody wants you here.'

Ed leans down and puts his face so close to mine I can physically feel the wrath coming off it. I want to cry and run away but I force myself to stay still, despite the trembling in my hands. 'Think anyone wants your coke-head shit of a boyfriend here either? At least I don't spend the night in the bathroom then come out and try and lamp someone. He's a fucking joke and you are too if you think he's interested in you. Fucking bitch.' I worry he's going to spit at me, but he barges past, bashing my shoulder with his own as he goes. I give a small yelp of pain because it hurts, but nowhere near as much as the truth.

26.

NOT THIS TIME

The first thing I do when I wake up, after peeing and having a quick perusal of Facebook, is ring Kate and offer myself up for her ire. I am barely into my fourth apology when she stops me.

'Ro, don't worry about it: everyone was drunk, me and Bob included – once it was over everyone started dancing again. I had the best time!' Then she hands the phone to Bob who repeats the process.

I'm happy she's happy but no less furious with Matt. Not only did he embarrass us both, I could hear the edge to Kate's voice when she said his name and I know my friends will all be talking about him amongst themselves and he's not going to come out of it well. I hate that my friends hate him now – I'd rather they hated me.

The last time I saw Matt, he was being hauled off the dance floor. After my run-in with Ed I went straight to the toilets to dab at the mascara that had smudged with the tears I couldn't stem, and have a debrief with my reflection in the mirror; when I came out, Ollie ran up to me to say he'd put Matt in a cab home so he must have been in a state. I left not long after myself; the party was starting to wind down and then Lisa yelled at me, so I treated myself to a cab home. I take a sip of my second cup of coffee and several cleansing breaths, then ring Matt's number.

'Hey,' I say when he picks up.

'Hey,' he groans in reply.

'How are you feeling?'

'Not great.'

'I'm not surprised . . .' I wonder just how much coke he put up his nose. He was drinking too, which made everything worse. 'So . . . it didn't end too well last night, did it?'

'I can't remember very much.' I hear the rustle of his duvet as he shifts around – it's almost midday and he's still in bed.

'You remember what happened at the end, though?'

'The end?'

'When you got into it with that guy?' Now I am starting to wonder if we are, in fact, having the same conversation.

'Oh Rosy, for God's sake . . .' Matt sighs so heavily I can almost feel his breath down the phone. 'Yeah, I probably could have left it, but you shouldn't have been flirting with him.'

I want to explain to Matt that there are no circumstances under which my behaviour could be described as flirting; I also want to assure him his reaction wasn't warranted even if I had been and I want to tell him that if he was so drunk and coked up that he cannot recall doing it, he clearly has a serious problem for which he should seek professional help. However, because I am so utterly incredulous that I am required to say any of this, the best I can manage is, 'I wasn't flirting,' in a weak, thready voice. I have so much to say I don't know how to begin.

In reply, Matt says: 'You obviously can't handle your drink.' Which makes me wonder if he can hear me speaking at all.

Matt doesn't say anything after that. This is what Charlie used to do to me and I recognise the same right-eous, punitive streak in Matt as the silence drags on, becoming ever more intolerable: he will give his final mandate then shut up, all in an effort to prove to me that his opinion is flawless and cannot be bettered, even if it is entirely misguided. I won't let Matt treat me like Charlie did. I refuse. 'Look, I'm sorry if . . .'

'Don't worry about it.' Matt shuts me down immedi-ately, meaning, of course: *it's your fault, but I'm being the bigger person here.*

Reality says: *You know all he heard was your apology, right?*

Then Matt sighs again, but something is different. This is not anger – he sounds resigned. Something is wrong. 'Look, Rosy, after last night . . . I saw a different side to you . . .'

Suddenly, panic is rising up through me like bile – these are the type of words you use to break up with someone.

'Hey, Matt, look,' I say, a little too pitchy, a little too fast, 'we both overdid it a bit on Saturday and things just got a bit messy – that guy just grabbed me, I didn't know what to do but I can see what it must have looked like so it's no wonder you were angry. But it was nothing, absolutely nothing. You're the only one I want to be with.'

Reality says, *Really?*

Careful, says my Self-esteem, *you don't want to end up alone.*

Matt says, 'Mm . . . I don't know, it just seems like there's a lot of drama going on with you.'

'No, there's isn't, I promise: maybe I've been a bit stressed out by work and stuff but that will all calm down . . . I'm sorry.' The line goes quiet. My anger is still there but it has been submerged by fear. I can't believe how fast this is happening.

'I'm not sure things are going to work out between us.' Everything is silent again but this time it's mainly in my own head. No, no, no, no, no – if I keep repeating it in my mind, maybe Matt will change his. He was supposed to apologise and go out of his way to make it up to me – not break up with me. This is all wrong. This wasn't what was supposed to happen.

'You're going to throw everything we have away because of one night? Matt, come on, please . . .'

'Rosy, I think it would be best for both of us if you don't beg.'

Suddenly, everything is quiet again.

*   *   *

Have you ever been on public transport and been so engrossed in whatever you're doing – reading a book, or playing on your phone – that you look up and suddenly realise you've reached your stop? Whether conscious or not, something usually rouses you; you look up, think, shit, I'm here, and know you have just seconds to leap off before the doors will close and you'll be trapped. Such a dramatic departure will be embarrassing but it will be outweighed by a swell of relief you feel as the train pulls away, knowing you're not on it.

It was when Matt said the word 'beg' – that's when I looked up.

27.

WILD MAN

I know when 2K are coming back from play: a boisterous, writhing mass of mini-beasts swarms towards the door, at which point Seema steps out and wrangles them into a calm, quiet line of children. They spend ten minutes cross-legged on the carpet (I couldn't envisage how thirty bodies would fit into such a small area until I saw it happen for the first time; I had underestimated how small a six-year-old is) whilst Seema takes them through the afternoon schedule ('It's a ploy to let them decompress,' she told me last week, 'otherwise they would be mental') and as she comes to an end it is my cue to take Dax next door. We have come a long way, Dax and I, over the last six weeks. Whereas once he couldn't look at me, now he turns to find me when it's time to go and he trots along beside me to the reading area. He's been creeping closer and closer to me with every passing week – often it's all I can do not to trip over him.

We've also got some serious banter going on. Last week, for example:

Me: Hey Dax, how are you today?

Dax: Fine.

Me: That's nice to hear – Miss Khanom told me you were painting farm animals this morning, was that fun?

Dax: Yes.

Me: Which animal did you draw?

Dax: Mm . . . (*gives it serious thought*) a cow.

Me: Ah, brilliant – cows are one of my favourites. So, shall we start our reading for today?

Dax: Yep.

I find it very encouraging.

Dax shows me his new book: it's another title featuring our fearless children and their fucking dog – it's the dog that always lands them in trouble. Each time Dax arrives clutching another story, in my head I beseech the kids to leave the stupid dog at home, but they never learn.

'This looks good, what do you think, Dax?' I chirrup.

'Yeah.' It's not a comprehensive critique but I consider it a step up from nothing whatsoever. Dax opens the first page. That's the other thing: his reading is getting so much better. He is markedly quicker and his accuracy is soaring; he reaches page five with just one mistake.

'*Oh – no – said – Griff – come – back – Peppy,*' he reads. At the end of the passage, I stop him and point to the page. 'Dax, you see this little mark here? The one that's a line with a dot underneath?' Dax follows my finger to the exclamation mark in the text. 'It means the character is shouting – like, *"Oh no!" said Griff. "Come back, Peppy!"'* Dax rereads the line. His intonation stays the same.

'One step at a time, eh?' I say. I want to hug him. I would if it weren't specifically prohibited.

With our twenty minutes up, Dax goes back to the classroom whilst I fill out his feedback form (I'm starting to run out of superlatives) and wait for Billy to come through the door.

I was lying in bed last week, thinking about reading with Billy and how dull his books seem to both of us, and it occurred to me that there must be a market for exciting, engaging children's stories to which kids can relate . . . I have therefore decided to write one. The story is going to centre around two young boys (based on Dax and Billy, except I can't call them that so I need to come up with alternatives, Rex and Sticky, something like that, except good) and they are going to solve mysteries that crop up at school, unwittingly aided by friends and their kindly teacher Miss Dana; Rex will act as the voice of moderation to offset Sticky's daredevil nature. I've taken to carrying my notebook with me everywhere I go so I can jot down ideas: I write on the bus, I keep my notebook open beside me as I watch in the evenings and I place it under my pillow in case I wake up in the night with a plot twist. I've been working on a scene involving a river that the boys need to traverse in order to get a . . . I don't know, a magic key or something, and I've had it in mind that the Dax character would stand on the bank, commenting on the raging rapids and urging caution, whilst 'Sticky' forges ahead . . . I pull my notebook from my bag. Maybe they should find some stepping-stones . . .

When I look at the clock I realise I've been writing for ten minutes and Real Billy should be here by now. I get up to look through the door and see the children still sat on the carpet as Seema gives a lesson on ladybirds – maybe she asked Billy to stay. I didn't notice him when the class came in from play, is he definitely in school? Perhaps he's forgotten, or Seema has, although the thought of Seema forgetting anything, ever, seems unlikely.

The children leave the carpet in groups and head to their tables; as they get up, I spot Billy. I wait until he is settled then go over and crouch down beside him. 'Hey Billy, ready to read?'

'No.' He doesn't look up from his picture.

'Right . . . why not?'

'Don't want to.'

'Ah. OK. It's just that . . . I . . .' I have yet to learn how to reason with a six-year-old. Billy's body visibly tenses and he covers his work with his arm. Doing my best Seema impression, I say: 'Come on, Billy, it's time to read.'

'*No.*' His tone is firmer and tinged with anger. From the corner of my eye I can see Seema heading over. Shit.

'Is everything OK?' This is just her in – I know she knows it's not.

'Billy was just saying he's not too keen on reading

today!' I add a jovial laugh as though this is excellent news.

Seema folds her arms. 'Why is that, Billy?' I'm not certain Billy has a grasp on rhetorical questions yet for he shakes his head and stays silent, which I fear is poor judgement on his part. Seema draws herself up tall. I feel a bit scared. 'Get up please, Billy,' she says and there is no ambiguity at all. Billy hauls himself to standing as though his own body is weighing him down. 'Miss Edwards, why don't you go back to the reading table and get things ready, Billy will be through in a moment.' It takes me a second to register who Seema is talking to, so rarely am I formally addressed; her dismissal is decisive, however, and I slink back through the door – I'm worried that Billy is not the only one in trouble. I peer out from behind the glass and watch Billy as he stomps along behind Seema; she sits in her chair and positions him in front of her then starts talking and although I can't hear what she's saying, I'm getting the gist from Billy's subdued fidgeting. Eventually, Seema gestures towards the door and I dive down to the table and shuffle papers.

Billy stamps in, letting the door bang shut behind him. He throws his book onto the table, his body into the chair and folds his arms.

'Hi, Billy,' I say gently. He swivels his head and shoulders away from me as far as they will go. Like an owl.

'Sorry we've had a tricky start this afternoon, I can see you're pretty cross . . .'

'I'm not!' Billy shouts and flings his book onto the table; it falls open on the exact page where we last left off, which is pretty cool.

'Fine. Geez . . .' The 'geez' comes out involuntarily, under my breath – I used to do that with Charlie, too. Men can be infuriating at any age, it seems.

Finally, *finally*, after five minutes of wrangling, Billy decides that he will read after all. It is his most accurate and articulate reading to date. He stumbles twice, otherwise he correctly decodes all of the 'tricky' words we've been targeting so either he's been practising at home or hating me brings out the best in him. When I try to congratulate him, however, he ignores me or shuts me out by leaning on his left arm and obscuring his book; when I point out his excellent use of expression he brings it right to his face. Nothing I say helps, although a lot seems to make it worse. A quick glimpse of the clock indicates we are only seven minutes into our allocated twenty. I wonder if Billy can tell the time yet.

'That was fantastic,' I tell Billy when he reaches the end of the book, 'the best reading you've done yet.' Billy throws his book on the floor.

'Hey . . . mister! Pick that up.' God, I need to learn how to communicate with children. Of course, Billy doesn't move. 'If you don't pick that book up, I'm going to have to . . . I shall . . .' I look at Billy, looking at me, and have the awful sense that he is enjoying this. Can a six-year-old look arch? 'Right, fine, we'll just leave it on the floor, and then we'll see what Miss Khanom has to say about your book being . . . dirty. And when I come back tomorrow . . .'

'You're not *coming* back!' Billy yells, before he turns and flees into the classroom. Billy and I have had our ups and downs and there have been a few occasions where I've wanted to cry, but I've always managed to keep myself together. This is not one of those times.

* * *

Later, I am on the carpet organising the reading books whilst Seema is at one of the children's tables, drawing something out on a large sheet of sugar paper. I can't concentrate: I keep putting the Level Three books with the Level Sixes and confusing the orange band books with the red. From across the room, I hear Seema huff and when I look over she is rubbing something out.

'Hey, Seema?' I call over.

She looks up with frustration etched into her face. 'Yeah?'

'No, don't worry.'

'OK.'

I go to pick up the next book and see that it is *Race!* From the cover the polar bears are grinning at me, mocking me, especially the one in the natty scarf.

'Seema? Why does Billy hate me?'

'He didn't say that, did he?'

'Not in words.' I explain what had happened during our session, emphasising how angry he was – I have to steel myself when I come to relate his parting shot. When

I'm finished, Seema laughs. It's not quite the cosy empathy I'd been hoping for.

'He absolutely does not hate you,' she says, 'in fact I've never seen him so enthusiastic about reading. Every morning he tells me that he's been practising for you.' (I *knew* it.) Leaving the books in teetering piles, I pull up a chair opposite Seema. She says, 'Billy has some . . . issues at home.' She is choosing her words carefully, conscious of confidentiality. 'He has experience of being rejected by people he loves. He likes you but he's scared you're going to abandon him too.'

I know how he feels . . . except, obviously, he is a six-year-old child, facing the loneliness and hardship of a broken home whilst I am a happy, healthy, self-determining adult – it's not the most apt comparison. What I'm so ineptly trying to convey is that I don't think that fear of rejection goes away, whether you're six or sixty; it is the reason why love feels so terrifying, because once you find it – and that's not an easy feat in itself – there is always the risk it will go away. I want to be reliable for Billy and I am determined not to let him down. It would be easier if he weren't being a little shit, though.

28.

BIG STRIPEY LIE

Miss Comic Sans

So, it didn't work out with M – he turned out to be a bit crazy-bananas. The experience has confirmed that I am perfectly happy without a boyfriend, but almost everyone under thirty that I know is either happily ensconced in a long-term relationship, or is dating and *about* to become ensconced in a long-term, happy relationship and if I don't get in on the act I might be destined to spend Saturday nights alone until I die, or I fashion a life partner from a mop and a pumpkin and call him Dafydd, whichever comes first. But I like doing my own

---

thing. I value my free time; after work, I want to write my book, eat food, and/or do some socialising. Otherwise, I like to sit on my sofa watching *The West Wing* with my Bear and a packet of custard creams. And yes, I do know how pathetic that makes me . . .

I sit back from my screen and take a sip of coffee. Caffè Nero is quiet this afternoon: behind me, a woman coos at her crotchety baby, strapped into his buggy under layers of puffa, seemingly in awe of his strangled mews. A young guy by the window is tapping on his laptop just as I am (I clocked him when I came in: semi-fit but grumpy) and the only other patron (baby doesn't count as I doubt it's bought anything) is an elderly woman who has sunk into her armchair. She is reading the paper, leaning in to read the print and turning the sheets with shaky hands, whilst nibbling a scone with frustrating torpor. If I assume myself a writer, technically, these people are all in my office.

I turn back to my screen, open my email and reread, for the eighth, maybe ninth time, the message Sally sent in reply to the email I sent her three days ago, to which I attached two extracts of my book. Sally, my good friend Sally, who just happens to work in publishing. Beyond the blog (that has now amassed ten real-people followers, consisting of Mum – we agreed that my father should have limited access, to save him from my entry on procrasturbating – BF; The Couples; Harriet; Liam; Sally and a woman called Kirsty McDermott whom I don't know but what do I care: ten followers is a whole one follower more than nine) nobody has read my writing; it took me an afternoon to work up to pressing 'send' on the email, having already taken six days to prepare two 2,000-word pieces. Sally didn't give much feedback in her response, hence my constant rereading as I try to discern a nuanced nugget of opinion I may have missed.

Before she signed off, she suggested we meet for lunch. This in particular has confused me. Why meet? Why lunch? Is it because I am by and large a dreadful writer and she thinks it kinder to tell me over a sandwich? Does she have scathing critique to share? Or could it be simply that Sally's matched with an Austrian jet-ski instructor and she wants to invite me to the Medieval-themed wedding they're having next week? We've scheduled for Friday; I'm looking forward to it in as much as I always enjoy seeing Sally, otherwise I am dreading it. I close my email and return to my half-finished post. I don't know where to go with it. Maybe I'll get a muffin.

Facebook, Twitter, Buzzfeed, Instagram and Tumblr are desolate tundras of inactivity, at least since I checked ten minutes ago. I texted BF but she hasn't replied so now I hate her and will have to find a new best friend. However, there, tucked in the corner of my phone screen, is the Tinder flame, burning bright. The ghosts of Elliot, Jonathan, Patrick, Andrew, Doug, Archie, Max, Guy and Matt are telling me not to do it. I should finish this blog post and then get back to the book . . . write the fucking book . . .

. . . I reboot Tinder. They make it too easy to do that.

It's been a while since I've been active in the Tindersphere; things have changed. What is a 'moment'? And can you really now un-match a previous match-ee? Kids these days don't know they're born: in my day (about six weeks ago) you had no choice but to push through the awkward agony of phasing out an accidental Like-ee or anyone who, after three promising messages, asked for a picture of your tits . . . it's a brave new world. The other day, BF mentioned something about a *new* app that tracks your movements in relation to those of a potential suitor; I'm only just getting to grips with the fact people are writing mini-bios on Tinder now – a new app is too much.

The number of people on Tinder also seems to have increased ten-fold: for every right swipe, I must make about thirty left and I've Liked just seven men so far, four of whom would be worth matching with and two worth messaging. I should cast my net wide; when I know, I'll know; I should look at their photos and follow the rules . . . all the Tinder wisdom from the past nine months is spinning in my head as I swipe left, left, left. I am just going to do the same to Nick, 30, when I get my first match, with Jack, fortunately one of the two men I wouldn't hate talking to. I tap his face. His photos are unlike any I have ever seen; in every shot he looks . . . different. It's like he's yo-yoing in age, or each picture is actually a shot of a different brother. There's no skiing, surfing or dog holding either: in one he's wearing a suit on a summer's day; in another, he's donned a sombrero.

A third has him in a bar with an extremely pretty girl to whom I've taken an instant dislike. He is always attractive though, in every one.

I'm still Tindering when he sends his first message.

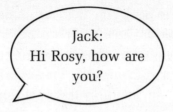

Jack:
Hi Rosy, how are
you?

Not original, but not offensive, misspelt or questionably legal either.

Rosy:
I'm OK thanks Jack,
just finished work.
How are you?

Jack:
That's early! What
do you do?

Damn – I shouldn't have mentioned work, of course he was going to ask about my job; do I say writer? I should stick to LSA, though it doesn't sound as impressive . . . but then hubris is a bitch. I wish I had the balls to make something up, like, 'I'm a magician's assistant' or 'I rear ferrets', but I would crack under questioning and Jack would think I was pathological.

Rosy:
I work in a primary school at the moment. Please tell me you do something exotic?!

Jack:
I'm sure some people think so; I work a lot of evenings though which takes the shine off.

Rosy:
Barman? Stripper? Night watchman? Now you HAVE to tell me . . .

Jack:
Ha! Not quite. I'm a doctor.

Is it shallow that I now fancy him more? To my mind, doctor equates to smart and compassionate; I'd take a doctor over a fireman or policeman every time. I must have had a hot-doctor experience that was as sexy as it was traumatic and thus deeply repressed into my unconscious. I should ask Mum.

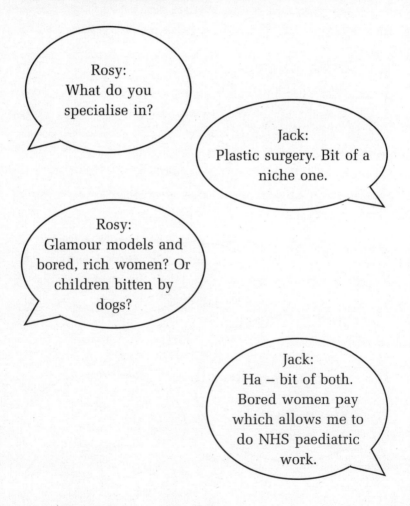

Rosy:
What do you
specialise in?

Jack:
Plastic surgery. Bit of a
niche one.

Rosy:
Glamour models and
bored, rich women? Or
children bitten by
dogs?

Jack:
Ha – bit of both.
Bored women pay
which allows me to
do NHS paediatric
work.

He is a doctor who fixes damaged children. Rosy: do not ask him to marry you. Don't even do it as a joke.

I text back to say his job sounds amazing, but ten minutes later I haven't had a reply. He's probably busy: maybe an emergency has come in and he's scrubbing up right now. He'll text back when he can. We seem to be getting on well, why wouldn't he? Although . . . maybe my stupid quip about those women offended him? They're still his patients, too . . . and I shouldn't have suggested he was a stripper; fuck, why do I do this? Me and my funny, funny jokes; it wouldn't kill me to just once drop the defensive armour and try being myself. Jack must have known I was kidding though, and if he didn't, I wouldn't want to be with someone so humourless. So screw him.

My phone beeps.

Jack:
I can't do this.

I ruined it. Great. Fuck.
No – fuck *him*.

> Jack:
> I'm not actually a doctor! I was joking around but you seem really nice so I can't keep up the lie!

> Jack:
> I'm really a musician! Sorry . . .!

Jack – if that is his real name – has lied to me, persistently; he's made up a false identity and fooled me into believing he is my dream man, making me look like an idiot in the process.

I like him even more.

*   *   *

Every year since we left university, BF and I have chosen one evening before Christmas and had a celebration. As we've got older, the Christmas traditions that so delighted us as children have been diluted in both our families: five years ago, my mother announced that she wouldn't bother with stockings for me and Bru any more; similarly, last year BF's parents opted for turkey crowns rather than, as her mother put it, 'go to the faff of getting a whole bird'. BF cried down the phone. So, because we both love Christmas and consider each other family, BF and I have created our own tradition of ordering Chinese, drinking cocktails-in-cans and watching *Miracle on 34th Street* in our pyjamas.

I've been hesitant to ask about Ed, but she'll be drunk soon and I need definitive assurance that he's gone.

'He's gone. Gone-gone,' BF says when I finally ask. 'He was definitely cheating on me.'

'You know for sure?'

'He told me.'

'He *told* you?' Initially, I am incredulous at Ed's rare display of honesty . . . but of course he told her. He couldn't just leave tortuous clues and wait until she confronted him to accuse her of being paranoid and hysterical like other men would; he needed her to know beyond doubt that he'd grown bored of her, that he'd found someone better than her to take her place. 'Hate' is a strong word, though it's not strong enough to describe my feelings for Ed. BF shakes her head. 'I actually thought I was in love with him – can you believe that? How are you even supposed to know? I don't know how you tell the difference between genuinely being in love with and just believing you are.'

Ah, the age-old 'am-I-in-love-or-aren't-I-and-if-I'm-not-why-does-it-feel-so-much-like-I-am' conundrum – it is something I have been thinking about a lot recently. After Matt, I feel like I can barely trust myself to know the red men from the green and not die when crossing the road. I thought I was falling in love with Matt; in hindsight, the disappointment of *not* being in love with Guy gave whatever I had with Matt substance it did not deserve. There were alarm bells with Matt, of course: the unregulated drug use; his casual disregard for things that mattered to me; the S&M hair-yanking, that was a big one . . . but I've been single for a while and out of love longer still: there comes a point where convincing yourself you're in love seems preferable to not feeling loved at all. It's not that you don't hear the bells – you choose not to listen. Perhaps it's related to age, but it seems like we are all carrying more baggage these days, making it harder to tell whether these early warning signs are minor foibles or blaring sirens from which you should run, screaming, leaving your possessions behind. The conclusion I have come to, fantastically reductive though it may be, is that you can't – you can't tell.

You can't tell if you're in love or if it just feels like it; you can't tell if the person you're falling in love with is going to fall in love with you; and there is no certainty, none, that the love someone feels for you is real, imagined or proffered in a mutated form that will see them up and leave twenty years on. But it is this jeopardy that makes falling in love so beautifully, dismally, addictively awesome and I think it is only when the love is over that you'll find out one way or the other. I know that the love I felt for Charlie was real because even after so long, even after he left me with all the pain, heartbreak and anguish that came with his departure, a part of me still loves him and always will. A very, very small part. A shard.

I relay my thoughts to BF, who listens in attentive silence, then says: 'Well, that's pretty . . .'

'Shit?'

'Yeah.' She dips a spring roll in the pot of plum sauce and pushes it into her mouth. 'One thing I do know,' she says, flecks of pastry shooting from her lips, 'is that I'm done. No more Tinder; no dates, no men, no massive head-fuck in the process.'

'I didn't mean you should just give up.'

She shrugs, grinning. 'I'll probably crack after a week. But, God – it's only once you're off Tinder that you realise how much of your focus it takes up; I've been putting off trying to get promoted all year because of dating, and then Ed, so that's my plan for the New Year: get promoted. Be happy.'

I never told BF about my conversation with Ed at Kate's engagement party. It has been a great sadness in my life to realise that some people, regardless of circumstance or personal history, are simply not nice. Ed is not nice. BF had to see that for herself before she would be able to let him go, but it's a monumental relief to hear that she has. 'It's a good plan,' I tell her.

'What about you then, now that Matt is gone? And he is gone, isn't he?'

I nod. If I'm ever worried that residual feelings for Matt might be surfacing, I need only replay the sound of him telling me not to beg.

It would be ridiculous to gush about Jack after one afternoon of messaging, and especially in light of what we have just been talking about. My phone vibrates in my bag; I glance down to see his name on the screen, as though he knows I'm thinking about him. 'I got chatting to someone today. He seems nice. It's nothing special.'

'Sure?' asks BF, eyebrows arched.

In the spirit of Ed's honesty, I reply with equal candour. 'No.'

29.

WOW

I've put on bronzer, but maybe not enough. I sweep an extra layer across my cheekbones and temples and add a stroke down my nose . . . I think that might be too much but if I wipe it off, it's going to take foundation and blusher with it – though should I have put on blusher if I've used bronzer? Shit . . . fake eyelashes would improve everything but they take north of twenty minutes to apply (excluding the habitual five minutes of crying and swearing) and I'm already running late: Jack and I agreed to meet at 8 p.m. and it's coming up to 7.30 now. I have been delayed by . . . sartorial issues. I had an outfit planned in my head (sex jeans, black top, low-heeled boots so I can wear thermal socks) but it looked boring and frumpy when I put it on and not in an edgy, Dalston kind of way; I went in another direction and put on a purple bodycon dress I'd forgotten I had but it looked slutty, and not in a high-class, girlfriend-of-Russian-oligarch Chelsea kind of way. With a total of twelve changes behind me, the thirteenth has been a return to my sex jeans/black top combo with a better bra and higher heeled boots that will have to do because I am running out of time. And clothes.

My first date with Jack will also be my first, first date on a Sunday night. His job has made it difficult to find a night we were both free – tonight was the first one we landed on. We've been messaging every day since we matched; yesterday we spent an hour swapping quotes from *The Job Lot* which is a show I genuinely like rather than one I've had to pretend to so that Jack might like me more. I also admitted my love for emojis and instead of laughing at me like he had every right to do, Jack used them to create a picture of a little boy looking up longingly at his lost balloon that was . . . beautiful. Jack is someone who can make emojis beautiful. It's all been light, inane stuff which has made messaging fun, but it's come at the expense of any serious getting-to-know-you stuff; now we're going to meet, we'll have to progress beyond the flippant back and forth for it to work. This means Jack might actually get to know me, my good parts as well as my bad, and if he sees my bad parts he might not like me after all.

He is already in the pub as I come through the door, sat at the bar in the blue shirt he described in reply to my panic text about my outift in case I didn't match up to my Tinder photos; I'm now confident that he'll recognise me but worried he won't think I'm pretty enough.

He looks at me as I come in and it's the strangest thing: I feel like I've seen him before, but in real life, outside of the Tindersphere; it's as though we might have been friends a long time ago, or I know how his voice is going to sound. He stands up. He is taller and more attractive than in his pictures: his brown hair is slightly longer and his brown eyes clearer, and the photos don't lend his face the kindness I can see as I look at him now. His half-drunk pint is resting on the bar, so he must have been early as I'm dead on eight o'clock. He seems nervous, or I do. 'I'm sorry I'm late,' I say, even though I'm not. He leans in for a hug, I go to kiss his cheek and the result is an awkward half-clinch during which I end up patting his chest.

'What would you like to drink?' asks Jack.

'A vodka and soda? If that's OK.' Jack turns to the bar and is being served as I hop up onto the stool beside his.

'How's your day been?' I ask as he hands me my drink and sits down. I am very conscious that we are not sitting at a table – it goes: Jack, space, me, with nothing in between us.

'It's been all right, thanks. My orchestra had its Christmas do last night and I felt a bit ropey this morning, but I'm OK now.' It doesn't sound like a brag about his hedonistic social life; he sounds almost apologetic.

'I want to know more about your work,' I say, 'your music. Not your medical practice.'

Jack shrinks by a third and he looks down at the floor before meeting my gaze. 'I feel bad about that! I couldn't resist and I thought you wouldn't believe me, and then you did . . .'

'. . . I loved it.' It makes me laugh to think about it now, and Jack laughs too; I've been laughing about it alone since Tuesday – it sounds nice to hear us do it together.

'I do want to hear about life as a musician, though.'

'It's really less exciting than it sounds.'

'To you, but I don't know anything about it and I'd like to.' From his bemused expression, I assume that talking about work holds all the thrill for Jack that I'd get from discussing my menstrual cycle. Still, he takes me through a typical day, which he says involves a lot of sitting around and playing the same phrase over and over; as he talks, I can see that like any job, his has its fair share of monotony; it's just so different from anything I've experienced and sounds so exotic that I can feel myself getting lost in his words.

'How have you ended up working in a school?' Jack asks me when I've wrung his job dry.

I say: 'I'm sort of . . . making some changes . . . in my life,' which is a translation from the original in my head: '*My housemate took pity on me.*' I take a (large) sip of my drink. 'I used to work in PR, but I had my appraisal and decided to leave.' That sounds like I was terrible at my job. 'Out of choice.' Nope, that's worse – that sounds like I got fired. There is a knot of anxiety starting to form in the space behind my stomach. I go to open my mouth, to say something that will (somehow) make this better, then Jack says: 'That's really impressive. I've always wished I was brave enough to make a big change like that,' and the knot loosens, just slightly. I am also struck by how grateful I am to Jack for saying that; my friends and family have been supportive but Jack is the first person to tell me he is *impressed*, in as much as one person can be by another leaving a job – I haven't been out saving orphans from peril or jumping double-deckers on a push bike. In truth, I wonder if I'm not a little bit proud of myself.

Jack says, 'I really admire you working with children, I'd be awful.'

'I doubt that.'

'No, honestly – I'd leave a door open and they'd all run into the road, or I'd leave white spirit open on the floor or something.'

'Why would you bring white spirit into a primary school?'

'You see!' Jack throws up his hands, making me laugh. 'Even hypothetically I'd be awful.' He takes a sip of his pint. 'Do you want to be a teacher then?'

'God, no, definitely not.' I think of Seema, responsible for thirty children in addition to the piles of marking and paperwork I see her ploughing through each week. I would never be able to achieve the levels of discipline she does – I can barely do it with one child. Although, that said: Billy and I had a breakthrough last week; we had a moment, like our very own supermarket Christmas ad. He arrived for our session quiet, calm and self-contained. I was alarmed. I concluded that he was either ill or had participated in an experimental body swap with a well-behaved classmate. It wasn't until the very end of our session that his behaviour made sense. He had arrived clutching two books, one of which he was adamant I couldn't touch (this was when I knew it was the real Billy after all) and promptly sat on it. He read well as always, and as we were getting up to leave, he grabbed the second book, took out something he'd hidden inside and handed it to me without a word. It was a Christmas card, made from carefully folded green paper with a picture of a robin in a Santa hat on the front (I think that was what it was) sitting amidst a snowy scene; inside, in red felt-tip, he had written: *To Rosy Happy Christmas!!! love Billy.* I didn't cry then; I managed to wait until I got home, where the card now sits front and centre on my dresser.

Jack frowns. 'Isn't working as an LSA an odd choice if you don't want to be a teacher?' I can't fault his logic.

'I needed to get back to work after I left my PR job, so initially it was just to have some money coming in . . .'

'Initially?'

'Sorry?'

'You said you "initially" did it for the money,' Jack queries, 'but it sounds like something changed?'

I say 'no' then 'yes' and then 'sort of', by which point Jack is looking confused/frightened. I say: 'I started to get quite involved with two boys I read with,' which obviously sounds much, much worse. 'No, I mean . . .' My ears are heating up. 'I mean, I really got to know them and I thought they could be good characters for a book . . .'

'Should I be ringing someone about this?' Jack laughs. Sort of laughs.

Jack becomes number eleven. I tell him about writing,

and I tell him properly; at this stage I have to – but I want to as well. I explain how Dax and Billy have now become Dexter and Bo and take him through the story as I have it (it doesn't take long). Jack watches me, listening intently but impassive; for someone with no interest in children this must sound excruciatingly dull. 'I'm not telling it very well.'

'No, keep going, I was just getting into it,' he urges.

I describe a conundrum Dexter and Bo are facing involving a ladder, some drawing pins and a stray goat. 'It sounds great,' says Jack charitably, pushing our empty glasses up the bar, 'though I'd have to question the health and safety practices of any school that allows students to roam free in lesson time.'

I laugh. 'Children won't, fortunately. If they like the story they'll accept the ropiest of plot twists.'

'So Bo is the naughty one then? Dexter sounds like the good angel on his shoulder.'

'Exactly.' I'm amazed that Jack gets it so quickly, and all from my shoddy explanation. He asks if I'm happy to drink the same again and heads to the far side of the bar to order.

Despite the sticky moment when he thought I was a paedophile, I feel like maybe Jack gets me, too. He is chatting away with the barman; he was the same when he ordered earlier, polite, warm and friendly. I really like that about him.

'There you go,' he says, as he comes back and slides my second drink towards me.

'Thanks. What are you drinking?'

'Oranjeboom.'

'What is that?'

'It's a type of beer; weird name, I know.'

'I'd make an idiot out of myself ordering that, I wouldn't say it right.'

'I'll teach you.' Jack smiles: 'So next round is on you, then.'

'Happily.' Jack wants another round. This means either a) he's enjoying himself and wants the date to continue or b) he's using alcohol as a crutch to wade through this unbearable evening and feels too awkward to end it. I'm gunning for the former. We're in a nice pub on a Sunday night – it's not hard to relax – but for me it's more than that: with Jack, everything feels easy. He shifts on his stool to get comfortable. Then he says, 'Have you thought about trying to get your book published?'

*   *   *

Sally and I met for lunch in Pret, just as we had months ago (albeit accidentally) when she had fired up my enthusiasm for Tinder and being alive in general; I wish I could attribute the venue to poetry, but really I couldn't think of anywhere else and I like Pret salads. Sal had ventured nothing more about the book extracts since her last email and seeing her in work mode – the sharp tailoring of her dark jacket in stark contrast to my sweatshirt with a soup stain on the sleeve – made me anxious.

'So how's it coming along?' she asked once we'd sat down.

'Fine. Brilliant.' She nodded but remained silent, so I continued: 'I'm writing this bit where Dexter and Bo get cornered by a giant rat, except the rat knows all this information they need. And the rat can talk . . .' I rambled on, which was preferable to silence but I could see Sally's eyes glazing over. I couldn't bear to ask her opinion out of fear she might give it to me; eventually I had to stop talking for breathing purposes at which point Sally said, 'Mm-hm.' Silence would have been better.

'You think my book is bad, don't you?' I asked.

'It's not that it isn't good . . . I like the teacher character . . .' Sally sighed and put her coffee on the table. 'Rosy, honestly: yes, it's quite shit. You write wonderfully but I don't think your style is suited to children's literature.'

You know that moment when you've quit your job, and you've upended your whole life, and you're sort of thinking that you could pursue your life-long dream, then someone with the credentials to know tells you that you are rubbish at your dream and you should cease and desist immediately and suddenly everything you're doing and have ever done is redundant, the whole world is against you and you're on the verge of crying or vomiting or flipping the table over in a rage, and ideally you'd do all three? I was almost at that moment. I could feel myself shutting down, diving inside myself for protection. But then Sally spoke again.

'What I wanted to talk about is your blog – it's fantastic. When you're writing as yourself the words flow, it's so easy and natural. If you want to write, that's what you should focus on.'

My mind was still in crisis management as Sally said this and I was slow to take it in; words like 'fantastic' jarred against phrases like 'it's quite shit' and 'you're a total failure, and should lose 5 lbs' (in hindsight, that was my self-esteem, taking advantage of the moment). And having spent the last couple of months so deeply intertwined with Bo/Billy and Dexter/Dax, I wasn't ready to let them go; I felt like I'd let them down, I'd failed to tell their story and they deserved to have it heard. The blog had been a dumb bit of frippery for which I'd been bashing out articles, fully formed, in half an hour at a time – it wasn't the genre-busting literature I wanted to write. This was where Sally saw merit?

'You should narrow your purview, choose a topic,' she said, speeding up as she warmed to her theme, 'write about something that really interests you. What's exciting in your life right now?' I think Sally sometimes confuses her life with my own: I told her nothing classifiably 'exciting' was going on, unless she saw something I didn't in going to work, writing a lousy book and evenings at home, eating pasta and trying to avoid Oona. She sat for a moment, tapping her manicured nails on the table as she thought.

And then she said, 'Are you still on Tinder?'

*   *   *

There are rules to cover every aspect of Tinder use, from who should be swiped where, to date conduct and managing expectations (in my paltry opinion, the entire experience could be distilled as this: dating can be rough, just as Tinder can be fun. Be kind, be respectful and be conscious that few people know themselves or what they're looking for, and that includes you). However, as far as I know, there are no rules about how to tell a Tinder date that you might be about to write a book about Tinder. Sally asked me to write extracts of two of the dates I've had so far. I chose Doug and Archie, not because they are archetypal – if Sally and I weren't already friends (or she had not recently had a date with a guy who, though initially insipid, took her back to his, suggested they got naked, then returned from the kitchen with a roll of cling film and an expectant expression) she might not have thought them true – but taken together they epitomise all the hopeless optimism that exists at the heart of everyone's search for love.

I don't want to lie to Jack, but neither do I want to fuel his paranoia that I've taped a dictaphone to the underside of the bar. I tell him about Sally, that she suggested I write some 'stuff' that's more 'personal' and that my 'personal stuff' will be considered in their team meeting on Monday.

'That sounds promising,' he says.

'My friend is pretty bad at her job.'

'Well, you tried.' Jack laughs, and it makes me laugh too.

I shift my weight and rest my arm on the bar. For all its novelty, spending an entire evening on a bar stool is not a comfortable experience; I've had one eye open for tables coming free but for a Sunday night, the pub is busy and the turnover is slow. The group closest to us have nearly finished their drinks; if any of them come up to order again, I'll tell them I saw mouse droppings by the beer taps or 'accidentally' punch them in the face.

'What would your dream job be?' I ask Jack. 'Or is music it?'

'I do enjoy what I do . . .' he speaks carefully and I can see that's he thinking. 'Maybe something football-related?'

'As in, playing?'

He shakes his head. 'No; journalism or analysis, that sort of thing. I've never really thought about it, to be honest.'

'It sounds like you're happy where you are.'

'Yeah – I probably am.'

There is a little bit of Liam in Jack: that same self-contained solidity – it's a sort of contentment at being in the present rather than racing ahead to the next thing, like I always seem to do; next job, next run, next date . . . Tinder thrives on this mode of thinking: *my last thirty-seven dates were horrific, but lucky thirty-eight* . . . It is such an immediate format that there's little incentive to pause from one date to the next, no reason to reflect on what might have gone wrong before you dive back into the Tindersphere. I'd always thought my own act-now-think-later-if-at-all freneticism was exciting and stimulating; if nothing else, I'd never get bored. I am, though: I'm bored of going on date after date. I want to be happy where I am.

Jack says: 'I think that table might be about to leave,' nodding to my fair bet group, 'would you fancy moving across?' So he's been watching the tables, too; this whole time, we've been just as uncomfortable as each other.

To make them definitely leave we hover beside the departing group as they don their coats then sit down at adjacent sides of the table so we're at right angles. No more flimsy stools for us: we've luxurious backrests and solid wood to lean on, we're going places, Jack and I.

'So you're quite into football, I take it?'

Jacks nods. 'Man United.'

'You'd fare well in my family.'

'There would be no problem with us getting on.' Having been enthralled just seconds ago by Jack's of-the-moment philosophy, I am suddenly projecting us both into a future that involves Jack chatting football with Dad and Bru whilst I help Mum clear the table from Sunday lunch. Back in this moment, the real one, Jack is telling me about his United lineage but I can't stop the fantasy playing in my head (Dad is calling Jack a 'good egg'; Mum gives me a knowing smile . . .); I have to make it stop, it's getting hard to focus.

'I take it you're not into football, then.'

'I'm not, I'm afraid.'

'Sport in general?'

'The gym, if that counts.'

'I'd say it does.'

Follow-up questions will mean having to admit that by 'the gym' I mean 'a brisk session once or twice a month' so I ask Jack what movies he likes. He reels off a list, some of which are seminal films I've heard of but not seen, but he mentions a handful I've not heard of at all. He turns the question back on me but my childhood staples (*The Lion King*) and heart-warming classics (*Forrest Gump*) receive a tepid response. 'We'd struggle to go to the cinema together,' he says, though my suggestion of going to different screenings makes him laugh. 'As long as you make the correct popcorn choice,' I add.

'What would that be?'

'Half and half sweet-salty mix.' I narrow my eyes. 'Why? Please don't say . . .' A grin spreads over Jack's mouth. 'You'd choose salt.'

'I don't see why *you* wouldn't.'

'It's like eating cardboard.'

'Except with so many more calories.'

Football, films and now salty bloody popcorn: Jack and I have barely anything in common beyond the fact we're both here, on this date. You can't like someone with whom you've no mutual interests; differences can be stimulating but relationships thrive on common ground, on experiences enjoyed together and the shared memories they create. Jack and I don't have the instant chemistry I had with Patrick and there's no suffusion of romance like there was when I was with Archie. We're certainly not caught in the haze of hormones and booze that led me into trouble with Matt, not after two drinks. If Patrick, Archie and Matt were dissimilar from each other, Jack is different from all three and, interests aside, our personalities seem mismatched as well: I am creative, inquiring and chaotic more often than not, whereas Jack seems reserved, quiet and thoughtful. So why is it, then, that I can't stop the same thought repeating over and over in my head: I like him. I like him. I really, really like him.

I take Jack up on his suggestion and buy the next round. When the barman asks what I'd like, I order a chaste Diet Coke despite the rum that's on offer. There's no reason, other than that I don't need or want any more alcohol.

'Thanks so much,' says Jack as I hand him his Oranjeboom (I pronounced it correctly, feeling pretty good about myself right now). 'I hope you didn't mind getting this one.'

'Why would I? Girls should buy one round at least.' I pause. 'Has that not been the case with your other Tinder dates?' Please say no: please let me be better than other girls at something.

'Actually you're only my second date so I don't have a lot of comparison.' I pretend to root around my bag for a tissue to give me time to think: Jack has only had two dates, of which I am one. It may be that Jack is exceptionally picky and I should feel honoured to have met his exacting standards; it may also be that I am on a date with a man 99.5 per cent of female Tinderites found repellent. Maybe his other date comprises the 0.5 per cent that realised this only *after* the date. Or maybe he's still dating her; maybe he was ambivalent before tonight but having met me, he's sure that she's The One. Maybe he's dating Naked Girl from the gym. Fuck.

'What about you?' Jack asks. 'Any horror stories?'

'A couple of good,' I say, 'a couple of bad.' This seems as close to the truth as I can get without lying. And in comparison to my friends, it's quite accurate: my poor, wonderful BF, whose time with Ed was far worse than any of the bad dates of my own; she's sick of it all now, I know, but her apathy will wane – I'll have her back in the Tindersphere by New Year. Kate and Sophie, insulated from it all, have no experience of Tinder and I hope they never will . . . but love is not a straight line: after five years together, Harriet and James have broken up. I'd thought it might have had something to do with the engagement party – I knew James was angry at Harriet for getting so drunk. But she confided in me that they'd been having problems for a while, and she'd only been drinking to block them out. And as for Oona . . . it will take an app more robust than Tinder to find her other half.

I need to change the subject; I don't think I can bear to hear about Jack's super awesome *other* Tinder date. 'I did see a guy who looked just like Gary Barlow on Tinder once,' I ramble. 'I got pretty excited – I thought it might actually be him, using an alias.'

'He's married, isn't he?' Jack wonders aloud. 'I did some session work with him a few years ago, he was a really nice guy.'

'Have you worked with anyone else famous?' I'm getting hot and over-stimulated – this always happens whenever I sense proximity to celebrities.

'A few . . .'

'So what you're telling me is that you're basically famous yourself. I'm on a date with a celebrity.'

'Yes, that is exactly what I'm saying.' We grin at each other.

We chat more about Barlow, which leads on to a dissection of Take That's back catalogue and in turn sparks a competition about which of us owns the most *Now . . .* albums, before Jack asks what I'm into now, and I wince. 'I have obscure taste in music.'

'Like who?'

'You're a trendy musician, I don't want to tell you.'

'Come on.'

I spend some seconds playing with my straw. 'I'm a mega Kate Bush fan.'

'That's not obscure, I love Kate Bush.'

'What?'

'I love Kate Bush.'

I am very aware that Jack is staring at me and I must be staring back; as I look, I am seeing something I've never seen before: I am seeing myself. That one thought, *I really like you*, is reflected back at me in Jack's expression and I recognise it, because it is my own. He is looking at me and telling me: *I really like you too*. I do not need to chase after his attention – I have it, here, right now. Neither must I pretend to be somebody else to warrant it: he is seeing me as I am, good and bad, messy, funny, failing and loving – and he hasn't turned away. I feel totally held by his gaze. He smiles at me, and I smile back.

*   *   *

It is freezing outside when Jack and I leave: a frost has settled on the windows of cars and it glistens on the pavement beneath our feet. I pull my coat tight and Jack hunches down into his collar as we are battered by a harsh gust of wind.

'Which way are you going?' he asks. The word makes me flinch: *going*.

'I'm getting the bus from around the corner. What about you – where are you headed?'

'It's probably easiest if I jump on the Tube . . .' He stops and looks round. 'It's just along this road, isn't it?'

'You need to veer right at the lights,' I say, 'or maybe you just stay straight . . .' I have to stop before I send Jack to Newcastle. 'Navigation isn't my strong point.'

'Don't worry, I trust you.'

'You probably shouldn't.'

'I'll take the risk.'

Dating is a risk, falling for someone is a risk; the whole love-seeking process is fraught with chance and uncertainty. To go on a date is to risk anything from mild disappointment to total, visceral, soul-destroying rejection; you have to expose yourself, in part at least, to stand any chance of one date becoming something more, and the risk of having someone tell you they don't like what they see is terrifying. There is also the risk that it *will* become something more; you can only get away with exposing yourself in part for so long. For the first time, ever, as far back as Charlie and further back still, I finally see it: I am a risk, too. I am not the only one having to be vulnerable here. I wonder if Jack really does trust me – I would never want to let him down.

'Thank you for a really great night,' he says.

'Thank you, too.'

'I hope you've had a good time.'

'I have.'

We are facing each other, standing close for warmth. If we're going to kiss, shouldn't we do it now? He's not leaning in, but nor am I . . . should I? Would he want me to? I don't think he'd reject me, I am 89 per cent confident that he doesn't find me physically repulsive, but bar a brief hand-brush back in the pub, we've hardly touched each other. We fall into an awkward laugh which absolutely does not make the situation ten times more awkward than it already is.

He says: 'Come 'ere,' in a gruff, jokey voice and pulls me in for a hug.

'Iff had mmeally gffet igh oo,' I say into his coat.

'Sorry?' Jack pulls back so I am looking up at him.

'It would be good to do this again.' I say it quickly, before I lose my nerve. It is my version of a kiss.

Jack says, 'Yeah . . . maybe.'

Oh God. Oh holy fucking crappity shit bag . . . I've got it all completely wrong. The look back inside – I thought I saw something but I've totally misjudged it. Like the total, mind-numbing idiot that I am, I thought Jack liked me, but I must have decided this for myself, and then he said he liked Kate Bush and . . .

'No!' Suddenly, there is panic in Jack's voice. He pushes me back, holding me by the shoulders at arm's length. His eyes are huge, wide and round with alarm. 'I didn't mean . . . I was trying to be funny again . . . I'd love to see you again.'

'Oh.' This is my totally inadequate way of expressing the sheer relief that has flooded every inch of my being.

'No, no, no – I was joking, because we've been joking around all night and . . . you know that? You know I was joking, don't you?'

'Mm-hm.' The knot in my gut is back, but this time it's pure shock – I am amazed at how disappointed I was, and how happy I am now. The intensity in Jack's voice and in the way he is looking at me reminds me of myself as I broke up with Guy, when I needed him to believe my words.

'Shall I call you tomorrow?'

'I'd like that.'

'Great. OK. I'll call you tomorrow.' He hugs me again, tighter this time and when he lets me go, the air seems colder than it was before. We say goodbye, Jack and I, and I turn and set off for home. *Tomorrow. He's going to call me tomorrow.* I double check I'm going in the right direction. I am.

But Jack doesn't call the next day.

He lied.

He calls whilst I'm still on the bus.